Praise for *The New Global Student*

"If we want our kids—and our country—to thrive in the global economy, we need to follow the excellent advice in this inspiring book."
—Bill Bartmann, Billionaire Business Coach

"This book is chock-full of fresh ideas."
—Peg Tyre, author of *The Trouble with Boys: A Surprising Report Card on Our Sons, Their Problems at School, and What Parents and Educators Must Do*

"*The New Global Student* recognizes the truth of the American kindergarten through college education conveyor belt—it is preparing children for the last century's economy. . . . This inspiring guide shows the way to prepare students for full, satisfying, and self-directed lives. Parents owe it to their children to read this book."
—Bob Compton, venture capitalist and executive producer of the documentary *Two Million Minutes: A Global Examination*

"*The New Global Student* offers an adventurous, grab-life-by-the-collar alternative to the traditional teenage rat race. Frost's lively prose and the students' eye-opening testimonials make this unorthodox guide a brisk and pleasurable read."
—Dan Brown, author of *The Great Expectations School: A Rookie Year in the New Blackboard Jungle*

"Depressed about college applications and costs? *The New Global Student* will lift your spirits. It's smart, practical, and fun. I guarantee it will make a difference."
—Peter Benson, Ph.D., author of *Sparks: How Parents Can Help Ignite the Hidden Strengths of Teenagers*

"Maya Frost may sound like a wacky mom who yanked her family somewhere south of the border. But once you read her engaging, witty, and, above all, practical book, you realize: She's you . . . if

you only took a step back and considered what kind of life would really help my kids, my bank account, and my family's future?"

—Lenore Skenazy, author of *Free-Range Kids: Giving Our Children the Freedom We Had Without Going Nuts with Worry*

"The globalization of higher education is shaping a new borderless innovation economy in which talent, opportunities, and resources can come from anywhere. *The New Global Student* provides a timely manual for those with the foresight to ride these waves of change and opportunity."

—John Kao, author of *Innovation Nation* and chairman of the Institute for Large Scale Innovation

"Frost's book serves as a refreshing antidote to the uninspired, expensive, and challenge-averse educational offerings of the day. Never have students and parents needed its bold, possibility-affirming message more than now."

—Bill Farren, founder of Education for Well-being

"Some books inspire, some inform, others convince or rouse the reader to action. *The New Global Student* does all this while being funny, smart, and a joy to read. In the midst of the whirlwind of stress and expectation that surrounds parents and children as college approaches, Maya Frost's voice whispers: *There is another way.*"

—Dale McGowan, editor of *Parenting Beyond Belief* and coauthor of *Raising Freethinkers*

"Maya Frost is like Dr. Spock for a new generation of paranoid parents. . . . This irrepressible book blows open doors and gets you moving in a whole new direction. Truly a lifesaver."

—Karen Maezen Miller, author of *Momma Zen: Walking the Crooked Path of Motherhood*

"Get your hands on Maya Frost's *The New Global Student*. It will open your eyes, get your heart pounding and your mind racing, and maybe set you off on the adventure of a lifetime."
—Eric Maisel, author of *Creativity for Life*
and *Coaching the Artist Within*

"With wit and wisdom, Maya Frost gives us a refreshing look at opportunities unknown to many of us. She offers a bold new way to help our kids discover their passions, develop their talents, and become successful leaders in our ever-changing global economy."
—Jim Fay, cofounder of Love and Logic Institute, Inc.

"A terrific resource . . . Maya Frost firmly validates a parent's choice to give their children a chance to experience life in another culture."
—Robin Pascoe, author of *Raising Global Nomads:
Parenting Abroad in an On-Demand World*

"Thank God for Maya Frost! *The New Global Student* should be on every parent's reading list, it's so refreshing and is packed with information. It's a road map for families who don't accept the status quo."
—Michelle Lamar, author and entertainment
editor for CafeMom

"Maya Frost's unconventional approach to international education got me thinking about new avenues—particularly to address my own teenage daughters' interests. As I read *The New Global Student* I found myself sharing its concepts with other parents whose children would like to pursue nontraditional paths for learning about the world and engaging in it."
—Homa Sabet Tavangar, author of
*Growing Up Global: Raising Children to Be at
Home in the World*

THE NEW GLOBAL STUDENT

Skip the SAT,

Save Thousands on Tuition,

and Get a Truly International Education

MAYA FROST

THREE RIVERS PRESS • NEW YORK

Published in the United States by Three Rivers Press,
an imprint of the Crown Publishing Group,
a division of Random House, Inc., New York.
www.crownpublishing.com
Three Rivers Press and the Tugboat design
are registered trademarks of Random House, Inc.

Library of Congress Cataloging-in-Publication Data
Frost, Maya.
    The new global student / Maya Frost.
        p. cm.
    Includes index.
    1. College student orientation.   2. High school graduates—
Life skills guides.   3. Experiential learning.   4. Education and
globalization.   5. American students—Foreign countries.
I. Title.
    LB2343.3.F76 2009
    378.1'98—dc22   2008050476

ISBN 978-0-307-45062-3

Printed in the United States of America

Design by Leonard Henderson

10   9   8   7   6   5   4   3   2

First Edition

For my big brother Dennis—
gifted teacher, brilliant linguist, and passionate global citizen.
After nearly twenty years, I still feel your presence every day
and see your spark in the four nieces you never had a chance
to meet.
Paz, mi hermano.

CONTENTS

GRACIAS Y BESOS

I've always looked at the acknowledgments pages of books with a great deal of curiosity. Who are all those people? How did they contribute? Does it really take a village to birth a book?

Turns out it does—but not in the way I expected.

I have loved every minute of writing this book and have been so privileged to have the opportunity to do it in my own funky way.

❏ Thank you, Argentina.

I offer cheek kisses and red wine toasts to those who played a role in nurturing me throughout the half-year I spent working on this book from my living room sofa in Buenos Aires. This village includes my cheerful neighbors and my beloved polyglot group of friends from around the world who never failed to ask about the project during our many dinners and coffees together.

I'm so glad that there is not a single mega–English bookstore in the entire (enormous) country. Blissfully removed from stacks of best sellers, I was free to enjoy the writing process without worrying about competition or critics. What a blessing! (Of course, it made walking back into Powell's Books in Portland, Oregon, quite a shock.)

❏ Thank you, Google and the Internet.

I found my wonderful agent, Stephanie Kip Rostan of Levine Greenberg Literary Agency, online. I am indebted to Sophfronia Scott, the e-mail goddess who steered me in the right direction by putting me in touch with Heather Proulx, the delightful woman who became my editor at Random House/Crown. I have felt fully supported by Stephanie and Heather the entire time, even though I did not meet either of them—or even talk to them on the phone—until well after the book was written! Consider it a testament to the new way of collaborating globally. Many thanks for the virtual high fives.

In addition to the team at Crown, my global village has included intrepid students, savvy parents, enlightened educators, and plenty of thoughtful experts who cheered me on via e-mail. I am especially grateful to the scores of former exchange students who so enthusiastically shared their personal stories, and I thank all of them profusely for believing in this project. I send special hugs to those who were generous enough to tell their wonderful tales without ever caring if they were published.

❏ Big love to my family.

Every day I am more thankful for my mother, Elaine Stark, who struggled to help me pay for college, never hesitated when I told her I wanted to spend my senior year studying in nine Asian countries, never shed a tear when she found out I was having my graduation ceremony at Sigmund Freud's house in Vienna (and knew that she would miss it), didn't whimper when I got a job teaching in rural Japan just months after my return from Asia, lovingly handled the details of my wedding while I was living abroad, and somehow managed to be okay with the fact that I had my first two children on the opposite side of the Pacific from her Oregon home. Now that I am the mother of four independent young women myself, I know how difficult it is to step back and allow our children to pursue their own paths (especially when it leads to other continents), and I feel so fortunate that my mother was such a steadfast model of true maternal love.

My deepest appreciation is tied with a pink ribbon and presented to my four bold and beautiful daughters. This book could never have been written without their heart-wide-open honesty, shared wisdom, and hilarious feedback. I cannot express the depth of my love, awe, and gratitude. They are, quite simply, my purpose for being on this planet.

Last but certainly not least, I must thank my incredible husband, Tom. Every single day of the last two and a half decades has been a grand adventure, and I am so richly blessed to have him as my keeper of faith, partner in parenting crime, personal chef, business strategist, jester, walking buddy, navigator, and soul mate. Tom lured me away from my laptop with fabulous meals, dragged me out to a café at least twice a day, and talked me through every word of this book. I thank him for all of these things, but most of all, I thank him for my beautiful life.

TOP TEN REASONS

TO READ THIS BOOK

> I have never let my schooling
> interfere with my education.
> MARK TWAIN

This is not your typical college-prep handbook. In fact, *The New Global Student* is more like the **anti**-college-prep handbook.

You won't find any suggestions on how to write an impressive essay for university admissions. There's not a single sentence about how to boost SAT scores. And it's not an ode to bilingual preschools, immersion elementary schools, or international high schools.

Instead, this eye-popping how-to guide offers tips, tricks, and only-if-you've-been-there secrets to show frazzled parents and students how to *completely avoid* the traditional hypercompetitive path to that golden university diploma and surge ahead with flaming enthusiasm and red-hot qualifications for life (and work) in the global economy.

No angst about competing with others.
No pricey (or pointless) get-ahead strategies.

No mandatory high school hoop jumping.
No ridiculous quest for meaningless test scores.
No mindless pursuit of achievement for the sake of
    college admissions.
No blind faith in bland "international" labels on
    applications.

This is a whole new game—and the star players are already prospering in their chosen positions around the world.

Think globally, act locally? The new global student is thinking *and acting* globally. Fortunately, we're no longer locked into the place-based model of schooling, so we have no need to follow the same old rules. Instead of adhering to the outdated four-by-four plan (four years of high school plus four years of college), the new breed of American global student is getting a ragin' education on campus, online, on the road, and on *their* terms and timelines. Not only are they not obsessing about the name of their alma mater, they're figuring out how to blend a perfect brew of education options that will allow them to glide into the global economy with:

- sizzling 21st-century skills
- outrageously relevant global experience
- a sparkling college degree
- a blazing sense of direction
- a big grin on their faces
- and *no debt*

This is not just a how-to book—it's a *why*-to book. You'll see how those who step sideways are taking full advantage of the many unconventional opportunities for phenomenal intellectual and personal development. The smartest parents are already using this approach to save thousands of dollars while helping their kids get an off-the-charts education that electrifies them, maximizes their talents, connects them globally, and catapults them into the creative class.[1]

In these pages you'll find plenty of statements from experts, but more revealing are the extraordinary stories from students who have learned how to do things *differently* and zoom ahead just the way they choose. Although this book speaks to parents of high school kids, the concepts presented here will enlighten and ex-hilarate parents of students from preschool to grad school, along with educators, mentors, grandparents, employers, community leaders, and especially **students from middle school through college**.

Whether you're looking for ways to fast-forward through high school, study abroad cheaply, save money on college tuition, graduate early, or live and work outside the United States, this is the ultimate bible on the do-it-your-way trend that has students and parents across the country exchanging hearty high fives.

Not sure if you're likely to benefit from the information in this book? Let me help you decide.

Take a look at the following statements. Pay attention to how often you find yourself nodding your head in agreement.

1. I am ready to get calm, clear, and creative in order to **discover the best education options** available.

2. I am excited to focus on *learning* (not just achievement), and I'm looking forward to **less stress and much more inspiration** along the way.

3. I need to learn about ways to **save thousands of dollars** on college expenses without sacrificing quality of education or opportunities for personal development.

4. I am questioning the current SAT/GPA/AP approach to getting into college, and I can't wait to find out how to **avoid standardized measures**.

(continued)

5. I know how important it is to learn more about the world, and I need solid information about **the most inexpensive and beneficial language-learning and study-abroad options** out there.

6. I've already read enough books by admissions advisers about the college-application process. I want to **get the inside scoop from no-bull experts, barrier-busting students, and shrewd parents** that I won't find anywhere else.

7. I need to hear from students who have managed to **finish high school early** in order to dive into higher education (especially the global variety)—and how this has helped them move forward in numerous ways.

8. I am excited about looking beyond math and science to discover more creative ways to **prepare for the global workplace.**

9. I want to **spend time abroad with my family,** and I need honest advice from those who have done it successfully and can offer tips about handling the kids' education.

10. It's time for a change, and I'm looking for inspiring stories and practical tips to help me **get fired up in order to make bolder (and more meaningful) life choices.**

Nodding? Cheering? Great.

If this list roused even a little bit of rah-rah in you, keep reading.

You're about to meet the new global student. Get ready to discover just how simple it can be to turn typical U.S. kids—from small towns, suburbs, and big cities—into highly competent leaders ready to embrace the world and its many opportunities.

EYES-WIDE-OPEN EDUCATION

CHAPTER ONE

Creative, Not Crazy

OUR FAMILY'S STORY

FOLLOWING OUR INSTINCTS

> If we did all the things we are capable of,
> we would literally astound ourselves.
> THOMAS A. EDISON

In the summer of 2005 my husband and I decided to sell everything and move abroad. There's nothing too unusual about that these days—except that we had four teenage daughters at the time, and the youngest three were about to enter their freshman, junior, and senior years of high school.

This book is about the lessons we learned—and the loopholes we discovered—while shepherding our kids through high school, into college, and beyond. Luckily, we stumbled upon a number of **affordable, accessible, and stunningly advantageous strategies that American parents *anywhere* can use** to help their kids get both an enriching education and a perspective-shifting international experience.

Sweet bonus: We saved a couple hundred thousand dollars in the process.

We were not on a crusade of any kind and never once waved a flag bearing the name of a particular educational movement. Our exodus wasn't spurred by fear, exasperation, or legal problems; it was simply a matter of following our instincts in order to give our kids what we felt would be a series of amazing opportunities for more learning and creativity.

When others hear our story, they can't help but make assumptions about us. Some we find hilarious.

ASSUMPTION 1: WE HAD A TON OF MONEY AND/OR SERIOUS CONNECTIONS.

Hoo-boy! That's a good one.

Let me be clear:

- ❏ We did not have a corporate cushion or support system of any kind.
- ❏ We had never received a bonus or stock payout in our lives.
- ❏ We didn't have a windfall from a business we had sold or an uncle who had died.
- ❏ We did not know anyone who had done what we were considering.
- ❏ We had no contacts where we were going.
- ❏ We did not speak the language.
- ❏ We were staring at multiple simultaneous college tuitions.

Need some numbers? Our annual income was firmly planted in the five figures—*together*. We weren't exactly swimming in cash, but we were more than comfortable. Our lifestyle was lean by design— we were choosing to work less than we could have because we valued our time with our kids. Or at least, that was our story.

Anyone looking at our tax forms would have said we were wildly optimistic (that being the polite way of putting it) to entertain the thought that we could move abroad, figure out how to make a living, *and* afford college for our girls.

And yet we had this feeling that not only could we continue to make enough to live well but that we'd actually *save more money for college* by living abroad than we could by staying in Oregon. (Juicy details later, but suffice it to say that this turned out to be a fantastic college-savings plan that only the most astute and progressive financial adviser would recommend.)

ASSUMPTION 2: WE WERE ODDBALL PARENTS.

Quirky. They think we must have been the kind of people you whisper about at parent meetings or avoid when you run into them in the grocery store.

The boring truth is that we were nice, normal people leading ordinary lives.

There was nothing particularly noteworthy about us. We weren't wild-eyed survivalists seeking a place to hunker down and wait for the Big KaBlooey, nor were we adrenaline-junkie adventurers off to scale the highest peaks. We didn't have a dream of sailing around the world; nor did we have an irresistible urge to go out and save it. Reasonably well mannered and inconspicuously attired, we did not embarrass our kids in public—unless my husband wanted to have a little fun, that is.

You wouldn't have looked twice at us at Starbucks, I swear.

ASSUMPTION 3: WE WERE DISCONNECTED OR JUST PLAIN MISERABLE WHERE WE WERE.

Well, no more than most people living in suburban America.

We didn't rant about the failings of our education system or launch into tirades about the decline of modern civilization—at least, not in mixed company or without provocation (or a few beers). Staunch supporters of the public schools, we had a tremendous amount of appreciation for the many caring teachers and conscientious administrators who were so committed to our kids and their classmates.

Sure, we felt that people bought too much stuff, wasted too

much gas, and packed their schedules too full, but we tried to view this with humor rather than despair. (Tip: It's easier that way.)

For several years we had lived in a Portland, Oregon, subdivision located about five miles from the Nike World Campus, another five from a huge Intel industrial park, and just down the way from Leupold and Stevens, the world's largest supplier of rifle scopes. I jokingly refer to this particular Bermuda Triangle as "the belly of the beast," but I had lived there as a kid when the area was nothing but fields and it holds a soft spot in my heart. The subdivisions bear the last names of my elementary school classmates whose grandparents had farmed the land there, and I used to catch butterflies in the meadow where Barnes & Noble now stands. I've been known to get all misty just standing in the business book section; I have deep roots there.

ASSUMPTION 4: OUR GIRLS WERE ENMESHED IN A SCANDAL AT SCHOOL THAT NECESSITATED A QUICK EXIT TO PROTECT THEIR SOCIAL STANDING.

Sorry—no gossip here. Our daughters were doing quite well and were far from being considered weird by their peers; they were excellent students, had lots of friends, and were involved in a number of activities. It's fair to say that they were generally happy (keeping in mind that we are talking about teenage girls).

In fact, everyone we knew seemed *generally* happy there.

But we couldn't shake the feeling that there was something more *vibrant* out there for us. The richness of life isn't recognized in a rush-rush world, and though we were personally committed to keeping things as simple as possible, we were immersed in a culture in which being "swamped" was a sign of success and being "exhausted" counted as a personal virtue. Perhaps we were just too lazy to run on that treadmill, but we prefer to think that we simply saw how unnecessarily urgent it all was. Besides, our kids were going to be leaving home soon; we wanted to share one last pivotal blast.

* * *

We knew from experience (more on our minisabbatical in Chapter Eight) that we'd do more laughing in one day abroad than we would likely do in a month of living in Generica. The world is a zesty place, but it's easy to forget that when you're surrounded by clusters of nondescript cul-de-sacs and uninspired strip malls. I guess we were searching for more oomph in the form of jaw-dropping visuals, chin-trembling poignancy, and almost-pee-your-pants hilarity—and we didn't want to simply watch it on a television or movie screen.

Of course, we recognized that leaving our home and our country wouldn't be a bed of roses, but then, neither is making a living and raising kids in suburbia. Hey, if we were going to go through the struggle of daily life anyway, we might as well get some serious wow out of it. A little extra frustration seemed worth it if it ultimately led to unforgettable peak experiences for everyone.

Plus, we realized that it was our responsibility as parents (not the school's job) to move our daughters toward maturity and autonomy. We had two harebrained ideas.

- **Harebrained Idea 1** was that they needed to become **flexible** and **innovative** in order to be prepared for an exciting future full of all kinds of impossible-to-predict opportunities. Everywhere we looked, parents were intent upon providing secure, consistent living situations that would allow their children to have the same friends, schools, and activities throughout childhood. To us this seemed like a way to promote head-in-the-sand syndrome. Shouldn't we be helping our kids learn how to deal with uncertainty, feel comfortable as outsiders, make new friends, and thrive wherever they go?

  Or was this just plain *mean*?

  Instead of sheltering our kids from the world, we believed we ought to hang a loving life preserver around their necks and toss them into it. How could they learn to become creative and resilient adults without leaving their zip code? Let's face it: a suburban school setting can't be expected to serve as a training ground for flexibility and innovation, and a trend-worshipping culture isn't likely to inspire kids to think for themselves. It was time to take matters into our own hands.

- **Harebrained Idea 2** was that we wanted our daughters to develop **empathy** and **responsibility** in order to become upstanding global citizens. It seemed ridiculous to think that it wasn't our responsibility to teach our kids responsibility. Besides, modeling trumps teaching. Parents need to *embody* the qualities they feel are important. Portland's ethos had seeped into our souls; we wanted our kids to develop a sense of duty to others and a desire to work for the greater good of society.

But beyond this wish list for wow, wonder, and world citizenship was education. We needed to get that nailed before we could allow ourselves to get all excited about finding cheap airfares online or selling our stuff on Craigslist.

There was research to be done! Logical first stop: the schools.

Teachers were full of praise for our daughters but expressed concern about how they would manage to complete high school in a new country. They assumed we would be homeschooling, and we kept our mouths shut about the fact that we had a more play-it-by-ear approach; we couldn't say for sure what our kids would be doing until we got there and tried a few options. We felt like we had to be a bit stealthy about the move, and we did our best to avoid stirring up unnecessary resistance. Still, I was looking for at least a hint of validation, so I contacted a school administrator. The father of a couple of bilingual grown children bearing graduate degrees, he seemed like a good person to offer advice on incorporating global experiences with school requirements.

After patiently listening to me rhapsodize about pulling our three daughters out of the local high school in order to experience life abroad as a family, he sighed and served up a steaming plate of reality.

"I agree one hundred percent that what you're proposing could be a fantastic experience for your kids," he told me. "But frankly we're not really set up to support it at this point. There are virtual options, but none that work with our district. Things are definitely moving in that direction, but we're likely a decade away from having a seamless system in place that would allow your daughters to complete their requirements to graduate from this school remotely." He explained that we'd need to withdraw the girls from the district, and then gave me a couple of websites to check out. "Listen, I'm cheering for you, but this might be a frustrating process. You're going to have to be quite bold."

Hmm. It was clear that "old school" thinking still ruled, and we did not have a decade to wait for things to change. We needed an approach that would work for our kids *right now*.

We had a family meeting. Within minutes we were nodding and grinning. It was decided: we would walk away from the school district and its requirements and set out for new territory.

Good bye, Old School. Hello, Bold School.

Now, I'll admit that we had some advantages as we set about planning our departure. As small-scale entrepreneurs, jumping into things about which we are clueless is our modus operandi. My husband likes to invent things, I teach people how to pay attention, and we both enjoy playing with marketing. Consequently, we're good at noticing what's going on around us, coming up with creative ways to handle challenges, and convincing ourselves (and others) to try something new.

Our career teeter-totter has tilted toward cockiness more often than caution. Acting boldly is second nature to us. Still, we knew that being bold wasn't enough; we were going to have to get clever as well. It's a good thing that brainstorming happens to be our favorite family pastime.

Of course, we didn't have this book. *You do.* You're already *way* ahead of where we started.

Two points to remember:

❑ Things turned out to be easier than we'd anticipated.
❑ *Anyone* can benefit from a bold(er) approach to education.

The options in this book are well within reach of the vast majority of families considering sending their kids to college. You don't have to make any choices that cause people to question your sanity (though it *is* fun and highly recommended), and *you can certainly stay right where you are while giving your kids some great opportunities for a global education.*

All you need are the tips in this book.

However, it does help if you're a little bit of a rebel inside. The good news is that most of us are. In my work with people from around the world, I've learned that almost everyone has a thirst for beauty, freedom, and discovery—and a hankering for more *fun*.

Scratch the surface of any Dockers-wearing Intel guy, and you'll find a budding novelist. Get a Nike exec talking, and she'll admit that what she really wants to do is start her own design company. Chat with a soccer mom over a latte, and she'll tell you that she longs to spend a year cooking in Tuscany. The dad coaching your son's Little League team has a dream of taking his kids on a great adventure in the Amazon, and the barista at your favorite coffee shop is fantasizing about studying architecture in Prague.

Boldness is *in* us—and it's screaming to get out.

If my husband and I weren't modeling innovation and flexibility—not to mention a 'burb-busting case of boldness—how could we expect our daughters to develop these qualities for themselves? Showing them that we were willing to look like idiots on a regular basis in order to experience more beauty, freedom, discovery, and fun would give them a brand-new way to view adulthood and their own possibilities.

There are those who take mini-steps toward their goals, and there are those who prefer to pole-vault. We opted for the flying leap.

Sure, we expected to take a few tumbles, and we had some spectacular ones. (Don't miss the "Mutinies, Meltdowns, and Other Merriment" section of Chapter Nine.) But despite the inevitable mistakes and embarrassing moments, we knew that our daughters would thrive (eventually), and we felt that the move would turn out to be the best thing we would ever do for our family.

Once we'd made our decision, we couldn't wait to dig into the details. We gave ourselves six weeks. Each morning we leaped out of bed, bursting with energy and buzzing about the tasks to be accomplished.

Making our businesses virtual? Piece o' cake. Within a week, we'd set it up so that we could work from anywhere.[1]

The bigger challenge: figuring out how to do school.

Oh, wait. That part was pretty easy, too, once we got the hang of it. I'll share plenty of tips so that you won't have to make the same goofs we did.

Actually, the hardest part about leaving the United States was dealing with the naysayers. And there were just so *many* of them, each with their own detailed arguments, devastating facial expressions, and deafening silences. Basically, everyone told us we were crazy.

- ◗ Our friends asked us how we could sacrifice our kids' education for the sake of an adventure. They couldn't imagine how we could consider yanking our kids out of perfectly good schools solely because we had sprouted a midlife wild hair.
- ◗ Our kids' friends' parents felt we were being more than a little selfish for not letting our girls have a "normal" high school experience. Some were convinced that our daughters were

going to wind up in therapy for life in order to come to terms with their missed slumber parties, homecoming games, and winter formals.

▶ Our family members were worried about us taking our girls out of the country. Who knew what terrible fate awaited them beyond our nation's borders?

▶ And as I've hinted already, school officials, most of whom will tell you that it's not a good idea to move across *town* when your kids are in high school, shook their heads and said we might be sabotaging our daughters' chances of getting into any top colleges.

We were feeling like very, very bad parents.

Fortunately, as entrepreneurs, we'd had a lot of practice ignoring seemingly sound advice; "They just don't understand our vision" is our motto. Pros when it comes to brandishing false bravado (another by-product of being self-employed), we came up with some great ways to deal with the criticism and even had a little fun with it. (You'll love the "Snappy Comeback Cheat Sheet" in Chapter Nine.) After being painfully pierced by the first few barbs, we learned not to take it all so personally. It helped to remember that people have a natural tendency to respond to new ideas in defensive ways, and we figured out how to handle disapproval (and ignorance) with humor and at least a sliver of grace. After a while we relished our role as rebels.

And so during those final weeks of skillfully shutting down the doom-and-gloomers (carefully avoiding any mention of our midnight what-the-hell-are-we-doing conversations), we sold everything we owned except a few items that fit into a five-by-five-foot storage unit. With two bags each, we boarded a plane for the sunny South.

Sometimes you just have to follow your instincts.

THE RESULTS ARE IN

So, how did things work out?

Did our daughters hate us for depriving them of their
  proms?
Did they fall hopelessly behind their peers in the race to
  get into college?
Did they end up on a tropical beach somewhere with no
  inclination to do anything but smoke weed all day?
They seem to be turning out all right.

❑ **Taeko** (our oldest daughter) spent her junior year of high
school in Chile, entered a liberal arts college in Canada at
eighteen with enough credits to start as a junior, spent a
summer working virtually as a research assistant for a Bill
and Melinda Gates Foundation project while living on a tropical island, graduated with a BS (and honors) in psychology at
nineteen, traveled around Latin America for several months,
flew to New York, and despite having no connections, got a job
as a health educator within days, beating several candidates
with graduate degrees and a decade of experience. (Secret
weapon: fluent colloquial Spanish and a killer condom-and-
cucumber demonstration.) As part of her personal mission
to prevent sexually transmitted diseases and unplanned
pregnancies, Taeko is finishing up her master's degree in
urban public health while working at a nonprofit community
health clinic in Harlem. She's twenty-two.

❑ **Tara** spent her junior year of high school in Brazil, graduated early, took college courses online while living with the
family in Mexico for a year, spent a summer studying in Germany, enrolled at a university in Canada for a semester, and
spent several months studying Spanish in Argentina. Despite

(continued)

her continent hopping and major changing, she earned her bachelor's degree (and honors) at an Oregon university two years ahead of her high school classmates. During her final year of studies in communications and Spanish, she did an internship at the Mexican consulate, taught at a nonprofit that offers Spanish lessons for preschoolers, and served as a mentor for Latino youth. Interested in cultural awareness and media literacy, Tara is juggling two internships in Manhattan: one at a leading Hispanic brand-communications agency, and one in MTV's international division. She's twenty.

❑ **Teal** spent her junior year of high school on exchange in Brazil and then joined the family for a new adventure in Argentina. She finished high school online, took intensive Spanish courses at an Argentine university, worked with an American writer to develop her expository skills, studied privately with a Canadian professor in world history, and transferred to a liberal arts university in Canada as a junior at eighteen. She's been both a TA (teaching assistant) and an RA (resident assistant) and will finish her degree in sociology and Spanish shortly after she turns nineteen. Unsure of where she wants to live but looking to work and save money while perfecting her language skills, Teal aced two interviews (in three languages) and accepted a position as a multilingual events coordinator for Norwegian Cruise Lines upon graduation.

❑ **Talya** never attended high school in the United States. Instead she moved with our family to Mexico and was the only foreigner in her all-Spanish private high school. After a very eventful year, we decided to move on. (Find out why in Chapter Nine.) Knowing the value of buy-in, we asked her where she'd like to go next. "Buenos Aires, Argentina," she declared, after due diligence. We packed our two bags each and headed to the "Paris of South America," where she studied Spanish, worked with private tutors from around the world, and attended a small American university with students from a dozen countries. She was awarded a very nice scholarship/grant package when she transferred to a private university in upstate New York with enough credits to be a junior, and she snagged a TA position (and a profile in the college newspaper) within her first few days on campus. She's seventeen.

None of our daughters ever submitted an SAT score. They never dealt with the typical senior-year stress of getting into college. They skipped the angst about GPAs, never took a single AP course, and ditched the drama of waiting for those fat envelopes from colleges to arrive. They had *zero* contacts in the fields they are pursuing and, like many of the global students you'll meet in this book, have been making their way based on their own experience and enthusiasm rather than on personal introductions or their university's reputation.

Educating four kids must have cost a fortune, right? Well, you can't do it for nothing, and we certainly could have chosen less expensive options (or grabbed a bigger slice of the financial aid pie), but we've kept to the budget we set. *Total* cost to us for *each* daughter's kindergarten-through-bachelor's-degree education: about $35,000, including *all* travel, study abroad, tutors, and college expenses.

None of us has any debt. Everybody seems pretty happy about that. During each year that we lived abroad, we were able to save enough for one daughter's education expenses. The old SIP (Save, Invest, Pray) approach to paying for college can work fine, but I think you'll find the new HAB (Have A Blast) technique far more appealing.

Contrary to what you might think by looking at the timelines, our girls haven't been on a joyless head-down race to finish school. They simply learned how to work smart, eliminate repetition, maximize opportunities, and be their own advocates. There's nothing remotely robotic about them; they've learned to navigate the bumps in their paths, and they're thrilled to be in complete control of each step. "I LOVE my LIFE!" is our daughters' most frequently expressed sentiment these days.

This is the part where you say, "Oh, those poor girls! They rushed through school and probably didn't have any fun at all."

Yes, they've worked hard, but they've attended their share of high school events, experienced college dorm life, and even managed to squeeze in a *few* memorable good times outside the traditional school environment.

Collectively, our daughters have:

- climbed the green peaks of Machu Picchu
- gone snowboarding in the Andes
- danced for days during Brazil's crazy Carnaval festivities
- camped with friends under the stars in the Atacama Desert
- danced in the Nebuta festival in northern Japan
- snorkeled in the turquoise waters of Bermuda
- kayaked among whales in the South Atlantic
- celebrated in Venice on the day Italy won the World Cup
- attended all-night raves with sixty thousand others in attendance
- hiked the glaciers of Patagonia

and much, much more.

(But damn—they did miss a prom or two.)

What about the poor parents? Did we slave away while living in a shack in a third-world country in order to pay for all of this?

Not a chance. My husband and I have a simple yet surprisingly luxurious lifestyle in the very cosmopolitan city of Buenos Aires, Argentina, deservedly one of the world's top tourist destinations:

▶ We enjoy relaxed, months-long visits with our daughters.
▶ We own our beautiful (but small) home outright, and it's perfect for exchanging with others anywhere in the world we'd like to visit.
▶ We are blissfully car-free.
▶ We have become valued members of our community and enjoy a rich social life with a wonderfully diverse group of friends from many places.
▶ We have creative work that we love and complete freedom to arrange our own schedules.

But those are simply perks. What matters most to us is that our kids have developed a comprehensive and compassionate world-view, fluency in at least one foreign language (if not two or three), a strong sense of their passions and talents, and a sizable set of skills and qualities that will enable them to find opportunities for engaging (and reasonably well-paid) work anywhere they choose to go.

So are we crazy . . . or creative? You be the judge. This book will help you see your own comfort zone and decide how far you'd like to stretch it.

Listen, I apologize if this section sounds like the scary beginning of the gaggiest holiday newsletter of all time. I'm using my girls here as the first examples (they're used to being guinea pigs), but I promise that you'll meet plenty of other students with whom I do not share blood ties.

I'd also like to point out that Tom and I are laughably imperfect parents and our girls cringe at the thought of being held up as beacons of hope for their generation, and that's the point: **there's no need for perfection, and no reason to choose someone else's path**. It's so much more fun (and ultimately far more beneficial) to discover our own best options, so in this book we're going to do some serious lightening up in order to release our grip on the one-way mentality. Laughing shakes and stirs a nice little chemical cocktail in our brains (more on that magic ball of goo in Chapter Six), so we'll make sure to do plenty of that while learning how to guarantee that our kids are global and grinning.

Every single day we feel grateful that we decided to trust our instincts, and I wrote this book to encourage other parents to trust theirs. No matter where you are or what you're considering, I'm offering facts and lessons learned in order to help you envision the possibilities for your own family. You don't have to take my word for it. You're about to read:

❏ remarkable stories from students who have learned how to get a kick-ass education *their* way
❏ pep talks from those who've spent a year abroad during high school—and how the experience changed them forever
❏ surprising advice from experts about the advantages of doing things differently
❏ tales of tears and triumph from my daughters
❏ straight talk from those who have found ways to study abroad—and get full credit for it—for pennies on the dollar
❏ no-holds-barred accounts of the ups and downs of living abroad—from the perspective of both parents and kids
❏ a clear explanation (courtesy of my formerly cranky husband) of the savings and relief you can expect if you choose to leave your U.S. lifestyle behind.

My hope is that you and your student will consider stepping off the traditional track—if only for a few steps—in order to explore enriching ways to discover more about the world. And the pot of gold at the end of the rainbow will be that you watch your kids soar beyond anything they'd ever imagined for themselves.

Your student's potential is far greater than you realize. The beautiful part is that you can choose to offer them love, guidance, and the occasional kick in the keister in whatever way you feel is most beneficial. There's no need to squeeze them into a mold that is suffocating. Breathing is *good*.

I have a hunch that we have something in common. I knew there was a way to help my kids open their eyes and really see the world—and their possibilities—with greater clarity. And yet it wasn't showing up in the standard approach to parenting, going to high school, and getting into—and through—college.

I was longing for something . . . *different*.

I promise you'll find that here.

> **Old School:** earnestly staying within the lines
> **Bold School:** happily scribbling wherever you go

HIGH-FIVING VS. HAND-WRINGING

> A reform is a correction of abuses; a revolution is a transfer of power.
> EDWARD GEORGE EARLE
> LYTTON BULWER-LYTTON

We're not going to wring our hands about the state of education in the United States. You see, we prefer high fives to slumped shoulders. It's so much better for your frame of mind, not to mention your posture.

Instead of focusing on what's wrong with our system, we're going to celebrate the fact that we have an enormous amount of freedom to choose from a tantalizing smorgasbord of education options. Our task is to encourage students to grab a plate and fill it with their favorites.

I know that what I have to say in this book isn't likely to be praised by university officials, educrats, study-abroad program coordinators, or those who've just spent a pile of money on their kids' education (my condolences). That's okay. I'm not beholden to anyone, nor am I trying to win any popularity contests. My intention is to embolden students and parents who are ready for a change. Sometimes all we need is a story or two to give us the courage to try something new, and my goal is to offer a bit of inspiration along with valuable information.

Prefer to participate in a happy education revolution rather than a heated debate about education reform? I thought so. We're about to summit the old-school peak and skip along the trail toward a much **more joyful and personalized approach** to learning and success.

Whew! Don't you feel better already?

So put your climbing gear away and relax. There's no hurry. There's nobody coming up behind you, nor is there anyone racing *ahead* of you. This is a completely different kind of path, and you'll find it far less crowded and far more congenial than any you've encountered. It's got its own pace, and there's no rushing allowed.

❏ **Smart Move**: The single most important thing parents can do to help their student prepare for a global future is simply *slow down* and step back in order to see the big picture.

We'll get to the tips, stories, and resources soon. But right now there are a couple of things you should know about why this approach works.

Let's begin by looking beyond math and Mandarin.

> **Old School:** fretting about the obstacles blocking education reform
> **Bold School:** celebrating our freedom to participate in an education revolution

CHAPTER TWO

Beyond Math and Mandarin

WHAT "GLOBAL" REALLY MEANS

> I love my country, but I think we
> should start seeing other people.
> SEEN ON A BUMPER STICKER
> IN PORTLAND, OREGON

Plenty of people believe that the United States is the best place to get a global education. Of course, most of them are bringing their global perspective *with* them when they arrive from other countries.

It's true that the United States remains the top destination for international students looking to study abroad (India and China send the most students here), but that's only because we had a good head start.[1] Lately, we Americans have been cruising on our world-class-college reputation rather than focusing on attracting the best talent. Post-9/11 visa restrictions dramatically reduced the flow of international students into the United States, and by the time we realized we'd better open the nozzle, other countries had seduced those top students through innovative recruitment efforts. Most U.S. universities continue to cling to the old fly-and-flyer approach to international recruiting—flying administrators around the world to pass out flyers at college fairs and to do meet-and-greets with study-abroad officials. Meanwhile universities in Australia, Canada, and the United Kingdom have strategically surged forward by relying on in-country agents abroad to promote their programs. U.S. university officials are squeamish about this, thinking the use of agents a tad unethical (you'll see the humor in this once you read Chapter Seven), but there are plenty of ethical ways to help bright and motivated young people find their way to our universities. While we dither, they're choosing non-U.S. options, and this affects the diversity on our college campuses and the opportunities for our students to connect and collaborate with those from other countries.

Okay, so maybe Americans *are* a little distracted when it comes to getting great (not just wealthy) students to come to the U.S. Perhaps we're concentrating on *other* aspects of global education, like sending a huge percentage of our college students abroad. Wait, no—that's definitely not happening either. (You won't believe the numbers—I'll share them in Chapter Seven.)

Curious about the latest buzz on students flowing hither and yon, I set up a Google Alert for "global education" and related terms. Each morning for months I'd read through the announcements about education conferences, scan through the university press releases, and browse study-abroad blog posts from every corner of the globe. It seemed that everyone was talking about global education but not in ways that had much to do with U.S. students or parents. In fact, other than a few references to cross-cultural literacy programs, collaborative online projects between classes on opposite sides of the world, and the distribution of solar-powered laptops, the phrase "global education" was almost universally attached to profit-oriented partnerships launched by universities (American and foreign) with an eye toward expansion. Most blurbs were nothing more than bugle calls for more prestige or a shapelier bottom line.

This really cranked my shank. If the majority of conversations about "global education" revolve around charging triple tuition from international students or buffing up a U.S. university brand by building campuses in the Middle East, who is watching out for the best interests of *American students and parents?*

There's a lot of talk about the value of a global education, and numerous U.S. college administrators are tooting their horns about their emphasis on internationalization. But even though it might *seem* like every college is scrambling to prepare students for the global economy, American universities are actually dropping the blue and green ball; not only are they falling behind in attracting international students to create a more diverse campus setting, they're actually *decreasing* their efforts to help more U.S. students gain a greater understanding of the world in the classroom.

A study by the Center for International Initiatives at the American Council on Education indicates that the percentage of American universities that require a course with an international or global focus actually *fell* from 41 percent in 2001 to 37 percent in 2006. Less than one in five U.S. colleges has a foreign language requirement, and less than 40 percent of institutions made specific reference to international or global education in their mission statements.[2]

Chest thumping. Lip service. But not a lot of *actual* global education goin' on.

❏ **Smart Move**: Savvy parents know better than to rely on American high schools or colleges to provide a truly global education for their students. They actively seek opportunities for international learning *beyond* the high school classroom or college campus.

Even if all American universities were to tilt their course requirements in a more global direction, enrolling in a few international studies or foreign language classes is not the same thing as becoming an educated and engaged global citizen. Those who are going into debt for the next decade to get that "global education advantage" deserve to know the difference.

Most educators acknowledge that students today need to be prepared in new ways to meet the challenges of the future, but they differ regarding the most crucial areas upon which to focus. Do we zero in on:

- more math and science?
- more foreign languages?
- more tech training?
- more international branch campuses for U.S. universities?
- more study-abroad programs for college students?
- more rigor to meet international standards?

Plenty of detailed business plans and school policies are being drafted in conference rooms around the world, but they aren't likely to help you or your student in the immediate future. You see, the vast majority of the "new" approaches to global education are heavily reliant upon old models. Whizzy tech tools aside, the plans themselves are anything but innovative.

Think of it as Old School 2.0. International schools are telling parents about how their curricula prepare students for the "global jobs" of the future. High school students are being required to sign up for more language courses in the name of "global education." College students are being steered toward packaged study-abroad programs to give them an edge in the "global economy." Consultants are offering to help college grads attract the interest of recruiters from "global corporations."

These are all generally helpful efforts, but there's nothing *new* here. In fact, even our best global education programs come across as a bit tired, like a past-her-prime beauty queen parading around in a sequined "global" banner.

Global this. Global that. What we need is a shot of global *authenticity*.

These "global" cosmetic enhancements fail to recognize the need for *actual va-va-voom experience* over résumé padding. Classes in math and Mandarin *alone* will not guarantee that our young people will be ready for a more multidimensional working environment, and painting them into a corner isn't going to help them develop the talents that will enable them to flourish in the ways they find most satisfying. The math-and-Mandarin approach—one that emphasizes particular subjects of study as the key to creating a more global student (not to mention a more robust economy)—is a superficial strategy for addressing a very complex challenge.

Let's see—as parents, do we tackle reform . . . or play with revolution? In this book we'll be choosing Door Number Two and looking into the heart of the matter—the need to help our kids develop an ambidextrous gift for mental gear shifting and a border-blind global perspective by ***spending time abroad in meaningful ways***.

What's meaningful? Well, that's for each student to decide, and just to get some ideas popping, we'll hear stories from those who are discovering their own sense of meaning. Let's kick things off by listening to how Ryan Hastreiter is doing it.

BOLD STATEMENT

I was sixteen when my life of traveling started. My parents did not believe I was truly interested in going to another country for a year, and to be honest, I had my doubts about the level of my commitment too. We were concerned about how it would affect my college plans and didn't really know how things would work out when I returned as a senior. The funny thing is that I see this recurring pattern that the decisions I doubt are the ones that take me to where I want to go.

I was selected as one of fifty students in the state to receive a scholarship to study abroad in my choice of location: Taiwan. I was dropped head-first into a school of

(*continued*)

nine thousand boys jabbering away in a language I did not understand in a climate of the most intense heat and humidity I had ever experienced. At that point I definitely thought I had made the wrong call. However, a year and a half after that original conversation with my parents, armed with my proficiency in one of the most difficult languages to master (Mandarin Chinese), I arrived back in the United States.

During my senior year of high school I attended courses at a nearby community college at no cost, thanks to a dual enrollment program. I aimed my credits toward a business major—I figured that business and Chinese would be a strategic combination. Thanks to those credits, I entered the University of Oregon with junior standing, two years ahead of my classmates. During my first year and summer of college, I worked for a Taiwanese electronics firm. The opportunity was amazing—great pay and perks (free dinners, flights, hotels) and travel to exciting places. I had the chance to put my university coursework and Mandarin skills to use in the United States, Taiwan, and Hong Kong. The one thing I missed while working in Asia was being outside—mainly, to go whitewater kayaking, a passion I had developed while attending U of O.

Once again I felt doubt, this time about choosing to stop working for the company in Taiwan. It seemed so perfectly suited to my major and my skills, but it wasn't for me, so I went against conventional wisdom and went to work as a marketing intern for a water-sports retailer in Colorado. The next two summers could not have been better. I was playing—as well as working—outdoors and getting paid good money for doing exactly what I wanted to do.

My kayaking skills developed to the point that I was

invited to help a Gear-for-Good donation campaign on the White Nile River in Uganda, Africa, while kayaking some of the wildest whitewater in the world. When I arrived at the river and scouted the first Class V rapids, I had that recurring doubt and thought, "Boy, this was a bad decision." But riding the insane whitewater, meeting the friendly Ugandan people, and sharing the adventure with a handful of the world's top kayakers (and truly outstanding individuals) were absolutely peak experiences for me. After I returned to the United States, I was offered a position in product development at Nike, then got promoted to the global retail projects division. I'm having a great time and discovering new ways to blend my interest in business and Chinese with my passion for outdoor recreation.

Between my seventeenth birthday in greater China and my twenty-second birthday in Uganda, I developed skills that can be gained only from spending significant (and intense!) periods of time connecting with people in other countries. I'm grateful to have learned Mandarin, but I also know that in the long run it's best to be flexible and open to the most interesting opportunities that come my way. When I feel doubt, I will know to head in that direction. College was great conceptually, but practically my global campus taught me the most.

Is Ryan still grinning at Nike, or is he kayaking the Great Bend of the Yangtze River in China—or both? Find out by reading the updates on the students profiled in this book at www.NewGlobal Student.com.

Being good at something shouldn't be the only reason to choose it as a career, and chasing an idea about becoming "globally competitive" might mean losing out on the most gratifying life experiences. There's a lot of global blah-blah out there, but we're going to sink our teeth into what matters most: a definition of "global" that goes beyond politics or profits.

❏ **Smart Move**: Parents and students need to embrace a definition of "global" that encompasses the notion of becoming *knowledgeable of, connected to, and passionately engaged in a world without borders.*

Let's run with that.

> **Old School:** seeing "global" as a brand of profitable ventures
>
> **Bold School:** seeing "global" as an invitation to connect

BACKING AWAY FROM THE EVERYBODY'S-DOING-IT CLIFF

> Collective fear stimulates herd instinct.
> BERTRAND RUSSELL

Know any juniors in high school? Take a close look. Most of these students and their parents are gearing up for the ooh-pick-me college admissions contest.

They're signing up for SAT-prep courses. Going to college fairs. Hiring tutors. Scouring books for tips on writing that sure-thing entrance essay. Some are even paying consultants to create the ideal student package.

Everyone is doing the *same* things and trying to get into the *same* schools. Students are putting together lists of accomplishments that are nearly identical. GPA. AP courses. SAT scores. Academic honors. Sports. Clubs. Community activities.

Yawn.

When you were a kid and you wanted to ask your parents for permission to do something you knew they weren't going to be too thrilled about, you probably pulled out the ol' "But all the *other* kids are doing it!" line.

And how'd that work for you?

Chances are, your mom or dad responded with lightning-quick parental reflexes in the form of this retort: "If all the other kids were jumping off a cliff, would *you* do it too?"

Now we find ourselves in an interesting position as parents who are encouraging their kids to *do the same things as everyone else.* We know this isn't such a brilliant move. If we slow down for just a minute, we'll realize that this is, in fact, a rather ill-advised strategy.

If you were vying for a coveted position in your field, would you set out to make sure you were doing *exactly the same things* as the other candidates for the job? Would you focus on holding the *same* offices, heading up the *same* committees, performing equally on the *same* skill tests, and getting recommendations from the *same* managers as your rivals?

No, you wouldn't. Because if you really wanted to get the attention of the committee looking for that prime candidate for the job, you'd make sure to *stand out* among the applicants. You'd shine your high beams on what makes you uniquely qualified for the position so that those interviewers would take one look at your résumé and say, "Wow! Now, *this* one is interesting!"

And yet when it comes to our kids, we give them a very narrow range of motion. They are jammed into the "perfect college candidate" locker and told that they must be better than their peers by somehow surpassing them in all the same categories.

Now, there's nothing inherently wrong with competition. It's what keeps us pushing, learning, and achieving when we'd rather take a nap. But there's a difference between *creative* competition and *mindless* competition. All too often we throw our kids into the academic ring and tell them to just keep punching (and getting hit) instead of showing them how one left hook can end the whole thing early without all that blood and bruising. Without a clear strategy we squander time and energy. School becomes a dull march instead of a creative cha-cha toward—and beyond—that high school diploma.

No wonder a quarter of all U.S. ninth graders aren't graduating with their high school classmates.[3] It's not necessarily that the courses are too hard—it's that the *future* looks too hard. When students are told that they will need at least some postsecondary education in order to be successful in life, they start to see a difficult struggle ahead. To those who are already falling behind in the ninth grade, that road to success looks impossibly long and arduous—the process is intimidating, the odds against succeeding overwhelming, the costs astronomical, and the actual learning completely irrelevant to their lives and interests.

We lose the students who sink like stones within the system—and that is tragic—but we also lose the students who dog-paddle without ever discovering and exploring their own talents and interests. There's too much emphasis on making our kids reasonably good at everything when they would be better served if we helped them *maximize their gifts* while soft-pedaling their shortcomings. Our current system tosses kids of all abilities together in the same learning cycle, and we end up with thousands of students immersed in a head-thumping agitation process that washes the curiosity, creativity, and individuality right out of them.

A critical part of raising kids is making sure to raise them *up*. Rigor can be useful, but only if we employ it as a way to elevate rather than denigrate. We need to resist getting locked into the standardized variety of rigor and choose instead to promote high expectations for each individual and an enthusiasm for learning that sparks both industriousness and imagination. Efficiency? Oh, I'm a fan. But just because one way seems to produce acceptable results doesn't mean another way won't blow your socks off.

When it comes to education, insisting on one path to a high school diploma/college degree/career thrashes the intrinsic thrill of learning right out of those who might dance happily (and diligently) along another trail that suits them better. We can't afford to lose *any* students, so let's skip the thrashing and take a gander at that beautiful rainbow of choices arcing over the horizon.

No other country in the world offers so many outstanding education options to its citizens, but instead of raising a toast to our vast array of choices, we waste way too much time arguing about which one is best. Old-school thinking drags us down at a time when we must use our formidable frontal lobes for a higher purpose; wearing blinders as we desperately race alongside others is *so* last season.

❏ **Smart Move**: Parents who are passionate about learning rather than pigheaded about the "right way" to get an education are far more likely to help their kids find their very best options for intellectual and personal development.

Let's stop drawing lines in the sand and start celebrating our right to choose what will inspire and ignite each student. Get ready to leave the mindless competition behind and start exploring a world of exciting learning adventures.

Old School: mindlessly competing against others by doing the same things
Bold School: mindfully doing things differently in order to maximize our greatest gifts

SHIFTING FROM "WHAT" TO "HOW"

> Happiness belongs to the self-sufficient.
> ARISTOTLE

You've heard the adage "It's not what you know, it's *who* you know."

Well, in our flattish and Googley world, it's no longer either of those things.[4] After all, nearly everyone with an Internet connection has access to the same content, and thanks to social networking sites and the ease of contacting others with shared interests or with opportunities to offer, we're no longer reliant upon the old-boy network or our alma mater ties to get a foot in the door.

Where you went to college used to matter more when you couldn't figure out how to get an interview at a given firm or organization and had to depend upon an introduction from someone or from an elite college name on your diploma. Now we are just a few online contacts away from reaching those who can elevate us, and job candidates who are bold and innovative are more likely to be snatched up than those who happen to be so-and-so's nephew or a fellow Preppy U alum. The playing field has leveled significantly with a few particularly spiky points of interest.[5] (You'll learn about them in Chapter Five.) Family ties and political pull matter only in an opaque world, and (thankfully) there is a trend toward more transparency and a shift from achievement that is bestowed (or bought) to that which is authentic and earned. This is cause for major high fives—unless, of course, you were counting on your cronies to help your kids get ahead.

The truth is that you don't want your kids to be looking to you to hand them a business card or make a phone call on their behalf. It's far more important—in both the short and the long term—to help them learn how to follow a thread and yank it when the time is right. There's no magic to it; it's an entirely learnable skill.

What a relief.

When we parents talk about global education, we're squinting our eyes and looking toward our kids' future employment, independence, and fulfillment. Yes, we want them to develop appreciation and knowledge of the planet and its people, but we're hoping this will enable them to do more than sing "We Are the World" while living in our basement. Our primo parental up-and-out strategy should be to help our kids understand their talents and to teach them how to generate ideas, research the heck out of 'em, and follow through in order to find great opportunities.

❑ **Smart Move**: Instead of *what* you know and *who* you know, stepping up in the 21st century will be more about *how* you know what you know and *where* you are willing and able to use it.

Who will rise above the rest? Those who:

- ❱ flex their learning muscles in new ways
- ❱ know how to apply their knowledge wherever they go
- ❱ don't need anyone to open the door for them

> **Old School:** counting on others to help you step ahead
> **Bold School:** relying on your own creativity to skip forward

RATE THE GLOBAL JOB CANDIDATES

> Flaming enthusiasm, backed up by horse sense and persistence, is the quality that most frequently makes for success.
>
> DALE CARNEGIE

Most parents believe that foreign language classes in high school and college will make their kids appealing as candidates for the global jobs of the future. But although language classes are necessary (and should be required in the earliest grades), they alone will not prepare students for jobs that require foreign language skills. The workplaces our students will be entering are more likely to need individuals who have learned their language skills in *experiential* ways (not just in the classroom). Not only that, but employers want to hire people who can serve as company (and country) ambassadors abroad, not just those who are able to translate e-mails or speak on the phone to clients from other nations.

If we want to help our students get ready for their future opportunities, we need to focus on the *how* and the *where*: *how* are they learning their language skills, and *where* are they able to use them? In addition, we must ask what *qualities* our students need to ensure that they will land those globalinguistic jobs and glitter wherever they go.

Nearly every travel experience can enrich us in some way, but not all time spent abroad is equal in terms of how it affects and advances us. Living independently as a local in one foreign country for three months trumps three short-term group trips to different destinations every time—and it's better for the planet too. A two-week house-building trip to Mexico, a three-week rain forest expedition in Costa Rica, a month-long painting workshop in Italy, or a six-week tour of temples in Japan can be an incredible experience, but it won't pack the same punch in terms of personal transformation or impress an employer who is looking for **fluency** in a language and **experience** living abroad.

❏ **Smart Move**: Bold schoolers understand that what matters most is not the number of plane tickets purchased or the number of countries on that destination list but the *depth* and *length* of those experiences abroad.

We can illustrate this point by playing the "Rate the Global Job Candidates" game. Imagine that you work for a company that is developing a department focusing on trade with Germany. Your firm is planning to open a small satellite office there, and your job is to hire someone to fill a local position with potential for rapid advancement and the opportunity to play a key role in the new branch in Germany. You need a presentable, hardworking individual who can speak German and is willing to be trained for a position requiring project management and a transfer to Germany within a year. After receiving a veritable flood of résumés, you select the top three candidates to interview. All of them are recent college graduates.

Let's have a look:

JACK

During middle school Jack spent a month in Spain with his family, and right after his high school graduation he traveled to London with friends for two weeks. He went to a prestigious university two states away where he majored in business and minored in German, was a member of a fraternity, spent a semester abroad in Germany with a group from his college, and went on a weeklong trip to China for a business symposium. He had a summer job at an office supply retailer and an internship with an accounting firm in his hometown. After graduating from college, he spent a month in Mexico with friends.

WILSON

After graduating from a private international high school (emphasis on French and German), Wilson spent a month in Germany with his classmates and a month in Italy with his family. He attended a university in Quebec, perfecting his French and continuing to study German, and earned a degree in international affairs. As president of his university's International Club, he went with several members on a two-week trip through France and Belgium and spent two weeks in Germany during spring break of his senior year. Wilson spent two summers working in his father's construction business and just completed a summer internship with a company that imports marble from Italy.

(*continued*)

KATIE

As a high school exchange student, Katie spent a year in Germany. She lived with German families, attended a German high school, and became fluent in German. While she was there, she traveled extensively throughout the country and went on a month-long coordinated trip through five European nations with exchange students from around the world. After returning to the United States, she finished high school while taking additional courses at a community college and spent a summer volunteering in Guatemala. Katie enrolled at a state university and earned her degree in three years with a double major in German and economics and a minor in Italian. She spent one summer working as a camp counselor at a local German-language immersion camp for kids and another summer in London as a nanny for the children of a German financial executive. Katie spent her second (middle) year of college taking courses in German politics and media at a German university while working for an environmental nonprofit organization. She lived in an apartment with two Turkish roommates and spent six weeks traveling on her own to reconnect with friends in Austria, Italy, the Czech Republic, and Greece. During her final year of college she worked as an intern for the German consulate. Katie is currently employed at a large publishing company, where she translates business articles from German to English.

Hmm. What do you think?

Assuming that all three candidate's interview well, which one stands out as the individual who:

❑ has the **most relevant skills**?
❑ could be **trusted to do an important presentation in German**?

❏ would best **represent your company while coordinating interviews and hiring new staff members abroad?**

❏ is **most likely to make contacts** that would enhance your company's success there?

❏ is most passionate about spending time in Germany and is therefore **most likely to be a good long-term investment for your firm?**

I'm betting my euros on Katie. Here's why:

1. **She is fluent.** Katie has shown that she has excellent speaking and writing skills in German.

2. **She is comfortable living in Germany.** Katie spent a total of two years there (one in high school, one in college), so we know that she can handle tasks such as getting a phone, finding an apartment, paying bills, and making travel arrangements— skills necessary for anyone moving abroad.

3. **She is interested in other cultures and has contacts in other countries.** This indicates that she would be helpful in a setting that may eventually include employees from various places.

4. **She has shown a desire to learn more than just the language.** Katie worked for a nonprofit, studied both German politics and media in addition to the language, and had to pay close attention to the business articles she was translating. This knowledge will be beneficial in establishing the company's presence abroad.

5. **She is independent and innovative.** She did not depend on the reputation of her university to give her credibility, nor did she assume that a study-abroad program through her college would be her best bet for language learning. She figured out her own ways to connect with others and to make money in other countries.

6. **She is confident traveling by herself.** She can find her way

in unfamiliar places and could represent your company in various settings.

7. **She inspires trust.** She was hired by a German executive to be responsible for his children in another country and was trusted to correctly translate articles for publication.

8. **She has been employed in a variety of settings,** including working with children in the United States and abroad, assisting immigrants and officials at the consulate, teaming up with German colleagues at a nonprofit, and translating in a busy office.

9. **She is consistently enthusiastic about Germany and the German language.** Katie has chosen jobs that allow her to deepen her skills in German while developing her ability to connect with different kinds of people. Reading her résumé, you get a sense that she would really love the opportunity to transfer to Germany and spend a significant amount of time there. And make no mistake: employers want to hire those who are passionate and excited about working for them.

You may think that Katie sounds too good to be true, but I assure you that both she and her résumé are real. (You'll be meeting more of her global-ready peers in the chapters ahead.)

It's critical for both parents and students to recognize that studying a foreign language, enrolling in an international high school, or signing up for a group semester abroad in college is *not enough* to get the nod from employers seeking talented candidates who are ready to hit the (foreign) ground running.

❑ **Smart Move**: Students need to focus on gaining hip-deep experience and cultivating big-grin enthusiasm. These qualities are far more valuable than a résumé laden with the same old bullet points bearing a "global" or "international" label.

We don't need a conference or a crystal ball to tell us what to expect in the next decade or two. Frankly, we need individuals who know how to *transcend* the traditional college experience, standard study-abroad program, and local-employees-only work-place. You won't find them napping in dull classes, trudging along during group tours, or twiddling their thumbs at boring desk jobs; they're out there beating bushes, looking under rocks, and dis-covering all kinds of thrilling ways to learn, travel, and work. While their peers are passing out more résumés, these young globals are juggling tantalizing offers and picking the ones with the greatest potential for *pow*.

How can we help our students go from bland to bold? Dump the emphasis on accumulating colorless accomplishments, and encourage the propagation of brilliant skills and exuberant initiative.

It's time to look at the **FACTS.** That's my handy-dandy mnemonic device to help you remember the **five key qualities** that will guarantee that students will be successful in whatever they choose to do in the wild and woolly world of global work. In addi-tion to being able to read, write, speak, calculate, and analyze pro-ficiently, bold future leaders share the following characteristics:

F IS FOR FLEXIBLE

- They **adapt quickly to their surroundings** and make new friends easily wherever they go.
- They **speak more than one language fluently**.
- They are **free—and eager—to travel or live abroad** and are not hampered by massive college debt, a lack of con-fidence, or insistence upon a particular lifestyle.
- They **think independently** and are not attached to a cer-tain "right way" of doing anything.

A IS FOR AWARE

- They read and **can discuss—intelligently—a wide vari-ety of subjects** ranging from economics to e-learning.
- They've lived abroad, **see their own culture with**

(continued)

greater clarity, and can represent their country in a respectful way.

- They've seen firsthand the inequities of the world and **show compassion and respect** for those who are struggling.
- They understand the need to focus on sustainable ways of living, and they **incorporate environmental awareness** in everything they do.

C IS FOR CURIOUS

- They **have a natural interest in a variety of topics** and enjoy learning on their own.
- They **know how to ask questions** in order to gain knowledge and create stronger connections with others.
- They don't wait for opportunities to appear—they **are actively engaged in research** in order to discover their best options for learning, travel, and work.
- They **know how to use a variety of tools** to both create and distribute information, and they continue to learn as new systems and gadgets are developed.

T IS FOR TRUSTWORTHY

- They know that in a global economy there are thousands of people who are willing and able to complete any given task, and they **recognize the increased importance of being dependable** in order to gain trust and greater opportunities.
- They **know how to collaborate with others** and can create a sense of community without the benefit of face-to-face meetings.
- They **hone their professional writing and speaking skills** and can convince others of their integrity and commitment remotely.

- They **complete their work on time** and to the best of their ability, and they stand by their work without making excuses.

S IS FOR SELF-DIRECTED

- They are extremely **good at establishing and moving toward their goals.**
- Their **work ethic and motivation are internalized**—they don't count on competition from their colleague in the next cubicle or sit-down sessions with the management to light a fire under their seats.
- They **can focus on the task at hand** whether they are in a work environment that is solitary and silent, social and distracting, or chaotic and stressful.
- They **have an abiding passion for what they are doing,** tremendous energy and enthusiasm, and a clear desire to improve their skills while doing their best work.

By now, you might be thinking, "Oh, crap. How is my kid *ever* going to get a job? He can't even get to school on time, and you're saying he's got to have these superhuman qualities in order to be successful at anything in the future!"

No worries. You see, *all* of the qualities I listed—

Flexibility
Awareness
Curiosity
Trustworthiness, and
Self-direction

will be developed naturally if you give your student a chance to step out into the world in *one very specific way*. I'll show you how.

But first, a little wake-up call.

Old School: going global by taking language classes or enrolling in an international school
Bold School: going global by gaining worthy experience abroad and generating visionary enthusiasm

GAME OVER: THE NEW WAY TO PLAY

> By the time the fool has learned the game, the players have dispersed.
> AFRICAN PROVERB

Two things about the American mindset are getting in the way of allowing our kids to lift off to new levels of learning that will ultimately allow them to change the world:

1. We are extremely competitive.
2. We tend to rest on our laurels once we reach the top.

Being competitive might *seem* like an advantage, but the problem is that we're not always selective about the areas in which we choose to compete, and we have a tendency to avoid collaboration if we have a chance to win. We can't help it—we've simply absorbed our culture's prevailing message. From the time we are very young, we are encouraged, guided, coached, taught, and trained to succeed by becoming better than others. We eat competition for breakfast ("Wheaties—The Breakfast of Champions!"), and "We Are the Champions" is the cultural theme song we just can't get out of our heads. And so we compete in everything we do.

It's fine to want our kids to be successful, but for their sake (and the sake of others around the world), we need to be far more **selective and intentional** about where we focus our own energy in the name of helping them fulfill their greatest potential.

It may seem odd that a competitive culture like ours would let things slide, but coupled with our cherished right to compete is a marked tendency to slip into complacency once we've reached the top. Consequently we've just lost the world's biggest game of "Red Light, Green Light" by taking too long to turn around and notice that those who were way behind us are now close enough to whisper in our ear.

There's no question that the United States is losing its edge in terms of educating its students for the global economy, and we cling to our denial of this fact at our own peril. Most Americans still believe we have the best undergrad education in the world, but even if this is true, it's small consolation for the fact that our college graduation rate slipped from first place in the world to fifteenth in only ten years.[6] And despite admirable efforts to alert the public to the need for thoughtful analysis of our approach to education—Bob Compton's must-see documentary *Two Million Minutes* has stirred up some spirited dialogue on this subject—the U.S. population in general seems unfazed by the fact that our country has slipped to the bottom of the pack of industrialized nations on international tests in math and science.[7]

We can't sit smugly on our at-least-we're-more-creative cushion either; U.S. student teams are consistently surpassed by those from other countries in the most prestigious innovation contests in the world, including the Imagine Cup, a Microsoft-sponsored competition among more than 100,000 students in one hundred–plus countries to explore new ways to address some of the world's toughest problems. (In the 2007 competition the United States didn't make it into the top three in *any* of the nine categories, losing out to innovators from Romania, Jamaica, Poland, Hungary, and Serbia, among others.)[8]

Some insist that Americans are just naturally more confident and so we'll always come out ahead. It's easy to feel like a winner within your comfort zone, but the point is that our kids, at some point, will be pushed *out* of theirs. If they've never been challenged in a different setting, how can they hold steady when things heat up?

Here's a test: throw a group of better-than-average college students from a dozen non-English-speaking countries (plus our champ from the United States) into a room, tell them to talk about world events, and see who is more informed, thoughtful, interesting, and respected by the others. It would be foolish to assume that our American ace will lead the pack—even though he's the only one speaking in his native language.

❑ **Smart Move**: Parents who shift their focus from athletics to academics and arts will do a much better job of preparing their kids for the global future.

Our students cannot skate through life in the global economy based solely upon their American charm (or passport), and though parents say we want what's best for our kids, we're far more likely to drive them to sports practices than to after-school math and science activities, arts programs, language classes, or events designed to give them a greater understanding of the world. Parents need to question where they're headed while driving that carpool and to become clear and consistent about making relevant learning a priority.

In addition, it's time for a new response to the growing competition from others. Rather than wrapping ourselves in denial or in red, white, and blue, we've got to become both **realistic and collaborative.** China and India collectively graduate *twelve times* more engineers than does the United States.[9] No matter how much our government or private industry might invest to steer kids toward math and science as careers, we simply cannot overtake these two countries in terms of numbers. Obviously this doesn't mean we should throw our hands in the air and avoid math and science altogether. Quite the opposite—it's critical that we find daring and downright sexy ways to inspire our students' best efforts in these areas. But concentrating on beating the Indian and Chinese students at their own game begins to look preposterous once we recognize that we're not even in the same ballpark.

Oh, sorry. I promised we weren't going to wring our hands. Ready to high-five?

Consider this: we've got a golden opportunity to *take advantage* of the way the tide is turning. Instead of getting all hangdog or harried about the future, we should be rejoicing (and strategizing) about the incredible circumstances that will enable students around the world to innovate and cooperate in unprecedented ways. Just as we want our kids to use their most tangible talents, our country can regain status and strength by exercising its most excellent traits. Historically, the United States has shown quite a flair for opportunism. Now is our chance to nudge it in a globally positive direction that benefits everyone.

No long faces allowed: we're completely capable of becoming global heroes rather than faded international champs. *Really.* It all depends on how we choose to respond to the challenges facing the world in the next few years.

China graduates more honors students each year than the United States graduates *students.*[10]

How do we react to this information? We can:

- waste time arguing about the numbers
- declare it a race to the finish and maniacally attempt to churn out more Mandarin-speaking mathematicians than China
- wave the American confidence flag and sing the praises of being popular and well rounded (as opposed to being skilled)

Or we can:

- **recognize that we have an extraordinary and vital role to play and start brainstorming (and smiling) about our possibilities.**

We get to choose.

There's a new way to play the global game, and we need to toss out the old cutthroat rules and learn the everyone-wins version. Our best strategy in the years ahead is to absorb and accept the world news and to see it as a catalyst for creativity. We all want our children to be excited about what they are learning, fully engaged in their good work, and fulfilled by their contributions to society. This does not require trouncing everybody else. It does, however, require parents to recognize the essential role we must play.

What exactly *is* our role? Our job is not to maintain our country's (dubious) dominance or even to ensure that our students have careers that are highly prized in the future. (They are likely to have jobs that have *not been invented yet*.) Let's get clever about helping our kids develop the essential skills and qualities they will need to live happily while collaborating with other members of the world community.

Do we need to get political about education? Absolutely. We have to work to ensure that all students have equal access to the education they need—regardless of race, location, or economic status—and we must define what is most important for our kids and find the best ways to teach them. It's time to rally around our most inventive and impassioned teachers and give them room to mentor others. But when all is said and done, your job as a parent is to get *personal*, not political.

Bottom line: Work for change, but please, oh please, *do not wait for it.*

I'm an optimist. I firmly believe that our education system will be radically improved eventually, but we simply can't turn this Big School bus on a dime. And so while that bus is doing a few three-corner maneuvers, it's our responsibility as parents and mentors to *make sure that our children or charges do not miss out* on their best opportunities to get a truly international education.

Our ed revolution can't wait for the lumbering pace of legislation—we need to kick it into high gear *now* and pursue it through both personal boldness and community barn raising. Read the news and then remember this: the world needs individuals who are skilled, innovative, energized, and compassionate. It's time to help our students realize their potential as valued and valuable global citizens no matter where they choose to live.

Let's play.

Old School: letting our we're-number-one mindset distract and disconnect us

Bold School: cheering for the global good by focusing on innovation and cooperation

FROM FRANTIC TO FEARLESS

CHAPTER THREE

Fego

YOU'RE SOAKING IN IT!

THE *ONE THING* PREVENTING STUDENTS FROM CATAPULTING FORWARD

> Being slightly paranoid is like being slightly pregnant—it tends to get worse.
> MOLLY IVINS

Okay, parents, listen up! It's time for a pop quiz.

I'm going to write one question on the board, and I'd like you to carefully consider your answer. Ready?

What's the *one thing* preventing your student from catapulting forward? Please take a moment to think about it.

(Cue *Jeopardy* music.)

Time's up. Let's see what some of you have come up with as an answer to this question. What's the *one thing* preventing your student from catapulting forward? Anyone?

Laziness!

Lack of focus!

Uninspired teachers!

51

Too many tests!
Too much stress!
Too many classes!
Not enough time!
Not enough money!
No sense of purpose!
No idea what they are interested in!
Fear!

Ding! Ding! Ding! The *one thing* preventing your student from catapulting forward is **fear.** Not his or hers—**yours.**

We've got a veritable royal flush of fears, and we're not very good about laying our cards on the table. In fact, according to Dr. Paul J. Donahue, author of *Parenting Without Fear: Letting Go of Worry and Focusing on What Really Matters,* there are *six* common fears faced by parents. Though he concentrates on the worries we have when our children are young, it's not too surprising to learn that those same fears keep us awake at night when our kids hit high school.

How are we fearful? Let us count the ways:

1. fear of letting go
2. fear of not doing enough
3. fear of taking charge
4. fear of slowing down
5. fear of unstructured time
6. fear of falling behind

As Dr. Donahue reminds us, "It's worth thinking about what our mission statement is as parents. Is it to create super athletes and students who achieve and get into fabulous colleges, or are we trying to help our kids learn to think and be independent and care about people?"

Good question.

Our fears feed upon themselves, and they are stirred up whenever we are surrounded by others who are fearful. "Parents and their teens applying to college can feel like they are in a fish bowl with their every move under scrutiny by the other kids and their families," Dr. Donahue told me. "They're hearing, 'Are you going to apply early?' 'Don't you love XX U?' 'What are your/your kid's SAT scores?' In that setting it takes a lot of courage for parents to not get caught up in all of it and to set an example for their kids."

When we're feeling afraid, we tend to look for active ways to ease our fears instead of simply changing our response to them. Getting our kids signed up for a new activity to flesh out their college applications feels more proactive than sitting down to talk to them about developing a healthy perspective. We need to model appropriate responses ourselves if we want our kids to relax.

At the same time parents may be legitimately worried about a student who is falling behind, or they may believe that they themselves are not doing enough to help. One of the hardest things for parents to recognize is that it's their responsibility to teach their *kids* how to take responsibility. As Dr. Donahue puts it, "There's nothing wrong with teaching kids to work hard and be ambitious, but by this age, that should be more internalized and kids should be chasing their own goals, not their parents'."

Letting go. Falling behind. Not doing enough. Unstructured time. Slowing down. Taking charge.

Which one is *your* favorite fear? If you're like most parents, you've got your own fear stew on the stove, and depending on the day (or the hour), it's likely to take on a particular flavor to reflect whatever's going on around you.

It helps to get familiar with the fears so that you can recognize them easily. In fact, simply seeing each fear with a neon label on it can really put things in perspective. Do you know your fears? Study your hand and prepare to slap down the appropriate card:

- Your daughter announces that she no longer wishes to participate in an activity to which she has devoted hours each week for the last few years. *Fear of unstructured time!*
- You overhear that your son's friend—a junior with a 4.0 GPA—has signed up for tutoring to help him improve his SAT score. You interrupt to get the name and number of the tutor. *Fear of falling behind!*
- Your daughter has been losing interest in her studies and her grades are slipping, but you're hesitant to talk to her about it because you don't want to seem like a nag. *Fear of taking charge!*
- Your son has decided that he wants to go to college on the other side of the country, and you're saying he should stick closer to home. *Fear of letting go!*
- You have been so worried about your daughter's chances for an athletic scholarship that you're exhausting yourself, her, and the rest of the family with an accelerated schedule of practices, camps, and trainings. *Fear of slowing down!*
- Your son is a voracious reader and has become a very articulate and thoughtful conversationalist. You keep telling him to join the debate team, get involved in student government, or do something that will help him look good when he's applying to colleges, but he refuses to get involved in any school activities and chooses instead to write a blog and post his opinions on various sites online. *Fear of not doing enough!*

Every day we are bombarded by news and cues that trigger these fears. We're being dealt every fear card on a daily basis. This fear is bad enough, but another sneaky little element is also gumming things up.

It's **ego.**

Oh, I know. Isn't it funny how we hate to be reminded that we have one of those? Well, it's true. Accept it. Now let's learn how ego affects the ways in which we cook up either calm support or crazed action.

How does ego fuel fear? Well, picture fear as this great big lightning bolt that comes along and zaps you right when you were minding your own business, just wrapped up in your own thoughts. Now, imagine ego as the serene outdoor soaking tub in which you have chosen to immerse yourself while thinking.

The fear alone is enough to make your eyes pop out, but ego makes the whole scene ever-so-much-more dramatic.

Fear. Ego. Let's call it *fego*. It's quite an electrifying combo. Fego is the driving force behind the multibillion-dollar college-prep industry. It's what motivates us to get our kids to take the PSAT as an eighth grader or to sign up our students for SAT-prep courses as freshmen. Fego makes our stomach churn when we hear about the neighbor kid getting into Princeton. It breathes down our neck when we're looking at summer camp or college websites.

When we let fego loose with a credit card, we end up with stacks of college-rankings magazines, vocabulary-boosting software, and essay-writing guides. We feverishly sign up our kids for three-week "service experiences" abroad that cost $6,000 and for anything else that will help us feel that we are being good parents by giving our kids their best chance to get ahead.

Yikes.

Most parents can accept the fact that they are afraid. Many will concede that they enjoy a good soak in the ego tub from time to time. But the hardest thing to admit is that we are terrified that we might be a *bad parent*. That's the big umbrella under which all the lesser fears take cover, and nobody wants to walk around with that dark canopy over their head.

Love—or fego? We get to choose the juice that runs our parenting machine. Love greases the gears, while fego flips the autopilot switch: we dive in and do something—*anything*—to avoid being seen as the slacker on the block. And whenever we pop into doing-anything mode, we're leaving our best intentions far behind and letting fear carry us—and our kids—forward.

Fego swallows common sense and lets out a big belch. When fear and ego converge, we become even more frantic to follow the path that everyone else is following. "They're all headed *that* direction! It must be the right one! We'd better hurry up and head down that path too! In fact, it looks like we're already late! *Run!*"

It's time to take a deep breath and *slow down*.

We're so manic about singing the more-is-better chorus that we're not taking the time to listen to the rest of the words. More of *what*, exactly?

We know in our hearts (and in our best moments, in our heads) that SAT scores and grades are not going to define our students' lives, but parents are wired for worry. Whether it's about test scores, crime stats, or health risks, worry runs like a current through our bodies, just waiting for that jolt of fego to fry our sensibilities.

Our fear—and more specifically, our fear-based behavior—is affecting our kids whether we recognize it or not.

We've all heard about "helicopter parents" and know those who hover over their children in an effort to shield them from the ickiness of life. And while this kind of protection can certainly create tentativeness, emotional immaturity, or rebellion in kids who never experience the bumps and bruises of growing up, it seems like a relative misdemeanor among parental crimes. But the problem is that **we are losing our ability to recognize the difference between:**

▸ *reasonable* concern

and

▸ *a hot-house parenting style* that severely limits our kids' confidence and ability to navigate in an uncertain world.

Hara Estroff Marano has been the editor-at-large for *Psychology Today* for seventeen years. She's seen her fair share of parenting trends and repercussions, but she's particularly concerned about the troubling shift toward overprotection. In her book *A Nation of Wimps: The High Cost of Invasive Parenting,* she presents a very convincing case that parental overinvolvement is crippling children psychologically and resulting in an alarming increase in mental issues in college students and twentysomethings out on their own for the first time. She suggests that this overprotection is taking its toll on parents and the future of our country too. Marano told me, "Swaddling our kids in bubble wrap prevents them from experiencing difficulties and developing the ability to adapt in unpredictable circumstances. In making life easier for their kids in the short term, parents are making it harder for them in the long term. In addition, they are depriving their children of meaning and a shot at deep satisfaction."

Children need to learn about real threats to their health and safety, but sometimes parents instill a deeper fear of the world through their comments and actions. Clay Collins grew up in an idyllic environment but absorbed his parents' belief that he was no match for the forces that intended to harm him. Only by defying the rules was he able to discover that he was capable of being out in the world on his own. He shares his story here.

BOLD STATEMENT

I was raised—along with 600,000 citrus trees—on my grandparents' nursery in rural Southern California. My mom yanked me from the school system because I had a learning disability called dysgraphia. I was failing most spelling tests while winning schoolwide spelling bees, and I was constantly scolded for "not trying hard enough" and "being lazy."

I learned many good things through my homeschooling experience:

(continued)

- Education can happen outside the bounds of a classroom.
- Artificial barriers do not need to be placed between socalled "learning environments" (school) and "living environments" (home).
- The value of a question is often greater than its answer.
- It is utterly miraculous that I can purchase the life's work of a great philosopher for under two dollars at a used-book store.

But growing up, I also learned about fear. My parents, as loving as they were, displayed a concern for safety that suggested the world was a very dangerous place. When I was young, my father would go downstairs a few times each night to check the house for potential threats to life and limb: fire hazards, gas leaks, and unlocked doors. Because of my parents' concerns, I rarely hosted or visited friends, and I was only occasionally allowed to walk around my decidedly safe neighborhood after sunset because I "could get shot for giving someone the wrong look."

When I was fifteen, I sneaked out of the house one night at two A.M. and just started walking; I felt compelled to do this. Four hours later a police officer picked me up and drove me home. I had walked through truly unsafe neighborhoods in a bordering city and had given people what I assumed was the "wrong look," but I wasn't shot at or kidnapped. I needed to prove to myself that the world was not always scary and that I could be safe while exploring it.

I tested out of high school a few months later and moved two hours away from my parents' home to cofound a software company. It was my first big step in learning to pull away from environments in which I didn't completely thrive in order to pursue situations where I could play to my strengths. In the three years following this move, I tore down so many of the fears I'd developed while growing up: fear of camping alone, fear of bicycling on crowded streets, and most important, fear of people of other races, sexual orientations, and religions. It was so liberating to debunk my fears, to see reality a bit more clearly, and to let my world grow just a little bigger.

My world grew by leaps and bounds several years later in 2004 when I spent several months in Ghana. I'd received a fellowship from the University of Minnesota's Human Rights Center to continue my graduate studies. This trip would make me the first person in my family to leave the United States since my parents spent four hours in Mexico more than twenty-five years ago. (It was their first and only venture out of the country despite living two hours away from the Mexican border.) My parents and grandparents always told me that "a book can take you anywhere you want to go," but I longed to see things for myself. Despite worrying that my parents would have trouble sleeping every night if I left for Africa, I checked my own fear and headed for Ghana.

During my stay I worked on a draft copy of a petition to the UN Commission on Human Rights. I also ate food from street vendors, swam in the Atlantic, danced outdoors with Ghanaians under night skies, and drank homemade gin served from a makeshift bar in someone's home. What impacted me the most, however, was a visit to a "slum" community of thirty thousand people living under threat of forced eviction. I witnessed malnutrition, children with scabies and dysentery, and families living in one-room roof-

(continued)

less homes. I was filled with concern for the people there and realized how very fortunate I was to have been so safe growing up in my citrus-scented sanctuary.

I've been on my own for twelve years now. My father still checks the locks several times each night. I've come a long way, however, since the night when I sneaked out of my home. I know what is beyond that locked door, and I embrace my freedom to experience it.

❏ **Smart Move**: Parents who set fear and ego on a high shelf are far more likely to become wise mentors rather than frightened protectors or crazed coaches.

Are you willing to accept that there are times when fear and ego interfere with your ability to be the best parent you can be?

Congratulations! You're ready for the next step. I've got a special technique for kicking fego in the groin—and I'm delighted to share it with you.

Old School: letting fear and ego influence our parenting decisions

Bold School: getting calm, clear, and creative in order to mentor our kids

PAGING DR. HOUSE: COMMON SENSE + BOLDNESS

> Common sense is genius dressed in its working clothes.
> RALPH WALDO EMERSON

If there's one thing I've learned from watching reruns of *House* on television (other than the Spanish words for body parts and obscure diseases), it's that sometimes the regular treatment options just don't work. Every once in a while it's necessary to try something drastic and counterintuitive in order to turn that terminal patient into a pink and perky picture of health. The same is true in education. If you've got an all-systems-are-shutting-down student who is failing to thrive, it might be time to get bold and pull a Dr. House—without the accompanying sociopathic behavior.

Of course, if you disconnect a smart kid from the traditional college-prep life-support system (aka high school), those who don't understand the advantages of doing so will look at you as though you have been popping way too many Vicodin. They see nothing but danger ahead: "His university options are crashing! He's losing pressure! More AP classes—*stat!*" But if you're like our cantankerous Dr. House, you are several steps ahead of those who are scrutinizing the symptoms listed on the whiteboard; you go ahead and order the surgery (removal from that particular school setting) or syringe (dose of excitement about a new learning challenge) that will save the patient by the next scene.

It's important to consider all conditions carefully. However, when a student is not only bored in class but *losing interest in learning*, it's time to call a code. We need to focus on common sense and mix it with our signature boldness. This is the secret serum that is saving thousands of listless students who are facing what can feel like a very gloomy prognosis: a few more years of a debilitating school experience.

Once again, it's all about the big picture. When we're feeling scared or hopeless, we stare harder at the only option we see. By stepping back, we can get a beautiful view of the entire forest instead of a single tree. Let's take a stroll through the education woods and see what we can learn about some of the most interesting trees we find there.

Here's a big shady one: grades.

Most parents recognize that it's a lot easier to get an A now than it was when they were in school. How many valedictorians were there in your graduating class? How many of them had a perfect grade-point average? It's not unusual to have more than fifty in large schools now—all of them with 4.0 averages or even higher, thanks to weighted grades.

My daughters were horrified to see that I'd received a few Cs on my first-grade report card. How crushing! Wasn't my mother upset? Did she try to talk my teacher into reconsidering the grade? How could I be a top student in the first grade (I was in the most advanced reading group) with a report card like that? I explained that everyone started with a C average and it was expected that your grades would improve once you actually, you know, *learned* something.

Starting with high marks is normal now, and it sets a precedent for perfection that is nearly impossible to maintain. If we start high and end up low, we're essentially telling our kids that they are *worse* than when they started out knowing nothing. And so to prevent disappointment, we keep things at a comfortable high. Our general disdain for mediocrity (often fueled by fego-wrestling parents) obscures the reality that *half of all students are below average*. Grade inflation and GPA worship result in unhealthy attitudes about achievement (and less interest in learning) and spark even more crushing humiliation for those who fail. Where's our common sense? If we don't grade realistically, we might as well drop grades altogether—and there are compelling arguments for doing so.

Here's a tree with a twisted trunk: homework.

Most adults recall having to do a fair amount of studying. And so if we parents feel that our schools need to be more rigorous, that generally translates into more homework, more memorizing, and more tests. After all, that's what *rigor* meant to us in those days. We expect schools to be tough, and we want our kids to work hard.

Parents are the ones driving the movement for more rigor without recognizing that it might be best to teach our kids how to work *smarter*, not just harder. It's easy to slip into more-is-better thinking and lose sight of the fact that what we really want is for our kids to learn how to learn in ways that are most *effective* and *relevant*.

Ah, now here's a tree worth a closer look: time.

Remember when you were in college? Consider how the actual work has changed since then. For one thing, we had to spend a lot more time getting the information we needed. We spent hours, days, even entire weekends in the library. Once we had handwritten our rough drafts, we spent hours typing up our reports. If we spilled coffee—or anything else—on those painstakingly prepared pages, we had no choice but to type them over again.

Compare that to the process of writing a college paper today. A student gets an assignment; does most of the research online, with the possible exception of a book or two; types up a rough draft on the computer; takes a break, then goes back to that same document to edit it; spell-checks it; then e-mails it to the professor directly. Done!

No searching through card catalogs. No climbing stairs to remote corners of the library. No swearing upon discovering that another student in your class has beaten you to the one copy of the book that is required reading for everyone. No waiting at the library counter to see if the book can be ordered from another library. No searching through microfiche to find information in the periodicals section. No trek through the night to return to the dorm, empty-handed and frustrated. Even the hours we spent physically preparing those papers and carrying them to class have disappeared in the whir of a laptop.

So when you think about the time that is saved every step of the way by the once-unimaginable shortcuts that technology has provided, you've got to ask yourself this: **why are students today spending the same number of years in high school and college as we did?**

And since they are, shouldn't they be learning *more* during that same period of time? If they don't have to devote hours to searching for information in order to complete their work—if it's all right there at their fingertips—isn't it possible that they could become more advanced in terms of critical thinking and knowledge of the world?

Well, *of course*. It all makes perfect sense. Our kids should be ling past us, full of excitement about what they're learning. After all, we've had decades to develop new teaching techniques, and we can now incorporate wondrous tech tools to make learning far more direct and interactive than when we were in school. Students today must be racing ahead of where we were in terms of learning. Right?

It doesn't seem to be going that way.

High schools now have more layers of academic requirements—not to mention disruptions in class time to deal with behavior and safety concerns, plus lengthy breaks to navigate the crowded hallways or long lines in the cafeteria—than a generation ago. The on-task time our kids spend actually learning in the classroom is less than when we were in school, due to logistics and management constraints.

For motivated students (or just plain impatient ones), the structure of the school day can sap enthusiasm for education. Many simply resign themselves to boredom, but the awake and curious students begin to consider ways to create more honest-to-goodness learning time while eliminating the bored-out-of-their-skulls waiting time. Now we're getting somewhere! This is exactly the kind of clarity and common sense we want to encourage. After all, our fired-up-for-the-future kids must be able to:

- recognize when their time is being wasted
- understand that they can make other choices
- get motivated to explore their options
- choose the path that will maximize their time and their opportunities for learning and personal development
- see fear and ego as obstacles that can be easily overcome
- develop confidence in their ability to move forward on their own

Many individuals epitomize the bold-school approach, and they've splattered their own education/career canvases in colorful and unique ways. One of my favorite bold schoolers is Joshua Davies. He has created a very enriching life for himself by following his instincts instead of traipsing along the tried-and-tired path to career success.

I met Joshua at the Spanish-language school I attended in Buenos Aires. He was there to improve his speaking skills, but unlike most of our classmates, he wasn't taking a break during or after college in order to go abroad. He was *getting paid* while spending months traveling in South America. Compared to some of the bold schoolers you'll meet later in this book, Joshua was a bit of a late bloomer in the travel department, but he made up for lost time; though he didn't leave the United States until he was twenty, he has wound his way through thirty countries in the last eight years. Joshua is not one to trumpet his personal success story, but I managed to pry it out of him. Here it is:

BOLD STATEMENT

I attended high school on Bainbridge Island (Seattle area) for my first two years. The teachers were nice enough, and to be honest, I had no real peer problems, but high school was just that: high school.

The curriculum was regimented with few real options for studying what I wanted, the classes were often geared toward the lowest common denominator and rather dull and easy, and most students spent the bulk of their time trying to do anything but study (not that this was an unwise reaction given the circumstances).

I'm not a complete bookworm by any means, but I hated the nagging sense that in high school I was really just biding my time. I was curious about everything, but I really wanted to be in control of my own learning choices. I didn't like the one-size-fits-none approach to education.

(continued)

Because of this, I participated in a dual enrollment program called Running Start as soon as I could (after my sophomore year). The credits I got at Seattle Central Community College counted for both university and high school, and though I was required to take a few courses to meet my high school requirements, for the most part I was able to choose as I liked.

I picked classes like international relations, art history, and abnormal psychology—subjects not offered at my high school. Beyond the freedom to make my own choices, the biggest impact on my life came from the tremendous variety of classmates I had—all ages, faiths, colors, beliefs, countries, and economic levels. It was a real cross-section, and the projects and discussions we had dwarfed what would have been possible in a largely homogeneous high school environment.

After two years of Running Start, I entered Bard College in New York. What I loved about the place was the focus on embracing a wide swath of subjects. Basically, we were forced to play—something that resulted in me completely changing my major while giving me a background in everything from Einstein to garden design. Though my parents were really great about covering my tuition, I had to work to pay for my living expenses. I picked the two best-paying jobs on campus: university tour guide and nude model in the art department. Odd, perhaps, but I had a lot of fun and paid my bills on time.

While at Bard, I did a semester abroad in India studying international relations, Hindi, art, and philosophy (which cost half the tuition only—nice savings there) and a summer semester in southern France to study art.

After graduation I entered a TEFL (Teaching English as

a Foreign Language) certificate program in Prague. I had a wonderful time teaching there, but when funds ran low, I took a friend's advice and headed to South Korea, where companies were paying all set-up costs (airfare, insurance, housing, furnishings). Someone fresh out of college could expect to teach twenty to thirty (absolute max) hours per week and easily have savings of $1,000 per month if not more. With the public school jobs in South Korea, even entry-level positions can come with one or two months of vacation.

After a year or two of teaching experience in South Korea, it is possible to get a job at a university—not at first- or second-tier schools, mind you, but the demand is high enough that if you present yourself well, it's definitely doable.

I didn't know about that in the beginning, however. So I taught at an institute for a year and used what I had saved to head to South America, where I taught and traveled for a year. From there I continued my circle, on to Europe and then back to South Korea, where I earned a master's degree in education in TESOL (Teaching English to Speakers of Other Languages) via distance learning from Shenandoah University. The master's program was surprisingly affordable at $12,000 total, and I paid it off in less than a year. It more than paid for itself by letting me get my first university job.

Here's what I love about this position:

** I have curricular freedom.
** The administration and students are great.
** I get five months of paid vacation each year.

(continued)

** I work twelve hours per week.

** I live in a beautiful part of Seoul in a very nice apartment that is subsidized by my university. (It costs me only $200 per month.)

** I have *savings* (after taxes and spending) of $20,000 to $40,000 per year. (I could save much more if I didn't choose to travel or opted to work overtime or off season, but I value my time off more than the cash at this point.)

I'm twenty-eight years old. I work less in a month than most of my friends work in a week. I travel nearly half the year. I'm not in debt at all and am well on my way to respectable savings. I truly enjoy the work that I do, have satisfying relationships with my students and friends, and feel grateful for the chance to live in this fascinating country.

TIPS AND ADVICE

1. **Do not put off travel.** The jobs are not going to disappear while you are away, and you can gain valuable skills while you're abroad.

2. **Never underestimate the kind of job you can get.** I've known plenty of teachers who sell themselves short when they could have much better jobs if only they'd applied. What have you got to lose?

3. **Round-the-world tickets are much cheaper than you expect,** as are travel expenses if you don't hang out in London and New York.

4. **Say yes to every opportunity put before you, even the strange ones.** Maybe you're tired that week, maybe you think you don't have time, but just say yes.

For my master's portfolio, I studied collaborative on-line education. When a friend asked me to do a short presentation at a local teaching conference on my master's findings, I was planning on saying no. I was nervous and uncertain, having never given a presentation of that sort, but decided, why the hell not?

I did my spiel, which led to being asked to be the new national webmaster of KOTESOL, which led to writing for *English Connection* magazine (KOTESOL publication), which was seen by a fellow teacher in Japan, who invited me to do an international student collaboration. As a result of that, the Korean government asked me to train incoming public school teachers, and Pearson-Longman invited me to join their international e-learning advisory board. Sometimes one yes can lead you to a series of incredible opportunities.

What's next? No clue—but I'm enjoying myself immensely. At this point I'm just grateful for everything and plan to continue to push my limits and see where that takes me.

Joshua could have stayed on the normal high school track, chosen to remain in the United States after he graduated from college, or opted for an expensive master's program that would have eaten considerably more of his income. He might have said no to that one presentation that ended up opening all kinds of doors. Instead, he decided to partake of the magic elixir of common sense and boldness.

❏ **Smart Move**: Bold schoolers are actively engaged in exploring and pursuing options that allow them to leap forward and learn on their own terms.

Common Sense + Boldness. In the next section, you'll discover more about how a big swig of this tasty tonic can be very powerful indeed.

Old School: swallowing the bitter medicine of boredom and resignation
Bold School: sipping the sweet elixir of common sense and boldness

PUSHING THE CC BUTTON

> Community colleges are like economy cars. Sure, you might feel a little inconsequential driving one alongside those in their shiny SUVs, but while they're standing in line to pay a fortune at the gas pump and scraping for years to make their monthly car payments, you're cruising to your destination in a car that's reasonably priced and runs like a dream on very little gas.
>
> PARENT OF THREE FORMER COMMUNITY COLLEGE STUDENTS WHO ARE NOW SUCCESSFUL (AND DEBT-FREE) UNIVERSITY GRADS

High school dropout rates in the United States continue to increase; some urban districts have graduation rates well below 50 percent, and nationwide only about 70 percent of ninth graders will graduate with their class.[1]

This is scandalous! Terrifying! Disastrous!

Well, actually, it's illuminating—but only if we dial down the panic and start asking important questions. Here's one: **where are these students going after they drop out?**

Are students simply giving up on education, or are they dropping out in order to get the education they want in *different* ways? Statistics don't provide the answer because, in most states, students who leave high school are considered dropouts if they are going to community college, homeschooling, switching to a virtual school, or studying abroad. It's clear that students are leaving high school earlier and more frequently than in recent years, but we don't have an accurate account of what they're doing when they leave.

We do know that enrollment in community colleges is increasing at record rates—nearly half of all U.S. undergraduates attend community college—and many of those new students are under eighteen.[2]

I interviewed a dozen community college advisers across the country, and they assured me that yes, the number of younger community college students is growing, both those who enter dual enrollment programs that offer credit for high school and college simultaneously and those who graduate early and choose community college as their entry point for a bachelor's degree. In addition, these advisers shared their frustration regarding one of the biggest obstacles preventing more students from considering enrolling in community college early: their parents.

Ah, yes. It seems that fego rears its ugly head when parents consider community college for their kids, even when it may be a superior option for high school students fired up to begin college early. In my conversations with community college counselors, they kept referring to the "bumper-sticker mentality" that parents have about the university that their kids attend.

Well, I'm about to share some information that might help you stomp on that fego.

For one thing, while some U.S. parents are struggling to accept the idea of community college, both **China and India are sending educators and administrators to the United States to *study* our community college model.**[3] That's right. They are turning to *us* for help in overhauling their outmoded vocational school programs. Chinese and Indian educators recognize that we have developed an exceedingly effective way to offer low-cost education options to a diverse population. Progressive Chinese and Indian business leaders are seeing that community colleges would serve them by providing employees who have both vocational skills and a good academic foundation. Foreign ministries of education are praising the U.S. community college model as an example of *practical* education that helps students synthesize information from various sources while giving them the option to continue on to earn a bachelor's degree.

Huh.

Another thing to keep in mind: in many cases those who choose to teach at community colleges are doing so precisely because they are more passionate about sharing their knowledge about their subject directly with students than about working in a university setting that emphasizes research and publishing. It's simply not true that community colleges *by definition* offer a less valuable educational experience. Kevin Carey, a policy analyst with Education Sector, a Washington think tank, told me, "Because people tend to believe that quality means selectivity and vice versa, many implicitly assume all community colleges are worse than all four-year colleges, but in fact some community colleges are providing a superior-quality undergrad education compared to four-year institutions."

This is heartening to be sure, but rather than compare community colleges with state or private universities, what we really need is to understand the advantages of community college when compared with the junior and senior years of high school. For those on the global path, starting college early can be very beneficial, but blending high school and college courses may be the best option for *most* high school students, as described in Nancy Hoffman and colleagues' *Minding the Gap: Why Integrating High School with College Makes Sense and How to Do It*. There are plenty of pedagogical and social reasons for a student to consider segueing into college while still in high school, but we're going to focus on the *practical* reasons for doing so and how they relate to going global. Plus, I'll help you understand the hidden holes in the community college path that could trip your student in unexpected ways.

Let's look at how taking community college classes in high school can help your son or daughter:

▶ avoid the stress of the typical college-prep process
▶ save thousands on the cost of a four-year degree
▶ enjoy an advantage over older community college students seeking to transfer
▶ develop skills that will be helpful in a four-year university setting
▶ discover and define interests and talents
▶ increase the likelihood of getting desirable summer jobs and internships

and most important of all:

▶ **make room for a high school exchange or gap year**

Discover the Sneaky, No-Stress Way to Get into College

Not all high school students can—or should—switch from high school to community college. How do you know if your student is likely to flourish or flounder?*

Dr. Cliff Adelman spent thirty years at the U.S. Department of Education and now serves as a senior associate at the Institute for Higher Education Policy. "It's all about fit," Dr. Adelman told me. "The thing to remember is that community colleges reflect real life. You may sit next to somebody who looks like your uncle Bob. Now, that could be just fine with a seventeen-year-old who is raring to go, but it might not be the right fit for a student who is more comfortable in a high school classroom."

Taking community college courses in high school is an outstanding way to shave thousands of dollars off the cost of a four-year college degree, and many bold schoolers recognize that it also increases the flexibility needed to incorporate time abroad. However, students need to understand that a poor grade in a community college course may haunt them far more than a bad grade in high school. For those who "swirl" (the commonly used term for taking courses at a number of institutions prior to earning a degree), it's even more important to do well in classes than it is for those who stay in one place and never have to transfer based on their transcripts. Many colleges will not accept transfer students who have lower than a C average in previous college coursework. (Transfer student motto: "No Cs in CC!")

If your son or daughter is lukewarm on the idea of community college but doing cartwheels at the thought of quitting high school, hold steady. If they are not ready to embrace and fully commit to community college (or another very well researched and appropriate option), they need to stay where they are until they have a good plan. Dropping out and *then* figuring out what to do is likely to lead to disengagement and depression. Students need good advice from an admissions counselor and support from their parents before withdrawing from high school.

The happy news is that when it comes to applying to four-year universities, good grades in community college courses can compensate for lackluster performance in high school. According to Dr. Adelman, most four-year colleges and universities evaluate community college transfer students based on their coursework, credits, and grades. "In the transfer process," Dr. Adelman explained, "these are more important than high school records, type of high school diploma, or SAT scores, which community colleges don't require anyway."

Bold schoolers begin taking community college courses at fifteen or sixteen in order to jump-start college, avoid the stress of the traditional application process, save lots of money, and earn enough credits by the age of eighteen to transfer to a four-year university as a junior. Best of all, this buys time at a critical age to study abroad, which is *the most important element* in a global education. (Much more on this in Chapters Five and Six.)

Community colleges do offer some top-quality courses, but not all courses are equal in terms of preparing students for a four-year degree. *Course selection is of vital importance,* and students need to be guided by those caring community college admissions counselors in order to make the smartest choices. The savviest students get even more strategic by selecting courses that allow them to:

❏ **mix with the most motivated students**

and

❏ **connect with potential mentors**

Learn the System

Linda Jensen is the dual enrollment coordinator at GateWay Community College in Phoenix, Arizona. Each year she helps more than two thousand high school students enroll in community college courses. I caught up with her in June 2008, when she was busy helping students who were in the process of getting their dual enrollment credits transferred to the university they planned to attend. She told me the following:

INSIDER INSIGHT

This is the most rewarding part of the process because I get to talk to students who are committed, focused, and—more importantly—*asking the right questions*. Part of "doing college" is learning how to navigate the system, being resourceful, and asking questions along the way to ensure that you get customized care. This is one of the greatest lessons to come out of the dual enrollment program. When I go to high schools to promote dual enrollment and register students for courses, I get a lot of blank stares and very often follow-up calls from parents whose kids didn't catch the details of how this works. But by the end of

(*continued*)

their senior year in the program, these students have college credits *and* they know how to get the info they need to move forward. As a result, they are far more self-directed and confident, which gives them an advantage over their peers at a four-year university.

Successful transfer students get their community college adviser in their corner *from the very beginning* and learn how to build bulletproof transcripts that will get accepted without a hitch.

Step to the Front of the Transfer Student Line

High school students who begin college courses early are seen as more desirable transfer students than those who go from high school graduation to community college and then to a four-year institution. One simple reason: doing well in college courses with adults at sixteen is just more impressive than doing the same at eighteen.

In addition, the university door may swing considerably wider for younger transfer students (those who are eighteen or younger) due to the potential for more tuition payments. Several community college advisers told me that universities are counting on these younger transfer students to take longer to graduate due to their age (they may decide to finish right alongside their high school classmates despite being ahead in terms of credits) and their desire to experience (and pay for) more of campus life. Young transfers who fast-forward to make room for time abroad can take advantage of this and still choose to graduate early if they like.

Students considering attending community college anyway benefit most by *starting early* instead of waiting until after high school graduation.

Going to community college might give your student a leg up on the four-year university admissions process, but not every university is going to accept transfer students. Do *not* view community college as a launching pad to get into Harvard. The Ivies have plenty of students clamoring to get in and pay for all four years, so they're not very interested in accepting transfer students, even those from other Ivy League universities. Still, every year community college students sneak in the back door as transfers and get accepted to those top-tier colleges.

How are four-year universities responding to the flood of students trying to transfer and trade up from community colleges? Some universities have little incentive to accept transfer students from community colleges because, unlike freshmen enrolling directly out of high school, the transfers don't count toward an institution's graduation rate, ACT or SAT average, or retention rate. Chalk it up to competition—universities intent upon being ranked highly in *U.S. News & World Report* and other college lists need to play the game in order to plump up those numbers.

In other cases, universities are requiring extra classes for transfers—it's an easy way to get more cash—and many students in this position just suck it up and pay because they want to attend a particular school. Fortunately, pressure on universities to be both fair and transparent regarding the transfer process is increasing.

❏ **Smart Move**: Bold schoolers go *beyond* community college transcripts. They don't rely on being a young transfer student with good grades—they've got an ace up their sleeves in the form of time spent abroad and the skills that come along with that. (Examples ahead!)

Grabbing Great Internships and Summer Jobs

There's another reason for students to consider starting community college classes in high school: it may give them an edge in terms of gaining relevant work experience. Norma Kent, vice president for communications at the American Association of

Community Colleges, points out that the community colleges have strong ties to the business community.

INSIDER INSIGHT

One thing we hear from business leaders again and again is that they are looking for employees who bring relevant skills to the table. A degree-seeking eighteen-year-old with a year's worth of college credits is likely to stand out as a better candidate for those internships and summer jobs than a recent high school graduate who has never taken a college course. The key difference is that these students have already had to show up and challenge themselves in an adult setting.

Common sense, right?

Okay, so we've got a long list of advantages for those going to community college early, and yet for many parents, it stills feels a little risky. How do we know it will actually *work*?

It's time for a success story.

I'll be honest—I had my own worries about community college for my kids. Thankfully, I've emerged from my soak in the ego tub long enough to see what can happen when you release the idea that community college is a lesser option. In fact, once I'd dried off, I got to watch some fireworks.

I'm talking about the beautiful sparks and explosions that result when a student discovers a particular passion. Ftt. *Sssssttt.* **POW!** Tom and I witnessed the fireworks when our oldest daughter, Taeko, took a course at the local community college in order to fulfill a requirement for high school graduation. Here is her story:

BOLD STATEMENT

After spending my junior year of high school on exchange in Chile, I had no interest in going back to high school. I'd already experienced living away from home, traveling independently, and yes, even partying. I knew I wanted to pursue an education that would prepare me for a career in health care, and going to football games and planning senior prom wouldn't help me with that.

I decided to participate in a program that allowed me to take most of my classes at Portland Community College for both high school and college credit—double-dipping, if you will. I figured I would take all the basic 100-level classes in social and behavioral sciences and then transfer to a university. There's not much difference between an intro community college class and one at a four-year college, so it made sense to me to save money early and invest more in the upper-level courses later.

The majority of the classes I needed to take to complete my high school diploma were electives, but there was one required course I was definitely *not* excited to take— general eleventh/twelfth-grade health. I searched desperately for a class that would be more challenging, found a 200-level human sexuality course, and got permission to take it to fulfill my requirement. Little did I know that this one class would unearth my passion for public health!

Judy Zimmerman was a dynamic instructor who spearheaded a lot of the public health initiatives on campus. She introduced me to the world of sexual health education and political advocacy. I came across a Planned Parenthood internship position as a peer educator that provided training and hands-on experience—plus a paycheck! Although I was the youngest applicant, I was hired thanks to a lot of previous volunteer experience (at a rehab center, at a children's hospital, and as a Special Olympics coach) and my Spanish skills. That job provided me with a solid base for sexual health education and group facilitation.

(continued)

A year later, as a junior at Acadia University in Nova Scotia, I was amazed to see that my sexuality professor was using Judy Zimmerman's publication as a guide for her course. I felt like I was already ahead of the game! I became a teaching assistant in the psychology department, codeveloped Acadia's sexual health workshop series on campus, got a grant to write an honors thesis, and was lucky to get a job as a virtual research assistant that allowed me to spend a summer staying with my college friend's family in Bermuda.

Thanks to those community college classes, I was able to earn my BS (with honors) at the age of nineteen. Community college got me jump-started, and my Acadia profs had very high expectations and taught me so much about being meticulous in my research. I feel that being really challenged then prepared me extremely well for the work I'm doing currently.

When people find out that I graduated at the age of nineteen, they ask if I feel I was robbed of my youth. I tell them it's possible to get the full college experience in much less than the typical four years—and that I definitely did. I lived in a notoriously wild dorm my first year. (It had been an all-male dorm, and I was among the first women students to be housed there.) I took full advantage of absolutely every aspect of college life and had a fantastic time those two years. I went to insane hockey games with paint on my face, met some of my closest friends, and have many stories that are verbally padlocked! I got most of that out of my system. I left Acadia on the highest of high notes without ever hitting the doldrums.

I did overload on credits most semesters during those two years and the summer in between. It would have been a lot easier if I'd gone for a BA or hadn't opted to do honors. Still, it's definitely possible to fit everything in once you focus and do some planning. Most of my classmates had no idea how old I was until an article came out in my college paper right before I graduated. Of course, my close friends knew my age since I had been waiting to turn nineteen (legal drinking age in Canada) to go to bars with them!

The best thing that ever happened to me was landing a job as a sexual health educator and HIV counselor at a clinic in New York City. I felt like I had found my calling! Through my clinic I have counseled more than a thousand clients and given sexual health presentations to high school boys in the Bronx, male inmates at a maximum-security facility, and homeless heroin addicts. I have learned so much from living and working in Harlem these last two years, and I feel proud that I can help create programs to improve the health of those in my community.

After a year of working at the clinic, I enrolled in the master's program at the Hunter School of Urban Public Health, taking courses two nights a week. A good friend had recently earned her MPH at an Ivy League school and told me that if she had to do it over again, she'd skip the $50,000-plus in loans and go to Hunter, since its program is highly respected, very affordable, and the only one focused on urban health specifically. Thank God I listened to her! I realize that my particular passion and field of work may not be lucrative in the beginning, and having no debt will take the pressure off and allow me to work for nonprofit agencies. Extra bonus: My employer offered to pay for *all* of my tuition!

Working full time at the clinic, going to school full time in the evenings, and doing my master's practicum at a needle-exchange program is no easy feat. However, the

(continued)

fact that a lot of concepts and activities overlap reduces some of the workload. I love bringing what I'm learning in my classes directly into my work and vice versa. Many of my classmates are a decade older than me and have been working in this field for years. I feel fortunate to be able to learn from their experience, and I'm honored that they see me as a respected colleague. The contacts I'm making through my master's program are sure to help me in my future pursuits in health care policy.

I did feel that there was a stigma attached to going to community college, but I am so glad I didn't let my peers' judgment (or my own ego) prevent me from choosing what I felt in my heart would be right for me. When people find out that I am nearly finished with my master's, have five years of work experience in my field, and am supporting myself financially (in Manhattan, no less) at twenty-two, they find it hard to believe. I guess I don't think of it as being particularly amazing—it's just that I made choices that allowed me to continue learning about what interested me.

Sometimes people assume that I'm on a really hard-core competitive track. The truth is that I'm serious about my work, but I also have a lot of fun—hey, I'm in my twenties and living in New York City! My supervisors view me as a dedicated professional, but my friends think of me as the girl most likely to be hanging out on the roof or rounding up everyone to go out on Friday night.

I don't judge my life in terms of achievement. I am just happy to be doing what I love to do. I sometimes wonder what my life would have been like if I had taken that required health class with a bunch of kids in high school! I couldn't be happier with my choice to go to community college.

Parents of students for whom everything comes easily have two options: watch them coast or help them soar. Tom and I can't take much credit for Taeko's successes—all we did was encourage her to go abroad in high school, consider alternatives when she returned, and pursue her passion in whatever way she chose. A motivated student who sidesteps the traditional path can go from a run-of-the-mill A student in high school to a super-charged young adult leader very quickly. Sometimes the best thing a parent can do is offer a softly spoken word of advice and then stand back and watch the sparks fill the sky.

How can you and your student make the right decision about high school versus community college? Steven Roy Goodman is an educational consultant and admissions strategist who has worked with parents and students from around the world to help them plan for and navigate the transition to college. A co-author of the book *College Admissions Together: It Takes a Family,* Goodman emphasizes the importance of families assessing their needs and concerns when it comes to taking risks by doing things differently.

INSIDER INSIGHT

Taking the path less traveled will actually help in the college application process. However, there's a caveat: one's time needs to be spent with a purpose. The potential risks and advantages need to be weighed, and every family will have a different comfort level. It's one thing for a high school student to travel abroad for a year or take college courses, to explore their interests with a mentor or commit to volunteer work. It's another thing to drop out of high school and wander aimlessly with the hope that you'll look more interesting on a college application. The key is to understand what's important to you so that you

(continued)

can choose where to focus your energy and when to take risks. I tell students to find what they love to do, and then do lots of it. It's always a good choice for students to engage in activities that deeply enhance their intellectual development. The more enriched a student is, the more attractive they will be to a university.

Excellent advice, but pay attention to what happens when we read about the need for "intellectual development": the fego alarm goes off once again.

Intellectual development! That's the ticket! We'll make them smarter! We'll arm them with information! We'll make sure they memorize all of it!

This is where we start to lose sight of the forest. There are so many trees that it's easy to get distracted from our goal of encouraging the kind of learning that is most likely to help our students in terms of both intellectual *and* personal development. In fact, we get stuck in one particular little thicket that makes it impossible to get that bird's-eye view we really need.

Let's spend a moment in that thicket right now. Once you learn more about it, you'll be able to smile and walk right past it without a second glance. You're going to recognize the initials on these trees: AP, IB, and SAT.

Old School: viewing community college as baby food for those who don't yet have teeth for anything more substantial

Bold School: viewing community college as a power shake that boosts energy, increases clarity, and builds strength for those ready to blast forward

CHAPTER FOUR

AP, IB & SAT

OMG!

WHY ADVANCED PLACEMENT ISN'T SO ADVANCED

> Now, here, you see, it takes all the running
> you can do, to keep in the same place.
>
> THE RED QUEEN TO ALICE
> IN LEWIS CARROLL'S *THROUGH*
> *THE LOOKING-GLASS*

Right now a high school student near you is taking an Advanced Placement course with the hope of doing well enough on the standardized test to get credit for an introductory-level course in that subject in college. In fact, *some* students near you may be taking *several* Advanced Placement courses. It's become a point of pride among some college-bound students to cram as many AP courses as possible into their schedule.

In the race for rigor, the AP program has become the torch-bearer. Unfortunately, it is yet another instance of chanting the more-is-better mantra. The result is a dilution of both the quality of the courses offered and the benefits accorded those who do well on the required tests. To understand how this has happened, we need to know a little AP history. (Find out more at http: apcentral.collegeboard.com.)

1950s: The Advanced Placement program was developed in response to the idea that "high schools and colleges could and should work together to avoid repetition in course work and allow motivated students to work at the height of their capabilities and advance as quickly as possible." Administrators at a handful of elite private high schools and Ivy League universities worked together to develop standards for course work that would prepare students for college academics. Special advanced classes were developed that allowed high school students to get credit for introductory courses at participating universities if they scored a minimum of 3 (out of 5) on the final test. The program was implemented in a number of locations and the results were impressive.

1960s: The AP program trained teachers to offer these more rigorous courses in selected schools. More universities developed policies for granting credit to those who did well on the AP tests.

Things hummed along for a couple of decades.

1990s: AP went vertical. The College Board expanded the goals of the program by introducing Pre-AP programs, including AP Vertical Teams and Building Success workshops. Enthusiastic middle school teachers assisted in developing and implementing a sequential curriculum.

Then everything started to shift.

2000 TO PRESENT: College tuition went up. The "echo boom" (children of baby boomers) bulge produced more college applicants. Students began to worry more about getting into a good university and finding the money to pay for it.

Students and parents began to think of the AP program as not only a way to prepare for college-level work and save money and time by earning college credits but also as a means to impress admissions officials looking for the next academic all-stars and scholarship recipients. A generation ago only the brightest college-bound students considered taking these advanced courses, but many students now consider AP courses a must-have on a college application.

Parents began demanding more AP courses. More students (including those considered not so advanced) chose to add AP courses to their schedules. Some schools focused on enrolling minority or at-risk students in AP courses and partnered with programs that subsidized the cost of the tests or even paid students cash for getting high scores. Teachers made adjustments in order to cater to the general level and size of the class, and they devoted more class time to covering important information that would appear on the AP subject exam.

Seeing their B-minus classmates show up in their AP classes prompted star students to shift into overachiever gear. Looking for an edge, they signed up for two, three, or even four of these advanced courses each semester, even though the original intent was to give kids a chance to focus in depth on only *one* challenging college-level subject at a time.

Then the B-plus students felt like slackers if they weren't taking at least a couple of AP courses every semester. They saw their peers filling their schedules with AP courses and worried that they'd never be able to compete in the race to get into college. Students no longer saw taking an AP course as an opportunity to delve more deeply into a subject they found interesting. Now students took AP courses in clusters for the purpose of competing with others to get into college.

College admissions officers, seeing applications in which students showed a total of ten or more AP test scores, questioned how advanced these courses could be if students were able to take so many of them at once. They suspected that those who were packing in AP courses were good test-takers eager to win points with admissions officials. Some universities, recognizing the benefits (some financial) of requiring incoming freshmen to take more introductory courses on campus, decided that they would not accept AP scores for credit.

This trend, along with watching their college-bound students become exhausted by the competition to accumulate more AP courses, has convinced some high school administrators to drop AP from their curricula. Instead, they are opting for classes that encourage more thoughtful discussion and for extended essay writing instead of standardized testing. Essentially, they are going back to basics and abandoning the noxious notion of rigor as the sole watermark of an excellent education.

And that's where we are today.

Over a million students take thirty-seven different AP courses and sit for two million tests in twenty-two subject areas each year.

The Advanced Placement program, along with oh-so-delightful high school rituals like the SAT and the PSAT, brings in millions of dollars a year for the College Board. Hey, there's nothing wrong with a winning business model (wait—isn't it a *not-for-profit* organization?), but there's also nothing wrong with questioning the value of a program that's popular.

The first sentence on the AP homepage is: "AP can change your life." Well, obviously. Outstanding AP teachers are inspiring thousands of motivated students in high schools across the country. If you've been lucky enough to have a gifted teacher in your lifetime, you know how powerful it can be. But you don't have to take an AP course to be stirred by a great teacher, and I'd bet that even the most effective AP teachers (and there are many) would love nothing more than to be told to simply teach the material in the way they find most exciting rather than sticking to the AP course guidelines.

But hey, I'm no expert on the efficacy of the AP program. So I found someone who is.

Dr. Tony Wagner describes himself as "a recovering high school English teacher," but that's just him being humble. He has been the codirector of the Change Leadership Group at the Harvard Graduate School of Education since its inception in 2000, has worked for more than thirty-five years in the field of school improvement, and is a frequent keynote speaker and widely published author on education and society. After teaching high school for twelve years, he served as a school principal, as a university professor in teacher education, and as the cofounder and first executive director of Educators for Social Responsibility.

Dr. Wagner has a few things to say about the AP program. In fact, he published a book called *The Global Achievement Gap: Why Even Our Best Schools Don't Teach the New Survival Skills Our Children Need—And What We Can Do About It*, in which he devotes a chunk of a chapter to discussing why the AP program does not prepare students for college.[1]

Hooray! Now I don't have to.

Dr. Wagner's main concern is that the AP program is yet another example of focusing on *content* rather than *critical skills*. As he puts it, "Which is more important: memorizing the parts of speech or writing an effective essay? We can't teach and test everything. In today's world, it's no longer how much you know that matters; it's what you do with what you know."

Exactly.

We want our students to stretch themselves intellectually, and even if a student doesn't score well enough on the test to get college credit, an AP class might offer a better learning environment than a no-logo high school course. But we can't ignore the fact that both the College Board (which receives payment for every AP test) and the universities that are refusing to grant credit are ultimately taking advantage of students who are doing what they are told will be best for their academic achievement. Both students and parents need to realize that they are not necessarily getting what is promised by the term "Advanced Placement."

Bottom line: Many students are discovering that Advanced Placement test scores may end up being a very ho-hum line item on that list of high school accomplishments.

Where's the common sense? We've added too many layers—mostly of the green variety—when all we really wanted to do in the beginning was give students a chance to delve into richer learning experiences to help them develop their skills and prepare for college.

The AP program filled a void back in the 1950s—it rewarded motivated students with college credit for taking difficult courses. But times have changed. Now many school districts offer dual enrollment programs for little or no cost, making it possible for a student to earn an associate's degree by the time he or she is shaking hands and grasping that high school diploma.

Hmm. Tap into your common sense for a moment and ask: Wouldn't it be simpler and more direct for a student to get "advanced placement" in college by taking *real* college courses while in high school?

Of course it would. That would make *perfect* sense. And as we learned in the last chapter, that's exactly what an increasing number of high school students are choosing to do.

Another commonsense question: If AP high school courses are truly at college level, and we're pushing more kids to take them, why are we even keeping these kids *in* high school? It seems we're just giving them extra time to grow up before they step out into the Real World—or at least, the college version of it—by encouraging their extended stay at the Juvenile Suites Inn. For many students, it offers a perfect combination: the comfort and safety of friends their own age and plenty of structure and adult supervision.

But what about those high school students who are sitting in the lobby of that Juvenile Suites Inn, bags packed, ready to check out early and head to the more grown-up College Hotel? These kids have their noses pressed against the glass, but we insist that they remain in high school even if it seems to be dragging them down intellectually or depressing them emotionally.

Is this the best way to help these students "advance"?

Remember: the fact that college-bound kids in your student's school are signing up for multiple AP courses doesn't mean that's the only option—or even the *best* option—available. It just means it's a popular choice, and we know that busy, worried people tend to follow the pack.

❏ **Smart Move**: Wise parents become informed about the options available for advanced learning and help their students make their best choices based on *relevance, skill development,* and *optimal learning environment.*

First, ask the school counselor for advice and then go online and check out the programs in your area. In rural areas or in struggling schools, or in a district that has no dual enrollment partnership with a local college, AP courses (including online versions) may be your best bet. (Then again, maybe not. You'll want to check out the program that I recommend—despite its one flaw—in the next section.)

The bold-school approach encourages students to use their common sense to avoid getting sucked into the multiple-AP-course vortex. In a knotty world, common sense is a *necessity,* and your goal as a parent must be to teach your student to look at the big picture whenever possible.

We're getting a much better view of the education forest now, aren't we?

Let's take a look at the next tree in this achievement thicket. It's the IB.

> **Old School:** taking as many AP courses as possible prior to going to college
> **Bold School:** avoiding the AP program in order to dive into more relevant opportunities for advanced learning

TO IB OR NOT TO IB: ONE UNFORTUNATE FLAW

> The world is but a school of inquiry.
> MICHEL DE MONTAIGNE

What can you do to enhance your student's global perspective if you're living in the heartland of America? How can you encourage the development of your child's cultural awareness if he or she is going to a school that is a sea of sameness?

I thought you'd never ask.

If you want to give your student some seriously good global learning right in your local classroom, the International Baccalaureate Diploma Programme will give you reason to grin. (Learn all about it at www.ibo.org.)

IB was started in Geneva back in 1968 by a talented group of teachers from international schools around the world. Their challenge was to develop a single standardized curriculum that schools in other countries would recognize.

Back then IB wasn't focused on teaching global issues or cultural awareness. You see, the first IB students were the children of diplomats and expats abroad. These kids were likely to be bicultural and/or bilingual, and many had lived in numerous countries by the time they graduated from high school. So in the beginning the purpose of the IB was to make it easier for these students who were moving from country to country to prepare for college by offering them a curriculum and a diploma recognized by universities around the world.

Have you ever moved your family to a new state and discovered that your kids' new school had a different timeline for specific courses (fourth grade emphasis on state history, for example, or a special focus on a particular area of math during seventh grade)? Consider what it would be like to change *countries* every two years. For corporate executives and others who transferred abroad with their families on a regular basis, IB was a godsend.

The International Baccalaureate (IB) offers international education programs in more than 2,400 schools in 131 countries worldwide, including 800 schools in the United States.

Since 1968 the IB organization has expanded its mission statement considerably. It now reads like a pocket guide to global citizenship and uses phrases like "intercultural understanding and respect" and "compassionate and lifelong learners." The IB folks focus on providing a top-quality curriculum and support to schools that are willing to go through the initial self-assessment and subsequent accreditation processes (which can take up to three years). IB administrators respond to requests from schools (rather than courting them), and 90 percent of IB schools are public institutions; an increasing number of schools in low-income and underperforming districts are becoming IB accredited.

To earn an IB diploma, juniors and seniors must take courses in six core areas: language, second language, individuals and societies, mathematics and computer science, experimental sciences, and the arts. In addition, they must complete three core requirements:

- an extended essay of four thousand words that gives them the chance to engage in independent research
- a Theory of Knowledge course that explores the nature of knowledge across disciplines

▶ the CAS (Creativity, Action, Service) core, encouraging students to be involved in artistic pursuits, sports, and community service work that fosters their awareness of life outside the academic arena

I talked to Dr. Ralph Cline, director of global school services for the IB program. Dr. Cline had been an AP teacher for more than a decade before joining the IB organization, and he explained that there are long-standing ties between the two programs. "There's no rivalry, really—we're all involved in creating opportunities for more in-depth learning—but Advanced Placement is a testing service, while IB offers a comprehensive curriculum with a global perspective. We're different animals."

When I asked Dr. Cline what appeals to parents most about the IB program, he responded with a familiar refrain. "It's the rigor," he told me. "Parents are looking for a way to give their kids a top-notch education. Though the multicultural perspective isn't at the top of most parents' list, it becomes a very valued part of the experience for everyone involved."

Think of IB as AP's hip global sister. She may not be cheerleader popular, but that's because she's spent most of her time abroad—and has legions of international fans to show for it. IB hangs out at cool cafés where she reads voraciously, asks probing questions, and engages in thoughtful debates with others on a wide range of topics. Meanwhile AP is holed up in her bedroom, cramming for content tests.

The IB program is inquiry-based, meaning that it places more emphasis on *how* students learn than on *what* they learn—and remember, this is an essential part of a global education. "Most of the content we teach kids now will be irrelevant by the time they reach their ten-year high school reunion," says Dr. Cline, "so we focus on teaching them how to learn, which is a skill that will be valuable no matter what comes down the pike." The approach is, well, global: instead of studying U.S. history in a compartmentalized way, IB students study a particular region (North America) and gain an understanding of how the borders and cultures shifted over time by learning about geography, politics, economics, and social customs as well as historic events. At the end of the two-year IB program, students are assessed by their regular teachers plus an external team.

What about college credit? Most universities acknowledge the excellence of the IB program, and many offer thirty credits for an IB diploma upon admission. But that's not the focus. As Dr. Cline told me, "We're going for depth and breadth of knowledge and understanding. We concentrate on preparing students for day two until the day they graduate with a university degree and less on where they might score on placement tests or credit tallies that first day at college."

What's the advantage of the IB diploma for your student? It's a cohesive, skill-building, globally oriented two-year curriculum that is recognized around the world.

Okay, so what's the one unfortunate and ironic flaw in the IB program? Its strength—a global curriculum that requires two years of continuous study—is also its greatest weakness. The problem is that a student cannot choose to go on an exchange program as a junior or senior in high school *and* earn an IB diploma *unless* they happen to transfer to a school abroad that offers the IB curriculum. Most exchange programs do not allow students to pick their schools, and (as we found here in Buenos Aires) the required coursework at IB schools is generally done in the language of that country. So unless your student is already fluent in the language spoken there or enrolls in an American school, it's going to be nearly impossible to complete the program abroad. (American high schools abroad are not inexpensive; the one in Buenos Aires costs close to $20,000 per year, making it out of reach for all but the wealthiest locals and foreigners with corporate or diplomatic benefits.)

Does this really matter? Yes. *Definitely*. Here's why:

Many parents who are considering sending their high school student on exchange choose *not* to do so precisely because they feel the IB diploma is more beneficial. This results in countless students missing out on their *very best chance* to get a truly international education.

❏ **Smart Move**: For parents who are committed to having their son or daughter *stay in one place* and *attend one school* during the last two years of high school, the IB program may be the very best way to give students a more global perspective while developing critical thinking skills. However, in most cases pursuing the IB diploma limits opportunities to enroll in college courses early (except for evening classes or summer terms) or to go on a high school exchange—and these options are ultimately far more advantageous for students preparing for those globalinguistic jobs of the future.

Although the number of certified IB schools is doubling every five years, the program isn't growing as fast as it needs to in order to make the most positive impact on students across the country. The biggest obstacle is the backlash from those who question a curriculum that embraces the cultures of the world. Some conservatives have gone so far as to call the IB program "anti-American" due to its emphasis on developing a global perspective. The truth is that opposing a curriculum that can help our students become well-educated, thoughtful, and collaborative world citizens might itself be "anti-American."

Bottom line: The IB program, like international and language-immersion schools, provides a basic foundation for global awareness, and that's worth celebrating. But just as you'd be leery of boarding a 747 with a pilot who'd trained

solely on flight simulation equipment without ever flying an actual plane, you can't expect language courses and global emphasis to provide that *experiential* aspect that is so critical to your student's international education.

If you are a parent who is choosing schools that emphasize languages and multicultural perspectives, I salute you, but at the same time I must also shake you by the shoulders and remind you that *every other student in your kid's school has that same advantage*. What are you doing to help your student get the *experience* he needs to deepen and leverage his global education in the best way possible?

Don't worry. I've got a terrific strategy for you in Chapter Six, another one in Chapter Seven, and more in Chapter Eight. But don't skip ahead—we need to continue our stroll through the education forest first!

Next up: a particularly gnarly-looking tree called the SAT.

Old School: assuming that an IB diploma will prepare students for the global economy

Bold School: recognizing that the IB diploma is an excellent choice for high school students who are unable to enroll in college courses or study abroad through an exchange program

WHEN IT'S SMART TO SKIP THE SAT

> When all think alike, no one thinks very much.
> WALTER LIPPMANN

Remember taking the SAT? I do.

I got up early on a Saturday morning and drove to a high school about twenty miles away. I waited in line with hundreds of other high school seniors clutching two number-two pencils, entered the appropriate room based on the first letter of my last name, and spent the next couple of hours filling in my answer form.

Then I drove to the fabric store and worked until nine P.M. The test just wasn't a big deal. I didn't really think about it for several weeks. I wasn't nervous about getting the results in the mail—it was simply a step I had to go through in order to fill out my college applications.

It's very different today. Most students will take the test at least twice, and many will begin with the PSAT as freshmen or sophomores in order to "get familiar" with the test. Parents (you may recognize yourself here) will buy fat books full of vocabulary lists, and students will download materials online so that they can spend hours taking practice tests. Many will enroll in special classes or tutorials—costing as much as several thousand dollars—to boost their scores. And they'll sweat about the results, believing that even a few points could have an effect on whether they shine among other college applicants.

The Scholastic Aptitude Test is the oldest college entrance exam in the United States. (Read more about the SAT at www.collegeboard.com.) The newest version of the test, launched in 2005, is composed of three sections—reading, math, and writing—each scored on a 200-to-800-point scale. The 171 questions are mostly multiple choice, with one brief essay and ten math questions that require students to indicate the answer on a grid. The test is "speeded," meaning it is designed so that many test-takers will be unable to finish all the questions. In addition to the regular SAT, there are one-hour subject exams that are entirely multiple choice. The Educational Testing Service (ETS) is under contract to the College Board (yes, that same not-for-profit organization that offers the Advanced Placement tests) to produce and administer the SAT, and Pearson Educational Measurement is responsible for scoring the tests.

Interestingly enough, College Board officials recently announced that the new SAT is no better than the old one at predicting college success for first-year students. And in a rather unconvincing statement of support for the new test, Laurence Bunin, senior vice president of operations at the College Board and general manager of the SAT program, said in an interview with *The New York Times*: "The 3-hour, 45-minutes test is almost as good a predictor as four years of high school grades."

Almost as good. Which raises the question, why *bother*? But I'm getting ahead of myself.

The ACT was developed in 1959 by American College Testing (both the test and the organization are now known as ACT). After years of playing second fiddle to the SAT, the ACT is now America's most widely accepted college entrance exam. (Check it out at www.act.org.) While the SAT has focused on identifying the most academically able students for admission to the most selective universities, the ACT has always been more of an everyman test. It was developed as a response to the tidal wave of college applicants in the 1950s (thanks in part to the increased availability of financial aid). Devised as a tool to help students make better decisions about which colleges to attend and which programs to study, it also provided helpful information to colleges about the students they were admitting.

ACT is decidedly less mercenary than the College Board, but either way you slice it, the college-prep testapalooza is a lucrative gig. The quest for perfect test scores has completely colored the college-application process in this country, and everyone seems to have succumbed to test-prep fever.

Or have they?

Piles of books and reports have been written about the SAT and its shortcomings. Even the test-makers agree that SAT results are a poor indicator of college success for females and minority students. But instead of rehashing that old news, let's take a look at the trends that are going to be making the SAT and ACT an even *bigger* part of the high school experience but a *less important* part of college admissions.

Here are **five important points** about the curiously changing role of these standardized tests:

1. **There is a growing trend toward *reducing the importance* of SAT and ACT scores in the college-admissions process across the United States.** Close to eight hundred four-year institutions across the country (including many highly ranked private schools) now admit a substantial number of college freshman applicants without regard to SAT or ACT scores, and many more universities are considering doing the same. Some of these schools exempt students who meet grade-point-average or class rank criteria, while others require SAT or ACT scores but use them only for placement purposes or to conduct research studies. So the good news is that *an unimpressive test score will not prevent anyone from getting an excellent education.*

2. **There is a growing trend toward *requiring* the PSAT, SAT, or ACT in high schools.** The College Board is lobbying state legislatures across the country to sign deals (some for over a million dollars a year) requiring *all* students to take the tests. In exchange, the College Board will provide schools with information about each student's test scores and offer college-prep options targeted to students depending on their results. The ACT has a similar (and many insist, far superior) required-test partnership that focuses on examinations designed for each year and career-guidance options as part of the test-result reports.

3. **Community colleges *do not* require SAT or ACT scores for admission.** Students can enroll at a community college by filling out an application and sitting for a placement test that will determine their appropriate course levels.

4. **Most universities do not require SAT or ACT scores—or even high school transcripts—from *transfer* applicants who have at least one year of college credits**

when applying. A student can take community college or university courses (online or in person) for a year or more— even during high school—and enter a four-year university as a transfer student without ever taking the SAT or ACT. Universities are looking for signs of college readiness, and the best indicator of college readiness is decent grades in college courses!

5. **By avoiding the focus on boosting standardized test scores, students can concentrate on more relevant learning experiences.** For some students, simply knowing that they can skip the SAT or ACT—or at least disregard their test scores—is such a relief that they leap into higher-level learning with greater focus and a palpable sense of joy. Those who stop worrying about getting top test scores are free to consider internships, exchanges, and other opportunities for enhanced learning rather than spending their weekends hunkered down over a test-prep book.

Robert Schaeffer is the public education director for FairTest, the National Center for Fair and Open Testing. (Find lots of great info at www.fairtest.org.) He's the go-to guy for the media whenever it's time for a back-to-school story on admissions numbers or a new report on slipping SAT scores. (Note: Expect a *major* slide in average scores as the tests become mandatory for all students in more high schools.) FairTest focuses on ensuring that the evaluation of students, teachers, and schools is fair, open, valid, and educationally beneficial. One of the organization's key projects involves promoting test-score optional policies for college admissions, so thank FairTest when applying to any of the hundreds of colleges and universities on the list!

As FairTest's spokesperson, Schaeffer's role is to be the voice of reason amid the unwarranted emphasis on test scores as a be-all-end-all-benchmark that either ensures or shatters a student's chances of getting into a good college. As part of his effort to ease the frenzied stampede to test-prep centers, Schaeffer reminds parents and students, "The SAT is simply one of many elements that may be considered on the path to college."

❏ **Smart Move**: Parents who *deemphasize* SAT and ACT test scores are free to mentor their students in ways that lead to greater personal and intellectual development.

Low test scores—or even no scores at all—should not be seen as an obstacle to college admission. Breathe. Feel better?

We need to understand the trends that are shaping our state and district policies regarding these standardized tests. It's really a numbers game—or to be more precise, a business numbers game. Schaeffer spells it out for us:

INSIDER INSIGHT

The size of high school graduating classes is predicted to peak by 2009, thus limiting the potential growth of the markets for college-bound students. So the test-makers are seeking to expand the number of test-takers by getting governments to require that all students take their exams. ACT has such contracts in seven states, and the College Board has been lobbying states across the country to sign up for partnerships that would require students to take the PSAT as sophomores or the SAT as juniors. That is, rather than limiting the tests to the historic markets of juniors and seniors, the test-makers are trying to push their exams "down" to high school sophomores and freshmen. Obviously, if students take the PSAT as freshmen or sophomores, they can take it again as sophomores and juniors, then take and retake the SAT as juniors and seniors.

Once again we can see that those College Board folks are pretty crafty. They've got a surefire way to vastly expand the market for PSAT- and SAT-prep materials and repeat tests, as well as for the AP tests that those who enroll in more rigorous courses will take. It's a sweet deal for the College Board.

Of course, ACT and the College Board package their proposals for state legislators as high-minded attempts to encourage more students to consider college—and this argument is difficult to counter. It's true that students, counselors, and parents will have access to test scores early on, which may serve as a catalyst for more students to take advanced courses in order to prepare for college. Test proponents say that there's no harm in having students take the exams, and the test scores will inform all parties and inspire students to keep their options open. The problem with mandating the PSAT or SAT is that these standardized tests were never designed to serve as a measure of early high school learning or as a tool for high school counselors to place freshmen and sophomores on the college-prep track. The ACT year-specific tests are designed for younger students and may serve as better indicators than an early-bird PSAT, but the fact remains that focusing on required tests sucks time, energy, and money away from other efforts to engage students in more meaningful and relevant learning experiences.

Should Your Student Take The Test?

If your student's high school requires one of these tests, there's not much you can do about it except remind your son or daughter that the test isn't a gauge of their future success. The SAT measures specific skills—making calculated guesses on multiple-choice questions in a timed format—that don't have much to do with college learning or with life after graduation.

If your school doesn't require the tests, then celebrate! You can choose what to do. If your student has major test anxiety or is simply not a brilliant test-taker, take heart. He or she has *absolutely no need* to take the SAT in order to get a good education—but you might want to consider it anyway in certain cases.

▶ The PSAT, which many high school students take during their sophomore year, is used as a way of selecting **National Merit Scholarship** recipients. (Learn more at www .nationalmerit.org.) For years educators have suggested that the National Merit Scholarship winners list isn't exactly a shining example of diversity and equal opportunity. A writing section was added in 1997 as a way to boost test scores for girls, but the results of this and other efforts to increase test fairness are in dispute. Still, if you happen to have a kid who might be exceptionally good at taking tests, it could be advantageous to take the PSAT. Earning thousands of dollars for college by taking a test seems like a pretty good deal, so if you have any reason to believe that your student will perform well on the PSAT, then by all means give it a shot. (Most recipients get $2,500 and a chance to renew the award each year, and being a National Merit Scholar may lead to more scholarships from the universities at which they apply.)

▶ You may want to encourage your son or daughter to take the SAT just for the **everybody's-doing-it aspect**. Everyone will be talking about it, so if they want to take the test, fine. Be aware that if your student's school requires the SAT or ACT, those test scores are likely to become a permanent part of their high school record. Even if the test isn't mandatory, some colleges will require students to submit any score received on an SAT taken within the previous year. By not taking the test, your student can avoid that whole issue with ease.

▶ Sometimes taking the SAT is a personal thing. Your student may look at the tests as **interesting mental challenges** and at test scores as opportunities to understand more about the intricacies of measuring learning in meaningful ways.

Of course, it's difficult to maintain a balanced perspective when everyone around you is bug-eyed with test-score mania.

None of my kids submitted an SAT score, but three of them took the test. While their peers in Oregon were taking AP English, they were spending all day thinking and speaking in another language, so they wanted to make sure their native language skills were up to snuff after they returned. I give them credit for being curious and committed to focusing on what they may have missed while they were out of the United States—and for not getting caught up in the hype about the importance of their SAT scores.

Stuck on the Ivy League? Then get those pencils ready.

With tens of thousands of applications coming in, the most competitive colleges are looking for any excuse to toss one into the slush pile. A freshman application that is missing an SAT or ACT score is very likely to earn a big black X and disappear along with thousands of other not-what-we're-looking-for applicants. So, if you can't let go of the Ivy League, you've got to be ready to do the dance.

But for the rest of you—those who recognize that there are many excellent universities that offer an outstanding education without requiring an SAT or ACT score—it's time for a high five!

Now, isn't this a lovely forest after all? Things look so much better when we have this panoramic view of the entire education woods.

But I've got a very special tree to show you now. Not very many people know about this particular tree and its secrets. It's just standing here on the edge of the forest, quietly waiting to be noticed.

See the initials carved in its trunk?

Yes, this one right here.

We're looking at the GED.

> **Old School:** viewing the SAT as a necessary evil that is of paramount importance in the college application process
> **Bold School:** seeing the SAT and test preparation as largely irrelevant and mostly optional

THE ONE TEST THAT CAN CHANGE EVERYTHING

> He that will have the Kernel must crack the Shell.
> THOMAS FULLER

It's a sticky August afternoon in 1976. I gather with my friends on the steps of our small-town high school, giddy about starting my junior year and still flush from the triumph of getting my driver's license earlier that day. Tables are set up in the library so that we can register for our fall classes, but nobody's paying any attention to that now.

There is an electric buzz in the air.

There is News.

We learn that one of our classmates—a beautiful, vivacious sixteen-year-old cheerleader with top grades and a delightful sense of humor—is pregnant. Her boyfriend, a popular recent graduate, is preparing to head off to join the navy. The two of them have just returned from Las Vegas and a cheesy chapel wedding and will be leaving for California within weeks.

We are blown away.

Some of us have gone to school with her since kindergarten. She is the most beloved student in our class. We always picture her as our homecoming queen, our prom queen, our valedictorian, and everything else—not because she is one of those evil types you see in teen movies but because we're truly proud of her. She really deserves the recognition; she is a remarkable girl.

We don't know how to respond, but as usual, our friend is bubbly and full of laughter. She puts us at ease by sharing funny stories about the wedding ceremony. She talks about her parents' reaction, what it feels like to be pregnant, and how excited she is to move to California with her new husband.

Someone asks her what she's going to do about school. A bright student who has always dreamed of going to college, she has only finished her sophomore year. Is she going to try to go to high school in California?

"Actually, I'm done. I went to the community college and took a test. I got my GED. I'm finished!"

There is an awkward silence. We know how difficult it must have been for her to do this. After all, she is a very intelligent girl, an accomplished student. And she took the *GED*! Feeling embarrassed for her, we nod and stare at our sandaled feet.

The way we see it, getting a GED is even more humiliating than getting pregnant and having a Vegas wedding at sixteen.

Eventually the talk turns to wedding rings, baby names, and departure dates, and a rousing discussion ensues about who will replace her as a varsity cheerleader.

But I am still dazed by what she's said.

She's *done*? *Finished* with high school? Just like *that*?

I can't get it out of my head.

Of course, I know about the GED. Everybody does. That's the test that pregnant girls and failing students take when they can't finish high school. It's what the pizza place in town asks for when you're trying to get hired as a night manager. Many of the local kids end up getting their GED if they are having a hard time their senior year for some reason.

But *this* girl? She is just not the GED type. She lights up a room by simply walking into it. She is Going Places. I can't picture her taking that test.

And yet she has. The rest of us will be struggling or napping through two more years of high school classes. She is *done*.

It occurs to me that I could take the GED too. I could take it and *run*, skipping two years of high school! But I'm not brave enough. I mean, what would I *do*? I want to go to college, and everybody knows that getting a GED is like stamping "loser" in bright red letters on a college application.

At least, that's the way we sixteen-year-olds viewed it back then, back in that small town.

Fast forward.

It's a sticky August afternoon in 2007. My sixteen-year-old daughter, Talya, is taking a test in a room along with others who are hoping to earn their GED certification.

She's not pregnant. She's not failing. She's not vying for a job at the pizza place.

She's going to college. *Early.*

After checking online to see what material would be covered, she spent a couple of months preparing. For her, this meant brushing up on her English skills since she'd spent the previous two years speaking Spanish. She earned a perfect score on the writing test and scored in the 99th percentile overall (meaning the 99th percentile of high school seniors nationwide—not just GED test-takers).

Once she had her GED certification, she was able to enroll in an American university in Buenos Aires. While her classmates back in Oregon schlepped through AP courses during their junior year of high school, she participated in passionate debates in a world religions class taught by an animated Hungarian professor, sat at the center of the finger-pointers as the only American in her U.S. history course, and had her English compositions worked over with a fine-toothed comb by her Harvard-educated American professor. She learned about other perspectives through discussions with her classmates from Argentina, the United Kingdom, Kuwait, Pakistan, and Lebanon. Each one of her freshman courses had fewer than ten students—and her bio lab had only six. (Total cost for the year: $5,000.)

But what did her high school friends in Oregon think when she told them she got her GED? They were stunned. They felt kind of embarrassed for her and sad that she was going to miss the best years of high school. They didn't know what to say.

And she laughed all the way to college. She was *done*.

There are sure to be people (like me) who associate the GED with a failing student they remember from high school or the girl who got pregnant and dropped out. The challenge is to rise above the critical judgment of the relatively clueless and embrace the opportunity to rocket ahead of them, smiling all the way.

But . . . the *GED? Seriously?* How can taking the GED possibly allow anyone to stay alongside—let alone pass—those on the perfect 4.0/super-SAT track?

The GED offers distinct advantages to those who are ready to blast through high school and blaze ahead as bold schoolers. It's just hard to clearly see the benefits of the GED when we're dripping and sizzling with fego. So let's shake off the fear ("Will my kid be serving fries forever?") and the ego ("No child of mine is going to take the GED!") and look at the GED as a tool for transcending the traditional focus on transcripts.

More than 16 million people have taken a GED test over the last sixty years.

The General Educational Development Testing Service (no, it's not the General Equivalency Diploma, though that's a common misperception) created its first test back in 1942, when the United States Armed Forces Institute asked the American Council on Education to develop a battery of tests to measure high-school-level academic skills. (Learn more at www.gedtest.org.)

In the beginning the GED was used as a way to help returning World War II veterans who had dropped out of high school in order to enlist. Those returning to civilian life were interested in taking advantage of the GI Bill to go to college, but they needed to complete high school first. After spending months or years on the battlefield, hanging out with high school students wasn't particularly appealing to the veterans. They'd seen and done more in their young lives than their hometown peers could imagine, and they certainly weren't into the social hooey of high school like the Sadie Hawkins dance or the graduation ceremonies—they just wanted to get the diploma and move on. The GED was the perfect solution, and thousands of veterans used the test as a way to jump-start their new lives.

In 1947 the GED became available to civilians when New York implemented a program to award its high school diploma to those who passed the test. Gradually more states adopted the GED as an alternative for high school students interested in joining the workforce early. In 1973 California became the last state to join the GED testing program. GED tests are offered in more than 3,200 locations, including more than 100 international test centers.

> In 2007 a ninety-seven-year-old woman became the oldest candidate to receive the GED certification.

Over the years there have been four generations of the GED. The first tests reflected an industrial era in which a high school diploma was sufficient for most jobs. Now candidates are more likely to cite education instead of employment as the reason for taking the GED.

> Average age of all GED candidates: 25
> Percentage of candidates aged 16–18: 30
> Percentage of candidates who are male: 59
> Percentage of all candidates who have been out of school for one year or less: 30

Many people assume that the GED is a simple exam that has been specially developed for low-performing students.

Wrong.

First of all, the GED tests are designed so that only the top 33 percent of all U.S. graduating seniors will be able to pass them. The folks at the testing centers make it very clear that it's not easy to just stroll in and ace the tests without preparing. In fact, in many states candidates are required to participate in prep sessions prior to taking a single test.

In addition, though the GED certification used to require that the student achieve a passing score on one all-inclusive test, it is now divided into *five* separate tests that are generally taken on different days. The tests cover science, language arts/reading, social studies, math, and language arts/writing. In 2006, 68 percent of those who completed the GED test battery passed by earning an average score of 450 or greater on five tests and a minimum score of 410 on each.

The most recent statistics (for 2006) indicate that only about 3 percent of current GED candidates are sixteen years old at the time they take the tests, mainly because many states have a compulsory school requirement for all students up to the age of seventeen. I was curious about how an influx of young GED test-takers might affect the administration of the battery of tests. I talked to Robert MacGillivray, the former deputy executive director of GED Testing Service, who pointed out that testing requirements vary from state to state and it's important for families to check with their local GED testing center for details. Depending on where you live, it may be possible (or not) to get a waiver to take the tests earlier than the minimum age.

MacGillivray told me that young students differ from older GED candidates mainly in speed. "The younger candidates tend to be more confident and finish the test much more quickly," MacGillivray explained. "They're used to taking tests because they've been in school more recently. An older candidate, on the other hand, may not have taken a test of any kind for years, so they're likely to be more cautious. If a mixed group seems intimidating for older or even younger candidates, testing centers can choose to offer test sessions specifically for younger test-takers."

Why should a perfectly happy high school student go the "Good Enough Diploma" route?

Well, any student who is perfectly happy—and who is challenged and thriving—in high school shouldn't go for the GED just because it's available. It is not intended as a first choice for those who want to complete high school, nor is it a ticket to slide.

However, in many cases the GED could be an ideal option. It provided a satisfying solution to the challenges Talya was facing by allowing her to:

- **avoid wasted time due to transcript issues.** Because of the change in hemisphere in moving from Mexico to Argentina, Talya arrived midway through the school year and would have had to sit through several months of the year she'd already taken *plus* spend three more years in a local high school, a distressing and time-wasting prospect.
- **study alongside older students with whom she had more in common.** Talya was doing very well in her intensive Spanish classes at a local Argentine university with mostly American college students. She had the confidence, skills, and motivation to keep up with those who were several years older than she was.
- **get "credit" for material she had learned outside class.** Talya had been spending several hours a week working with tutors, including an American attorney who guided her studies in English literature and an Argentine biologist who introduced her to postdoc scientists who were conducting research in the bowels of the science museum. The GED option allowed her to avoid chasing transcripts, concentrate on learning, and show the knowledge she'd gained through self-study.
- **dive into more advanced work.** Many students are fully capable of handling a college-level course without having

taken an advanced course in that subject in high school. History, sociology, psychology, anthropology, and even many science courses in college present basic material that is needed to understand the concepts addressed, so previous exposure is not necessary. (What matters most: good reading comprehension and study skills.)

In Talya's case, earning her GED certification allowed her to continue her education in the most immediate, challenging, and fulfilling way possible.

More students are finding that the GED can help them get direct access to excellent educational opportunities. **Take a look at the face of the new GED candidate:**

◆ International students

Many high school students who come to the United States from other countries choose to take the GED as a way of avoiding the transnational transcript dance. It's a lot less frustrating—and less expensive—than duplicating, translating, certifying, and FedExing documents across the world and back numerous times.

◆ Students who have moved during high school

Some students choose the GED if their new high school would require them to repeat courses they have already taken. Because every school is different, finding a perfect match between two similar courses can be difficult. Students balk at spending time taking a class that is very close (but deemed not quite close enough) to one they have already completed, and instead of devoting a semester or two to tidying up their transcripts, they'd rather take the GED so that they can enroll in college courses immediately.

(continued)

Homeschooled students

These students are choosing to take the GED at sixteen or seventeen so that they can enroll in college early. They tend to be very self-directed and focused on academics, and earning their GED certification allows them to connect with other young college students who are making their education a priority.

Students enrolled in virtual schools

Online courses are giving students of all ages an opportunity to complete or complement their studies. While many online students choose to take the SAT and enter university in the traditional way, those who are ahead of their high school peers may opt to skip ahead by simply taking the GED.

Elite athletes, actors, artists, or musicians

Those who are involved in elite sports or other activities that require a great deal of training or travel may take the GED in order to avoid being expelled for missing too many days of high school.

Students with medical issues

The GED is a good choice for those who have been ill or hospitalized after an injury or surgery and must be away from school for long periods of time. Some GED test centers have special arrangements allowing candidates in hospitals or rehab centers to take the tests on site.

Students who have lived or studied abroad

As more and more students choose to study abroad or focus on an opportunity that takes them away from their high school for several weeks, months, or even years, GED certification is a convenient way to allow them to complete the requirements they need to enter college.

Do four-year universities accept the GED as a substitute for a high school diploma? That depends. Most public institutions accept the GED on freshman applications, but private universities are less likely to accept it unless it is accompanied by other traditional entrance materials (like SAT scores) or is part of a transfer application. College-admissions directors are looking for students who show initiative and follow-through. They are more likely to see taking a battery of five GED tests at the age of sixteen in order to enroll in college courses or to spend a year abroad as a plus, not a minus. However, applying with a GED certification *alone*—with no college credits to transfer and no convincing story about why it was the best choice—is a much more problematic strategy.

Bear in mind that I'm not recommending that a young person take the GED tests in order to enroll as a full-time residential student at a four-year university early and move into a dorm at sixteen (although this may be a viable option for some). Instead, I'm suggesting that those who want to take community college or university courses instead of the offerings at their local high school can move forward by taking the GED series *as part of a plan* to transfer to a four-year university at eighteen as a sophomore or junior.

❏ **Smart Move**: Parents who rise above their fear and ego can see the power of the GED to liberate motivated students and lift them to new heights.

The GED may be the best choice for your son or daughter, but first you must learn about *all* options for students in your area.

Thousands of kids have had their fill of homeroom classes and spirit assemblies by the age of sixteen and are ready to focus on learning in a more mature environment. If a dual enrollment program isn't available or practical for your student, the GED *plus* college courses could be a very advantageous combination.

I'm delighted that Talya got her GED certification, and so is she. While her Oregon classmates were taking AP biology during their junior year of high school, she was taking Biology 201 in college. She was thrilled to be learning more about herself and her interests while earning college credit and associating with older students.

If your student is completely happy in high school and is taking the most challenging and relevant courses while finding ways to earn college credits through IB, AP, or dual enrollment, that's great. But if your son or daughter really isn't into high school (or worse, is feeling stifled there) but is excited about *learning* and going on to college, you may want to consider opening the GED door to higher education.

Old School: viewing GED certification as a last resort for low-achieving students

Bold School: seeing GED certification as a beneficial tool for motivated students who are ready to start college early

CHAPTER FIVE

Meet the New A Student

ARTFUL, ADVANCED,

ATYPICAL, AND ADVENTUROUS

> To hell with facts! We need stories.
> KEN KESEY

THREE STORIES OF A STUDENTS

What type of students will thrive as bold schoolers? Well, that's what's so great about this approach—*any* student can benefit from a more expansive education! Whether you have a kid who has always done everything by the book or one who has been a rebel from the time she was a toddler, rest assured that this strategy offers advantages to everyone.

Rather than thinking of a certain type of student who might do best by doing school differently, consider the key ingredients that characterize this eyes-wide-open perspective. You see, a new kind of **A** student is getting attention these days—and we're not talking grades.

Bold schoolers aren't obsessing about their GPA. (That's *old* school.) Instead, they're looking at the **A**s that will guarantee that they'll stand out by magnifying the skills, talents, and interests that make them unique.

These students understand the value of an education that is:

Artful: *skillful or clever in adapting means to ends; ingenious.* Pasting together a strategic educational collage of methods and mentors ensures that the experience is both *individualized* and *intentional.*

Advanced: *embodying ideas, practices, and attitudes that are more enlightened than the standardized, established, or traditional.* Seeing beyond the traditional path invites innovation and allows students to go through high school and college in a *truly* advanced way. *Advanced* refers to both depth and speed—in general, bold schoolers find ways to go deeper sooner and to do so in ways that are both *informed* and *inspired.*

Atypical: *not conforming to type; unusual.* By doing school differently, students open new doors to learning and discover a wide range of options. Those who define their own high standards instead of following the crowd are seen as *independent* and *imaginative*—two qualities that will distinguish 21st-century leaders, especially members of the knowledge-based creative class.

Adventurous: *inclined to undertake new and daring enterprises.* Bold schoolers who take chances in order to move forward in exciting directions blast through old patterns of thinking while developing wisdom and becoming *intrepid* and *indomitable.*

You need not pick only one of these, and not all of these **A** qualities are necessary. Your student may head in a particularly artful or adventurous direction, or she may choose a quick/deep/ quirky combo that is both advanced and atypical. Selecting even *one* of these themes will provide a framework for a personalized education that will set your student apart from the pack, and concocting a perfect mix of all four will result in an even more enriching experience.

Artful. Advanced. Atypical. Adventurous.

The key to success for these new **A** students is a sense of *being fully involved in their own education.*

There's something you should know about bold schoolers in general: they're modest. They are much more likely to be low-key than loud-mouthed about their personal trajectory, and they're used to not getting much recognition. In addition, they're too busy getting a wildly creative and personalized education to feel dejected about the fact that nobody is organizing a special assembly in their honor.

Bold schoolers are infused with a sense of gratitude; they use words like "fortunate" and "lucky" a lot. Even though they have had to struggle more than their peers, they don't have a chip on their shoulder, and they are quick to thank others for even the tiniest morsels of assistance or encouragement.

I find this extremely refreshing, but it also makes me want to cry. I feel like gathering all the bold schoolers across the country for a big group hug. The truth: bold schoolers are likely to have *far* more impressive personal and academic accomplishments than your garden-variety high school graduate with a shelf full of trophies, team photos, and certificates—and they've earned theirs without any awards ceremonies or yearbook photos to mark the occasion.

Bold schoolers are so used to downplaying everything that it takes a bit of prodding to get them to open up, but they are genuinely thrilled to have a chance to help others who might be struggling the same way they were. The three individuals you are about to meet aren't into grandstanding. They agreed to share their stories here only because (1) I begged them, and (2) I promised them that readers would be appreciative rather than judgmental. Please prove me right.

Let's begin with Gabrielle Wallace, a delightful bold-school poster girl. She found my blog about living in Argentina and contacted me directly (a bold-school basic) while researching places to stay during a planned trip to Buenos Aires. I had just posted about the fact that I was writing a book about alternative education, and she mentioned that she might have some thoughts to share. Indeed she does.

BOLD STATEMENT

At the end of junior high my English teacher realized I was disappointed in school. It's not that I didn't like learning; I just didn't like school. I really enjoyed doing creative writing work in her English class, but I was not happy in the public school environment. It felt like jail to me—a controlled institution that I couldn't leave (I wasn't rebellious enough to skip school), strict rules that didn't make sense to me, and an uncomfortable social environment (I had recently moved from Hawaii to Indiana and had to form a new social circle). She told me, "Don't worry. Next year you'll be in high school, and everything will be better."

I wanted to believe her, but after the first few months of high school, I was very disillusioned. It was disheartening that I could not work at my own speed, and I longed for even a moment of individualized attention. I started adding up the minutes in the school day that I thought of as "wasted" time. I just felt that I could accomplish so much more if I studied on my own.

At the end of my first semester of high school, I found Grace Llewellyn's *The Teenage Liberation Guidebook: How to Quit School and Get a Real Life and Education*. I was really inspired! I discussed my frustration about high school with my parents. We went to an open house for a private school (my parents realized they couldn't afford tuition) and attended a homeschool convention (it turned out to be mostly Christian fundamentalist families hoping to avoid teaching evolution). At that point I felt totally discouraged but continued to do research on my own.

I read about how others had studied at home, taken the SATs, participated in sports and activities outside of high school, and been admitted to colleges just as any other student might. I begged my parents to allow me to leave high school and start homeschooling right away, but they said no. They had too many worries that I would not receive a traditional education and that they didn't have any time to assist me. They were concerned that I wouldn't be able to get accepted to any college and that it might be illegal for me to stop going to school. So, feeling dejected, I finished the rest of my freshman year of high school, receiving grades ranging from As to Cs.

After that school year my family and I moved to Minneapolis. There I found the PSEO (Post Secondary Education Option) program that allows a high school student in good standing to take college courses for credit. I read and reread all the rules and figured out that I could register with the state as a homeschooled student and take as many college courses as I could handle—*for free*. Once again I begged my parents, and this time, since I had a solid plan with structured courses, they agreed.

My morale and grades skyrocketed! That school year at Normandale Community College (NCC) I completed fourteen general studies courses, including English, Western history, French, human biology, art, and more—and received straight As.

I was so grateful for that program. I could not have
(continued)

made a better choice for the change in my education. My age, fifteen, was not an issue because I was relatively mature, and there were other PSEO students from area high schools as well as other young college students.

Actually, dropping out of high school was a positive experience socially. I had been stuck in a circle of girls I can now identify as very bad influences. Leaving that setting allowed me to reconstruct my identity and create a new group of friends from among my college classmates.

I wanted to continue at NCC under the PSEO program, but the next year my family and I had to move again, this time to Maine. I found out that in Maine the GED can be taken only by those age eighteen or older. I wasn't about to go back to high school after a great year of college! So my mother and I made a trip back to Minnesota for a week so that I could take the GED tests there, where the minimum age is sixteen. I passed and applied to the University of Southern Maine as a transfer student at sixteen.

I thoroughly enjoyed my classes at USM! Although I had wanted to get out of high school as soon as possible, I wasn't in a rush to finish college—I absolutely loved being a student in that setting. I got involved in political activities, acted in a play, made the scholar-athlete list four years in a row, and participated in Model United Nations debate conferences as a delegate and chairperson. To pay for my tuition, I worked part time for the City of Portland in after-school programs. The city had an agreement with state universities that it would pay for half of its employees' tuition *plus* hourly wages.

I chose not to tell many people my age or that I got my GED, because I was afraid they would think I was strange. When I did share, people would usually say something like "Wow, you must be a genius!" I was embarrassed by that kind of attention because I knew it was not my IQ but my motivation that got me into college so young.

At USM I majored in international relations and received minors in Spanish and history. (I graduated at the age of twenty with a 3.33 GPA.) During my second year at USM I applied to study abroad through a university summer program in Cuba and got a grant that covered almost all of the trip's expenses. I spent two weeks at the University of Havana, and it got me hooked on travel!

After that I really wanted to study for a longer period of time in a Spanish-speaking country. I spent many hours in the study-abroad office looking through brochures of companies offering packages, including many all-inclusive programs with costs starting at $6,000 a semester and going way, way up. I didn't have that kind of money and I didn't want to go abroad with a group of Americans. Plus, I was interested in going to a third-world country, which wasn't really an option for most of the packaged programs.

So using my Spanish, I researched university websites in the Caribbean and South America. I decided on a university in the Dominican Republic—I had a few Dominican friends who could give me advice on their country, and I knew it would be a pretty cheap option. I made phone calls and sent e-mails to contacts I found through the university website and organized my own study-abroad plan. After staying with a Dominican family for a week, I was really lucky to find a studio apartment for rent right across the street from the university for only $250 a month! I was thrilled because it was so much cheaper than the host family housing that ran other foreign students at least $1,000 each month.

I took a Spanish proficiency test and tested into classes for native speakers, which allowed me to make more local

(continued)

friends than if I had been stuck in classes for foreigners only. The total for the semester's tuition as a foreign student was $1,200. (This international rate was four times more than a Dominican student would pay, but compared with the study-abroad programs it was dirt cheap.) I paid for this with savings from my part-time job. I had much more freedom and paid far less than the other foreign students and was completely happy with my situation. I even had homestay experiences with my new Dominican friends who took me home to their families on school vacations.

There were times when I was afraid that I wouldn't be successful in a regular class for native speakers or that I wouldn't find a place to live without the support of a study-abroad program. But the truth is that it really wasn't that hard. I felt grateful to be learning so much about living there. I gained so much trust in my own ability to thrive in a foreign environment.

After the Dominican Republic I returned to USM for graduation. Then I spent a month in Brazil attending a conference put on by the World Social Forum and studying Portuguese and capoeira (an Afro-Brazilian martial art I had been practicing for a year prior). I arranged a homestay through the WSF website and stayed for free with a female college student, Luiza, who lived with her mother. We got along very well, and she introduced me to many of her friends. We still keep in touch now, four years later.

I was going to stay in Brazil longer, but I returned to the United States upon receiving an invitation to interview for an English teacher position in Japan through JET, the Japan Exchange and Teaching Programme (www .jetprogramme.org). I was fortunate to be accepted and six months later traveled to Japan, where I taught English at a Japanese high school for one year. I could write a novel about that year—actually, I am working on that now! In Japan I got a great education in culture, language, and how to adapt to a foreign place (again). It was my first professional job as a high school teacher—ironic, as I had not earned an official high school diploma myself.

When I returned from Japan, I found a job as a Spanish teacher at a private Jewish school in Boston. (I am now a state-certified teacher for grades five through twelve.) I love working at a private school, where I have great freedom with my curriculum. I try to use that advantage to make my classes engaging for my students, and I am learning so much about how to be a better teacher. I can now see how limited class time and high student-teacher ratios can make it difficult to provide individualized attention!

I would never advise dropping out of high school just to run away from it. No matter what, make sure you are moving toward an educational goal. You have to do whatever it takes to make your education the best it can be for you personally. I was miserable in public high school, so that meant dropping out, getting my GED, and going straight to college. Maybe that's for you, or maybe you can find your own path.

You must be assertive and research your options because no one—not your teachers or parents—will know exactly what is best for you. You have to be very organized and motivated even when others discourage or doubt you, which believe me they will. Talk to your teachers in whatever subject most interests you to see what advice they have for you to further your education.

(continued)

If you're not happy with your situation, there is always another way of doing things. My best suggestions:

❑ It really helps to talk to people who have unconventional educational histories.
❑ Apply for all kinds of opportunities, no matter what the odds may be—you just might get what you want, like my job in Japan!
❑ Find out about options such as employers that pay for tuition.
❑ Consider studying abroad in a third-world country, and look into creating your own itinerary and arranging your own home stay.

Most of all, don't be afraid to follow your heart. When I share my educational history with people, the first question they usually ask is "Don't you feel like you missed out? Don't you wish you went to the prom?" My answer is unequivocally no and no. I think I did so well in college because I found an education that fit me and I truly wanted to be there. I feel lucky that I was able to discover wonderful ways to continue to learn.

There are many students like Gabrielle who have come up with their own A-plus plan that incorporates all the **A** qualities— artful, advanced, atypical, and adventurous—but her story is unique in terms of the challenges she was facing: she started at a young age (fifteen), her parents were reluctant to veer off the standard path, and she had very limited resources. Gabrielle was her own advocate, and she figured out how to finish high school early, earn money for college, study abroad inexpensively, and work in another country. At every point Gabrielle remained deeply involved in her educational experience because she was creating it herself. And you might be interested to know that, thanks to her savings from her year in Japan (and having no college debt), she was able to buy her own little condo in Boston (at age twenty-two) that she can swap during her summers off in order to visit other places around the world.

Gabrielle's story is inspiring, but it may also be intimidating to those who are interested in taking on a less daunting mission. Maybe your student has just one obstacle (instead of several) or wants to find an alternative to high school without necessarily finishing early or entering college ahead of schedule. Sometimes it takes just one bold move to shift everything into place.

Emily Montgomery just wanted to do what seemed reasonable— avoid repeating a year of high school that she had "missed" while abroad. She figured out how to get into a top college without graduating from high school *or* getting a GED. Here's her story:

BOLD STATEMENT

I attended a language magnet high school to study Japanese while my friend's father tutored me in Hungarian on the weekends. I soon became frustrated trying to become proficient in a language from a classroom setting. I also loved traveling and learning about other cultures. I had been to Hungary once before with my friend's family, and it was the first time I had experienced another culture not as a tourist but from a family setting. I wanted more.

A few of my friends studied abroad with AFS Intercultural Programs, and my family had also hosted two AFS students in our home in Houston. I broached the subject with my parents, who were undoubtedly hesitant about sending their sixteen-year-old daughter to another country for a year. However, my parents have always been

(continued)

extremely supportive and have tried to give me every opportunity to grow in my own way. So I signed up for the full-year AFS program, and instead of entering my third year of high school in Houston, I enrolled at a public school in Tiszaújváros, Hungary.

All of my classes were in Hungarian. I would copy down all the notes, but I obviously couldn't do work on the same level. I had my own Hungarian tutor through AFS and went to a music conservatory for the viola, where I joined an orchestra and took private instruction as well.

Studying abroad was a lot more than experiencing a new culture. It helped me learn about my own capabilities and strengths. Instead of living with an AFS host family, I arranged to stay with my friend's grandmother. She did not speak any English, so I had to learn Hungarian, and she gave me all the time in the world to do it. We cooked Hungarian dishes together, and I read *Harry Potter* aloud to her in Hungarian.

In Houston I had attended an IB/AP high school. I didn't want to exclude the possibility of getting an IB diploma, so I didn't even try to get any high school credits in Hungary. My plan was to take an extra year in high school—a junior year abroad and then a junior year and senior year in the United States.

But coming back to my home in the United States wasn't so simple. I had changed, my friends had changed (and were all seniors), and even some of my interests had changed. I had new energy for my schoolwork, but it wasn't the type of work I wanted to do. I longed to be able to come up with my own ideas and structures in a paper rather than write the magical formula that gives students fives on AP exams. I got involved with new activities, such as the Houston chapter of Amnesty International, and helped establish that organization at my high school. But still I wasn't happy about staying in high school an extra year.

In October of my second junior year (it would have been my senior year) my grandmother took me to see Wellesley, Mount Holyoke, and Kenyon colleges. I loved what I saw! Students were articulate and focused. I was excited by the discussions I heard both inside and outside the classroom.

I decided I would apply to these three schools. I didn't have backup colleges, because my backup was completing high school. I took my SAT tests, wrote my college essays, and went for interviews—all in a very short period of time. The most important part in gaining acceptance was making an argument about why I should go to college without completing high school. I think this actually helped me get into these colleges since the schools saw I had drive and initiative to pursue what I wanted in my education.

Ever since I had attended a Wellesley tea in Houston during my first year of high school, Wellesley had been my top choice. It was one of the few schools with a peace and justice program and also happened to have an accelerating candidate program that took one or two juniors a year. In my essay to Wellesley, I wrote about my year abroad and how it had opened my eyes to new ways of thinking and to my own strengths.

Wellesley let me finish something I had started in Hungary—exploring new cultures, political systems, and organizational structures. Since Hungary I've taken every opportunity to travel and explore. I traveled to India with a Wellesley grassroots study, studied abroad in Geneva

(continued)

for a semester during my junior year, and worked for the Senate immigration subcommittee. I finished my degree in political science (concentration in international relations) in four years, and currently I am working in New York with a financial services consulting company. I wanted to get a taste of the business world after my liberal arts education before pursuing graduate studies.

Hungary taught me that there are no limits to what I can accomplish, and it gave me some friendships that I still treasure today.

At first glance you might think that Emily didn't do anything too extraordinary—she ended up finishing high school at the same time as her classmates, went to college, studied abroad for a semester, graduated in four years, and is now working. What's unusual is that the confidence and self-knowledge she gained from her time in Hungary greatly influenced her later: she *knew* that she was ready for college and set about finding ways to get in. Emily found her open door and stepped through it, very persistently working toward getting into the school she dreamed of attending. Though she had some advantages—a supportive family and financial resources—what carried her forward was a clear sense of self-awareness and a level of perseverance that will continue to influence her life in the years to come.

Lang Van Dommelen didn't move around like Gabrielle or have to hound his parents to homeschool him, and he didn't have to be sly like Emily to avoid wasting a year that could be far more academically enriching. But he made one very bold decision that expanded his world exponentially. I'll let him explain.

BOLD STATEMENT

From the age of ten I lived in a small three-room log cabin in Bird Creek, Alaska. The house is off the grid, so we have no running water and use an outhouse. We have a generator to provide our power.

My parents started homeschooling me in seventh grade. The commute to town had become too much, and the private school I attended did not offer courses for my level. My parents made the decision to take both my sister and me out at that point, and we continued our Waldorf education at home. Waldorf education is described as "education for the hands, heart, and head." I learned my subjects in month-long blocks, and I wrote and illustrated all of my essays by hand in our lesson books.

I was doing art during my main lesson blocks but also apprenticing at a local potter's studio. I spent maybe eight hours a week there mixing clay, throwing pots, and firing kilns. During my last year of studying at home, I strayed from the Waldorf method and became more self-directed about my studies.

I heard about the Rotary Youth Exchange program from a family friend. I contacted my local Rotary Club that year about applying, but they had already selected a student. The next year I applied and was thrilled to learn that I had been accepted!

My predeparture experience was full of hope, exuberance, and despair. Every year Rotary District 5010 (Alaska, Yukon, and Russia) holds a youth exchange conference in a resort town fifteen minutes from my small town of a few hundred. Up until this point I had no friends who were going through the same emotional ups and downs
(continued)

that I was going through. At the three-day conference all the exchange students (those preparing to leave, those in the district from other countries, and those who had returned home after being abroad) would be present. I was excited but also very nervous.

There I was, this sixteen-year-old, extremely shy, quiet boy completely out of my comfort zone. Fortunately I met a wonderful girl there named Samantha who encouraged me and dragged me through the social gatherings of the weekend. At the beginning of the conference we were told our destinations so that we could connect with others who were from the same area or were heading that way. When I found out that I would be going to my first-choice country—Italy—I was ecstatic! At that point I had no idea that the challenges I would face in the months prior to my departure would cause me to make choices that were way beyond my years.

I went through my predeparture life, attending Rotary meetings and a district conference up until the first week of June, when I received a call from my district chairperson. He told me that Italy had pulled out of my exchange! (This is not a typical situation for Rotary, but it does happen once in a while.) I had three choices: I could pull out of the exchange entirely, I could go to Mexico, or I could go to Thailand.

I was stunned. I had spent the last three months reading about Italy and taking lessons in Italian! I had twenty-four hours to make a decision. After a sleepless night of agonizing, I chose to go to Thailand with a mission to learn and to make the very best of the situation. Though the change in destination really messed up a lot of the predeparture preparations I'd made, going to Thailand turned out to be the best choice of my life!

The whole year was hard. I struggled with host families, I struggled with the language, and I struggled with school, but I wouldn't have given up any of it for the world. My best, my most lasting memory of the entire year was the two-week period during which I became a novice Buddhist monk. For me, it was one of the biggest steps in "becoming" Thai.

The language was probably my biggest challenge. I spent hours and hours every day studying alone and then with my Thai friends whom I had recruited to help me practice. The exhaustion was ridiculous. I was completely drained. I would go home from school and just shut down.

I went to school for six months. At first I really struggled in my assigned classes. I would spend the vast majority of my class periods studying Thai. Later in the year I requested that I be able to move around a little more in order to study different subjects. This allowed me to take a Thai cooking class, a Thai dessert class, drawing, and Buddhism, and I also had a weekly lesson with a professor in Thai language and another about Thai culture.

While studying Thai during class and with teachers was beneficial, what really helped me was walking in the streets, going into shops, talking to vendors in markets, and hanging out with friends outside school. I made deals with classmates and had them teach me, and then I would help them with their English. I was able to get by in Thai by the end of the year.

I got to travel both alone and with exchange students. Personally I felt traveling alone gave me the opportunity to see more of the real country. I would take the third-class train and often would get off at random small villages and

(continued)

go to the local market or just explore. Traveling and seeing the way the people lived really helped me understand the culture and lives of Thai people.

Also I am a serious rock climber, and it turned out that my small town in Thailand is home to some of the best climbing around Bangkok. A group of rock climbers—a mix of Thais and British and French expats, some of whom had been teaching in Thai schools for many years—got together each week. They offered me a shoulder to lean on and provided great support and friendship during my time in Thailand.

I really began to feel at home during the last three or so months of the exchange. I was able to communicate, I understood the culture, I loved *my* king, and I began to feel Thai.

When I returned to Alaska, I had a few high school credits to finish and decided to complete the majority of my requirements at the University of Anchorage. (My father is a professor there.) I think that my exchange made me a lot more motivated in school. Plus, things seem relatively easy—everyone speaks a language I can understand!

My exchange changed the way I think about the world and what I want to study. I'm currently majoring in international relations and environment/society, studying French and working at a popular pub/pizzeria. I'm very interested in learning more about international aid and development. Thailand inspired me to develop a greater understanding of other cultures and look for ways that I might contribute toward building a positive future.

Lang went from self-study in a cabin in the woods of Alaska to attending a school in Bangkok, Thailand. He didn't let his initial disappointment (not going to Italy) interfere with his ability to recognize a fantastic opportunity, and he threw himself into absorbing everything he could in his new country. He even upped the ante by choosing to experience life as a Buddhist monk!

Notice that all three of these students used their own particular skills and interests to connect with others and to make friendships that transcended barriers. They recognized the power of connecting on the basis of shared passions and leveraged their opportunities for friendship and support.

But that's not the biggest thing they have in common.

What Gabrielle, Emily, and Lang share is the transformational experience of **spending a significant period of time living abroad at a very impressionable age**. This is an unsurpassable opportunity for optimal personal growth and ongoing global awareness. But beyond that it's exactly what our kids *need*—even if it scares the hell out of us. We'll be poking at that fear—and peeking at the ways it shows up—in the next section.

> **Old School:** showcasing hoop-jumping skills by getting straight **As**
>
> **Bold School:** showcasing passion, confidence, and creativity by being **a**typical, **a**dvanced, **a**rtful, and **a**dventurous

THE RIGHT TO A RITE OF PASSAGE

> Little children, headache; big children, heartache.
> ITALIAN PROVERB

Thomas Armstrong is a psychologist and author of numerous books on the ways we learn throughout life. In his most recent, *The Human Odyssey: Navigating the Twelve Stages of Life,* he describes the key characteristics and challenges specific to each step in the human life cycle.[1] Not surprisingly, the quality most strongly associated with adolescence is **passion.** In the second decade of life, our students are biologically wired to grow up and begin toying with their passion in the areas of social, mental, and—yes, here it is—*physical* development. This is exactly what freaks us out about our adolescents—we are worried that their passion will lead them to do crazy, dangerous, or terribly fun things. So we respond by doing all we can to limit their options in order to protect our students from themselves. "At this age our kids are like plants bursting through their pots, in dire need of being transplanted," Dr. Armstrong told me. "We have to release them from confinement and allow them to stretch while encouraging them to find appropriate directions for their growth. This is the only way they will get the opportunities they need to solve problems in order to develop their frontal lobes."

In addition to passion and pot bursting, adolescents have a deep longing to endure a **rite of passage** that will serve as a sign of liberation to themselves and others. Heads up to parents: you play an *extremely* important role here.

Ready for a revelation? According to Dr. Armstrong:

> Parents who have not created their own fulfilling lives are generally the ones most likely to restrain their adolescents from emotionally advancing into adulthood. Our own unresolved issues suck our adolescents into a state of unconscious dependence and immaturity.

Ouch! Well, if that shoe fits, try walking around in it for a while. You'll notice plenty of other parents wearing the same ones.

Really, you've got to feel bad for our students; in our modern culture there just aren't too many great opportunities for them to show the world their independence. Get your driver's license? Big deal. A new tattoo? Zzzz. Getting busted with your friends for some asinine (but memorable) incident? You can see how this might seem like an appealing option to a kid looking to distinguish himself. Without much leeway, it's nearly impossible to proclaim oneself an adult in truly exemplary style. We have our kids in lockdown at a time when their brain chemicals are cheering them on and telling them to break out of parental prison in outlandish ways.

We should know better than to do battle with biology.

For centuries cultures around the world have offered a pivotal journey as a rite of passage for their adolescents. Whether they were sent off on a vision quest, a jungle hunt, an apprenticeship, or a battle, young people were given the chance to separate from home and family, become immersed in a new place, and establish independence. Upon their return they were viewed as adults who were ready to stand on their own two feet.

From the 1600s through the 1800s well-to-do English families sent their sixteen-year-old sons (along with tutors) on an extended journey through Europe, known as the "Grand Tour." These young men (and women too, once train travel made it cheaper and safer) would visit landmarks, appreciate works of art in galleries and museums along the way, and learn about the ideas of great thinkers whose contributions shaped the cultural landscape. Back then the risks were much greater for those who traveled by carriage, train, or ship; it took longer to get everywhere, meaning these trips extended for many months or even years, and deadly diseases threatened those who explored distant lands. Still, despite the dangers, sending young men and women on a lengthy journey far from home was recognized by society as immensely valuable. Even those who could scarcely afford it made every effort to provide their sons and daughters with this profoundly life-altering experience that served to usher them into adulthood.

These days we've opted out of such momentous rites of passage in favor of multiple photo moments. Fear and lack of imagination have constricted our view of adolescents' possibilities; we limit them to three-hour events like sweet sixteen parties and high school graduation ceremonies and infuse these occasions with far more weight than is warranted. Let's face it: sweating alongside your friends in synthetic clothing—no matter how sparkly or voluminous—is a pretty pitiful excuse for a peak experience compared to, say, traveling through Europe for months. Even our students' travel opportunities tend to be digitally documented parties ("Spring break! WOOOO!") rather than personally challenging experiences that lead to self-discovery and a sense of true independence.

A few departures do feel like rites of passage. Joining the military has turned young people into adults for generations, but it's not necessarily the coming-of-age experience most parents want for their kids. Going off to college is a relatively clear mark of young adulthood, but the problem is that students go through it *en masse*. The Grand Tour, the apprenticeship, and the vision quest were primarily solitary journeys during which the young person had room to reflect. It was understood that growing up and gaining autonomy was a process that required *time alone* and *a separation from family, friends, and familiar ideas*. You just can't get that from sorority rush and beer pong.

Fortunately, there *is* a way to launch our kids into the world and celebrate their emergence as young adults. In the next chapter, you will hear stories from students who've been through a powerful rite of passage that exploded both their passion and their intellect: living abroad for a year before the age of twenty. Their parents kicked off those not-fulfilled-in-my-own-life shoes and conquered their fego in order to give the kids an exceptional opportunity for evolution. High five!

For those who embrace this journey, the rewards can be absolutely astonishing.

Get ready to go global.

Old School: protecting our adolescents from their passion and blocking them from attaining independence

Bold School: launching our adolescents by providing them with a significant and enriching rite of passage

THE BIG IDEA: GOING GLOBAL

CHAPTER SIX

The Boldest Advantage

A YEARLONG

HIGH SCHOOL EXCHANGE

THE MOST RECOMMENDED EXCHANGE PROGRAM— AND WHY IT'S THE BEST

> To travel is to discover that everyone is wrong about other countries.
> ALDOUS HUXLEY

Most parents flash me a deer-in-the-headlights look when I mention sending high school students abroad for a year. For one thing they can't imagine being away from their son or daughter for that long. Also, they are reluctant to fix what doesn't seem to be broken—their student seems reasonably happy just cruising through high school, and they don't want to rock the boat.

Once again the biggest blockade is fego: parents are worried about their kids' ability to deal with the experience—and may be even more worried about how *they* will handle the separation. Plus, they don't want to be seen as an uncaring parent who isn't bothered by sending their child to another continent for a year. Those whose identity centers on being a parent who does everything for their kids are the ones most likely to find the whole idea abhorrent—after all, who will *they* be if their son or daughter isn't there?

Sending your student abroad might be a big leap, but it makes all subsequent leaps seem like baby steps. That going-off-to-college day will be an absolute cakewalk by comparison, and you'll be one of the enviable parents who laughs at empty-nest syndrome. (Tip: It's way more fun than crying.)

I've had three tearful good-byes with my daughters when they went abroad during high school (and many more weepy farewells since then), and I can assure you that the sadness and worry you feel as a parent will be completely overridden by the thrill of seeing your child become utterly transformed into a young adult with a heap of remarkable skills that he or she could never have gained by staying home with you.

Has your heart been warmed by watching your student make a winning goal, give an eloquent speech, or take a bow following a musical performance? Small potatoes, my friend. You will never be more proud of your student—or *yourself*—than you'll be when you see what they've become because of your gigantic (if heart-ripping) gift of allowing them to have an adventurous rite of passage all their own. They'll look different, know and love another culture, have dozens of friends from around the world, and be completely at ease navigating in a foreign land that would drop you to your knees in a day. There's nothing more satisfying than watching your seventeen-year-old surpass you in terms of confidence and language skills.

But that's just *my* story. Here's one from Kelli Swanson Jaecks.

BOLD STATEMENT

In March of her eighth-grade year my sweet, bubbly daughter came home with a name and number of some person who had substituted in her English class that day. She told the kids that the local Rotary Club was still looking for a few students to travel that very summer to South Africa and Sweden. Brea was very excited, and so were we. We made the call that evening, and within a month, both Brea (fourteen) and our son Keston (sixteen) were signed up to travel independently abroad.

Brea was due to go to South Africa—alone—in three months' time. We threw ourselves into preparations, meetings, and research about how to get her there safely, obtain a visa, and find out about the family that would be hosting her.

We met with opposition from grandparents and friends, even her middle school principal, all voicing concerns about the dangers of South Africa: AIDS, the crime rate, and racial unrest. We could see the doubt and questioning of our judgment as parents, even from those who didn't verbally express it. We had to continually justify our decision by citing the great track record of Rotary Youth Exchange and claiming what we know to be true: the only way this world will come to true peace is for people—especially youth—to travel the globe. We're a lot less likely to go to war with those who have opened their arms and homes to us, and we need a critical mass of individuals who've been embraced abroad and who share a deep connection with those in countries around the world.

Brea spent five weeks with a wonderful loving family living in a suburb of Johannesburg. Yes, she saw homes surrounded by high iron fences to keep out crime. She saw armed soldiers guarding cars in the local mall's parking lot, and she saw poverty up close and personal. What could be wrong with exposing her to that? My husband and I fully believe in giving kids a chance to see the world as it is.

Our daughter came home lit up with the fire of travel

(*continued*)

and a new respect for other cultures. Her first words to us upon her return were "I am going to go on the yearlong exchange now!" And so Brea spent her junior year of high school in a small rural town in central Brazil. It was a fantastic experience for her.

My advice: That year, while she was gone and our son was in college, I started my master's degree program. This kept me too busy to be worried about Brea and allowed me to fulfill a personal goal. It turned out to be a great plan for everyone!

When Brea came home, she was a very independent, confident, world-aware young woman. The positives of international travel for young people far outweigh any negatives. Adjusting to change, sometimes filled with pain and conflict, is a necessary and exciting task for both the student and the parents. I am very proud of Brea and know that she is becoming an engaged and positive force for her society and the world. She is truly a global citizen.

I'm not going to sugarcoat this: it's hard to send your child away for a year. But though we long to keep our kids close, our grand parental sacrifice will give them a tremendous long-term advantage. Yes, the airport scene is sad, but within a month most parents have recovered beautifully from their initial what-have-we-done stage. And don't think it's only the moms who get emotional—Tom was a mess the week we said good-bye to Taeko when she left for her year in Chile. Here's the way he describes it:

I never really thought about how I would feel when our oldest daughter, Taeko, left on her Rotary exchange to Chile. Having been an exchange student myself, I was excited for her to experience some of the same things that I had. But the day before she left I was physically ill and could barely get out of bed, something that is very rare for me. At the time I insisted that it had nothing to do with emotions, but looking back on it (and having experienced the same thing when we sent two more daughters abroad) I am certain that it did.

We adjusted to having one less child in the house, but we thought of Taeko often and were captivated by the postcards, letters, and e-mails that started arriving after her first month away. The growth in her maturity was obvious and astounding.

Going to pick up Taeko at the airport after her year abroad was one of the most gratifying experiences of my life. The excitement started three months before she came home, and it grew and grew. Within minutes of reuniting with her, we could see that she seemed several years older than when she'd left. Getting reacquainted was an incredible opportunity to shift from a parent/kid relationship to a peer/peer relationship. It was a dramatic but very sweet and satisfying transition

I felt that my year of worry when she was gone as a high school junior was more than compensated for by the fact that she was completely capable of handling *anything* during her college years. Having our child come home a strong young adult able to take on the world *without* our help was a greater reward than any possible combination of grades, test scores, trophies, acceptances, or achievements I can imagine.

I could fill an entire chapter with testimonials from parents, but they'd all sound similar: "It was difficult at times, but it turned out to be an extremely important year for our son/daughter and we're so grateful that we decided to send him/her abroad." Even the hardships—no, *especiallly* the hardships—are likely to be exceptional learning opportunities for everyone. Still, it helps to know what to expect, and there are **two key points** you need to understand in order to make the most of the exchange experience:

First, no matter what program you choose, you must accept that every student will have a different experience, and in most cases, it will not be an easy one. The program coordinators, the destination, the host parents, the school situation, the student's personality, and a million other details come together to create the exchange experience. No program can guarantee that everything will go perfectly, and you should run away from anyone promising a silky-smooth ride. Be realistic and expect bumps. Count on the fact that at times your student will whine and/or cry and that you as a parent will lose sleep and/or hair. It helps to remember that you've already lost a lot of sleep/hair worrying about your student over the years, and that's likely to continue no matter where your son or daughter may be. Even in the most ideal situations—those in which the student is fully and lovingly supported every step of the way—the year will be challenging. That's the point!

The one thing most likely to sabotage a student's exchange is frequent e-mails or calls from parents who express sadness and concern. Those who *really* care about their kids will give them room and time to settle in without adding another layer of angst by flooding them with I-miss-you messages. This is precisely why the best exchange programs have a thirty-day rule: no phone or e-mail contact during the first month after the initial I'm-here-and-I'm-fine phone call. One wise and good-natured mother I know said it helped her to think of it as a *full-body* exchange—doing anything that would keep her daughter's head and heart back home while the rest of her was abroad would just be "messy for everyone." Sending kids abroad requires a bit of tough love—and a much bigger chunk of self-control.

❏ **Smart Move**: Wise parents understand that parenting isn't about simply keeping kids happy—it's about giving them opportunities to be truly challenged in order to develop fully as confident and compassionate young adults.

Those who surpass the milk-and-cookies role give their children a chance to discover their potential, and the rewards can be spectacular for both kids and parents. For one thing, if you do it right, your son or daughter will think you are the *greatest parent alive* for giving them the freedom to experience life abroad at this age. This is precisely what will get you through the not-so-great moments.

The second key point: **do not expect a yearlong exchange to be focused on academics.** In most cases, you will have no control over your student's school situation—and that's fine. Some students end up in very demanding schools, while others will find that school is nearly impossible due to the language barrier or completely lacking in rigor or organization (teachers not showing up, students not participating, etc.). Both extremes—and anything in between—can be very frustrating, but it's all part of the process.

Savvy parents recognize that students on exchange develop the Triple C qualities—*confidence, critical thinking,* and *compassion*—that will take them *way* beyond their classmates who are writing term papers back home. Sure, they might be missing AP English or pre-calculus, but these courses can't offer anything close to the same benefits as grappling with the personal issues that crop up during a year abroad.

Convinced enough to learn more? Well, here's the first wall you're likely to face: **how to pick the right exchange organization.**

Many parents who recognize the benefits of sending their student abroad get bogged down once they begin looking at the options. There are so many programs that it's easy to become overwhelmed by the research process and give up on the idea altogether. The hardest part is choosing a program without having some kind of personal connection to it. Perhaps you don't know anyone who has sent their son or daughter abroad for a year, and without a recommendation from someone you know and trust, you're hesitant to take the next step.

Please allow me to make this part a little easier for you.

There are literally hundreds of exchange programs out there but just a handful that consistently offer high school students great opportunities to spend a year living in another country with host families. Back in Chapter Five you read about Emily's participation in **AFS** (www.afs.org). The American Field Service was founded in 1914 as an organization dedicated to transporting wounded soldiers. Now AFS is a leader in intercultural learning and offers international exchange programs in more than fifty countries around the world through its network of more than 30,000 active volunteers. More than 325,000 individuals have benefited from the experience of studying abroad through AFS.

Another excellent program is **Youth For Understanding** (www .yfu.org), which began very humbly in the United States in 1951. At that time an American minister proposed to church leaders that teenagers from war-torn West Germany be brought to the United States to live with a family and attend high school for a year in an effort to heal the wounds of World War II. Since then YFU has grown into a network of more than fifty partner organizations and has offered exchanges to approximately 200,000 students around the world.

If you're considering sending your student abroad for a summer, a semester, or a year, AFS and YFU are excellent options.

There are many other organizations creating wonderful exchange opportunities for students, but I'm going to focus on only one. I have my own personal reasons for recommending it, but even if I didn't, I'd pick **Rotary International** (www.rotary.org) over all others, hands down.

FOUR BIG REASONS

▶ Rotary International's Youth Exchange program (RYE) is organized and supported by **an enormous network of volunteers around the globe.** Rotary is the largest organization offering cultural-exchange programs for high school students, and because there are **more than 1.2 million Rotarians in 33,000 clubs in more than 200 countries and geographical areas,** there's likely to be a Rotary Club member nearby and ready to help your student anywhere in the world they happen to be—including airports, clinics, and government offices.

▶ The Rotary Youth Exchange program offers an **unmatchable level of support to families and students.** In many cases the local Rotary Club will offer activities for months prior to departure (described as the "outbound" period), during the exchange itself ("inbound"), and even after the student's return to their home country (the "rebound" period). Though most exchange organizations require some kind of group orientation prior to departure, those with only one office for each region or country are not equipped to provide the ongoing support that the Rotary Club volunteers offer right in the student's home district. Many Rotary Youth Exchange students attend numerous events—from lunch meetings to long recreational weekends and excursions with many other students—before, during, and after their exchange. For this reason the Rotary experience is sometimes referred to as "the three-year exchange."

▶ Rotary International offers its **exchange programs at a considerably lower price than most other organizations.** Though it varies widely depending on each local Rotary Club and the hosting club in the destination country, on

(continued)

average families pay no more than $4,000 for the full-year program, *including* airfare and visa expenses. (Other programs range from $8,000 to $12,000 for the year, with some organizations charging $20,000 or more.) In addition, many clubs offer scholarships that cover most costs, and the majority of Rotary Youth Exchange students receive a monthly stipend (generally between $50 to $100) to help with basic daily expenses such as extra school supplies or activities.

▶ Rotary International **is committed to humanitarian work on both a local and a global scale.** Thanks to Rotary and its partners, *two billion* children have been immunized against polio, five million have been spared disability, and more than 250,000 deaths from polio have been prevented. Through Rotary programs, hundreds of thousands of committed individuals from around the world are studying conflict resolution, earning scholarships for international study, traveling on cultural exchanges, and helping their communities through service projects of all kinds.

There are two key differences between the application process for Rotary and the ones used by most other programs:

1. **It's very local and personal.** Instead of sending application materials and a deposit check to a regional or national organization office, each student applies directly through the Rotary Club in their own community and has face-to-face interviews with local members.
2. **There is a fairly long lead time.** In order to go abroad their junior year of high school, students should apply to their local Rotary Club during early fall of their sophomore year. Many students interested in going on exchange find out about the Rotary program too late to apply. Best bet: Check in with your local Rotary Club during your student's *freshman* year, but re-

member that students can apply even as seniors to go abroad after graduation. (They can't be older than nineteen during their exchange.)

> Rotary International is the world's first service club organization. Rotary Clubs are nonpolitical and open to all cultures, races, and religions. Rotary's main objective is service—in the community, in the workplace, and throughout the world.

Not every Rotary Club sponsors exchange students, and some do so only every few years. We ended up going through three different Rotary Clubs (all within ten miles of our home) in order to get our daughters sponsored. Some clubs are really gung-ho about the exchange program, and others focus on different projects. Look for a club that is very active and excited about helping your student have their best exchange experience. Clubs also vary in terms of the sponsorship amount. We paid less than $1,000 per year above the cost of the airfare and visa, but your local club might require a greater or lesser financial contribution.

What nobody tells you: parents of Rotary Youth Exchange students (especially those like us who have sent several kids abroad) share a wink and a grin because we know that sending our sons and daughters off on an exchange can actually *save us money* while giving them the most amazing year of their lives. It's true. Consider this: their food and other daily expenses are covered, and we're not paying for their summer camps, activity fees, gas, car insurance, prom dresses, or athletic shoes. If your kid goes to private school, you'll save thousands of dollars on that alone. Of course, all bets are off if you send your son or daughter to Europe with a credit card. (ATM/debit cards are definitely the way to go, and expenses—not to mention shopping—in pricier countries will add to your year-end tally.)

Full disclosure: Tom and I have never been members of

Rotary, nor has anyone in our families. However, we're grateful to Rotary for a number of reasons.

When I was in high school, I received a $500 scholarship from the Rotary Club near my town. After college I was hired to teach English in rural Japan at a group of schools owned by Grif Frost, a young man who'd been born and raised in Oregon. Grif had spent a year in France during high school as a Rotary Youth Exchange student, and after returning home for his senior year, he fell in love with Noriko Nomura, a Rotary Youth Exchange student from Japan who lived with his family for a few months. Eventually they got married, and the couple and their young children were living in Noriko's hometown on the northern tip of Honshu, where they had established English schools in four local cities.

At first I was the only single American teaching English within a hundred miles or more. That changed three months later when Grif's brother Tom arrived. Tom and I became teaching partners, spending sixteen hours a day working side by side and hitting the road together three days a week to astound kindergarten students and entertain adults with our physical and fast-paced Dynamic English classes all over the area. Growing up in small Oregon agricultural towns near each other and spending time in India (Tom as a Rotary Youth Exchange student when he was sixteen, me as a senior in college on a yearlong Pacific Rim trip through the University of Puget Sound) gave us a lot of common ground. You can guess the rest: we fell in love, got married, and lived happily ever after.

Rotary has been a consistent and enriching part of our lives ever since.

▶ Shortly after we moved back to Oregon from Japan, Tom's host brothers from India moved to the United States to earn their graduate degrees. One host brother lives about ten minutes from our former Portland home.

▶ A few years later Tom and I decided to take a three-month

sabbatical in order to return to India to spend time with his former host families there. It changed our family forever. (More on that in Chapter Eight.)

♦ We hosted RYE students while our girls were on their exchanges.

♦ When we lived in Mexico, our daughter Tara became good friends with RYE students from several countries.

♦ When we decided to leave Mexico, we let Talya pick the next destination since she hadn't had a chance to go on her own Rotary Youth Exchange.

♦ In Buenos Aires her best friend was a girl from Wyoming who spent her junior year in Argentina on a Rotary Youth Exchange and returned to attend college there.

That's a long way of saying that I'm a pretty big fan of Rotary in general and the Rotary Youth Exchange program in particular. However, that doesn't mean my reasons for recommending it are clouded by my personal experience. I cheerfully encourage you to do your own research, but you won't find a more comprehensive support program or more dedicated volunteers around the world who are committed to offering affordable intercultural exchange opportunities to students from all backgrounds.

I know what you're thinking: "Gee, I'm not sure about this. Isn't it good enough to send my student on a semester abroad during his junior year of college? Why not keep him here at home until he graduates from high school?"

Get ready for some stories.

Later in this chapter you'll learn why the *timing* of this experience is extremely critical and how sending your son or daughter on a yearlong exchange during (or right after) high school could be **the most important parenting decision you ever make.** But right now let's take a look at a few vignettes from the exchange students themselves. I think you'll find them rather inspiring.

Old School: thinking of the Rotary Club as a group of business owners and city officials who have weekly lunches with local speakers in your community
Bold School: thinking of the Rotary Club as an enormous network of more than a million members in 200+ countries and geographical areas focusing on global health, volunteer service, conflict resolution, and exceptional intercultural exchange experiences

"THE MOST AMAZING YEAR OF MY LIFE": STORIES FROM RETURNEES

> The longest journey of any person
> is the journey inward.
> DAG HAMMARSKJÖLD

Whether students choose to go abroad through Rotary, AFS, YFU, or any of a number of organizations, they all share similar stories and will say they feel an immediate affinity with any former exchange student they meet.

I've had the privilege of interviewing more than one hundred former exchange students, and while I don't pretend that this was an exhaustive study, the examples in this chapter are fairly representative. Undoubtedly some returnees don't go to college, find work with an international tint, or ever travel again—but I didn't come across any of them. Despite the incredible range of experiences they shared, nearly every returnee expressed the following:

❏ **My year abroad was extremely challenging at times.**
❏ **I learned so much about myself and the world.**
❏ **I made friendships that remain among the most important relationships in my life.**

> ❏ **My year abroad changed me profoundly as a person.**
> ❏ **It was the most intense year of my life. I would certainly choose to do it again, and I recommend it to every young person I know.**

These statements alone can't begin to convey the enormity of the experiences' impact on those involved nor the richness that these students can describe in intricate detail even many years later. In this section I offer thumbnail sketches from former exchange students. I have included *only* Rotary returnees, not to play favorites but to eliminate differences due to the program itself while revealing the wide range of experiences possible for students within a given framework.

Talk about advanced placement. Remember Katie, our winning candidate for the German job in Chapter Two? You're about to meet others like her, and you may recognize some recurring themes. To avoid repetition, I have removed references to the fact that many students managed to "CLEP out" (via the College Level Examination Program) of the requirements for the language they learned while abroad, leading them to get an easy head start on a foreign language major or minor. (Teal, our third daughter, earned a Spanish major by taking only *one* Spanish course at her final university, thanks to her year studying in Argentina—and the stellar transfer techniques you'll learn in the next chapter.) This is a clear example of the advantage of studying abroad during or right after high school, but you'll see in these stories that an exchange can be a year that keeps on giving in many ways.

LISA BARNES
HOMETOWN: WATERVILLE, NEW YORK
DESTINATION: LECCO, ITALY
YEAR: 1997–98 (AFTER HIGH SCHOOL GRADUATION)

I tell people that my exchange was the greatest year of my life, which started with the worst three months of my life. I wanted to leave Italy after the first month, but thankfully I didn't. If there had been a plane waiting to fly me home that first month, I would have been on it, but by the end of my exchange I was in love, singing pretty successfully in a band, and talking with my dad about moving to Italy permanently and changing my citizenship!

When I first learned about my destination, I was upset that I wasn't going to be living in a big city like Milan. I wanted to have that easy out of being able to find people who could speak English, and I hoped to be able to brag to my friends about the party life I would be living. Instead, I ended up in the middle of the mountains in a town where goats frequently crossed the road. As a result of being more isolated, I was immersed in the language and became fluent. I remain in constant contact with my many Italian friends.

I had deferred my enrollment to Ithaca College in order to go on my exchange, and my time abroad definitely changed my university experience. I was much more focused on my studies, I worked as an Italian tutor, was a TA for the Italian department, and earned a minor in Italian in addition to my major in corporate communications/advertising. I have used my language skills in several positions with both American and Italian companies.

The greatest lesson I learned as an exchange student is that I can make it through anything by believing in myself. My experience in Italy really allowed me to set high goals in life. I think every American teenager should be required to spend one year abroad.

KATI PROCTOR
HOMETOWN: RACINE, WISCONSIN
DESTINATION: MERLO, ARGENTINA
YEAR: 2003–04 (JUNIOR YEAR OF HIGH SCHOOL)

When I came back from my exchange, I didn't really understand that getting into college was something that one stressed about. I was amazed that some of my friends had people helping them write entrance essays. Heck, I wouldn't even let my mother look at mine!

I meant everything I wrote in my essays, whereas I felt like some kids just BS what they think will get them in. It was definitely a plus to be able to say that I had lived in a foreign country for eleven months where I didn't know the language to begin with and stayed with a family and went to a local high school!

I was accepted at several good schools and selected the University of Chicago, where I am majoring in Near Eastern languages and civilizations. My main emphasis is on Armenian, and I spent several months as an intern at the U.S. Embassy in Yerevan during the conflict in neighboring Georgia. My work in the consular office turned out to be quite exciting: I assisted in the evacuation of American citizens from Georgia, calling hotels to locate people and helping Americans who had to leave quickly without their passports. I held the elevator door for the president of Armenia, had a chance to see the prime minister during his visit, did a presentation for "American Corner" on college life in the United States, and have attended meetings and events at which I represented the embassy.

My exchange opened up the world to me and allowed me to see that I have endless opportunities to explore new places and study other cultures.

THERESE ENDERS
HOMETOWN: GRAND RAPIDS, MICHIGAN
DESTINATION: KALININGRAD, RUSSIA
YEAR: 2004–05 (AFTER HIGH SCHOOL GRADUATION)

True confession: my year in Russia was the worst year of my life— *but* I would choose to do it all over again because it was the most valuable experience I've ever had. I was able to find out who I really was when taken entirely out of context—away from my friends, family, job, church, and normal social setting. I realized that at my worst I could be incredibly lazy and indifferent. I learned that I needed to be responsible for my own happiness.

I had only one host family, and they were nice people, but they treated me like I was about twelve. Ultimately I learned to balance consideration for their wishes with my own sanity by doing little things like sneaking out in my Birkenstocks (which were forbidden due to an old wives' tale about bare toes and infertility) on nice days. There were no other exchange students anywhere near me; I did not take a single trip with other students or attend a conference, but the upside is that I came home pretty fluent in Russian.

I was extremely glad I used my exchange as a gap year before entering Michigan State University. While other students were freaking out about being away from home for a month, I was excited to be so close! My exchange definitely shows up in my life: I'm majoring in both Russian and international relations, and I spent a summer interning for a state representative. (I was told that it was my experience abroad that made me the top candidate for the position.) I've especially enjoyed leading the international student orientation at MSU—I know what it's like to be alone in a new country, and I want to help others the same way others helped me.

Recently, I spent a semester in the Czech Republic and had that "best experience of my life" that I was looking for when I went to Russia. Having been to Russia first made that experience all the sweeter; three months was like a vacation compared to a full-year exchange!

My year abroad was the hardest and most rewarding thing I've ever done academically, spiritually, and emotionally. My advice is to just go and let it be what it is but also be your own advocate. I highly recommend the Rotary program—they were generous in countless ways. I paid for my plane ticket and visa and that was about it. All things considered, it was the deal of a lifetime.

ADAM YOUNG-VALDOVINOS
HOMETOWN: CANBY, OREGON
DESTINATION: NIIGATA, JAPAN
YEAR: 2004–05 (JUNIOR YEAR OF HIGH SCHOOL)

My exchange in Japan turned me into a leader. I established a successful community service club that brought together a diverse group of individuals. I decided that if I could do that in a culture that wasn't my own, there shouldn't be any reason I couldn't do it in my own country.

Living in Japan inspired me to view the world from a different perspective, and I believe that that was why I was accepted by so many excellent universities. My SATs and ACTs were egregious by Ivy League standards (except for my Japanese SAT II), I never took a single AP course, and although I was valedictorian, it wasn't that impressive coming from Canby High School. I wasn't on academic overdrive my senior year, but I did pour myself into my extracurricular activities, and I think that Yale and the other schools viewed my passion and confidence favorably.

After my freshman year at Yale, I took a year off to live in South Korea, where I studied the language (my sixth), did volunteer work, conducted research, performed in a musical, and worked as a disc jockey for an international radio station. Now I'm in Beijing on a fellowship to spend a year studying with an intellectual community of about ten Yale students, ten Beida students, and eight Yale professors.

I don't know what the future will bring—I have learned to be very flexible. Life is a long hallway with all sorts of doors and windows, and if one opens up, I will probably jump in with no hesitation or regrets. Wherever I go, I intend to use all of my gifts and skills to be of service and to continue learning.

ERIN HENSLEY
HOMETOWN: TULSA, OKLAHOMA
DESTINATION: FRAUENFELD, SWITZERLAND
YEAR: 2004–05 (JUNIOR YEAR OF HIGH SCHOOL)

My exchange literally defines who I am. It's one of the first things I share about myself in any kind of "get to know you" conversation.

I grew up and gained so much from that experience that I cannot imagine the kind of person I would be without it.

I raised money for my exchange by sending letters to everyone I knew telling them about what I was doing and asking if they'd like to help me. Because of that and a little from my family, I had enough to go.

I got to travel a lot during my exchange! I met some of my relatives in Germany, went to Paris with my first host family, went to Tuscany with my friend's host family, went on lots of ski trips with various Rotary members and my school friends, and even went on a trip to South Africa with my last host family, followed by a three-week Euro tour organized by the Rotarians! I felt so lucky to see incredible places I never imagined I would visit.

I'm a student at Grace University in Nebraska, and after completing a summer internship in Switzerland, I am now spending my junior year in Austria improving my German and studying business. My world has expanded dramatically because of my exchange.

> ALAINA ZULLI
> HOMETOWN: RIVERHEAD, NEW YORK
> DESTINATION: IVANO-FRANKIVSK, UKRAINE
> YEAR: 1997–98 (JUNIOR YEAR OF HIGH SCHOOL)

Around the fourth month of my exchange, I fell into a period of deep homesickness that I had been sure I would not succumb to. I am so glad that my parents made me stick it out—the last three months were the best time of my life! It was spring, I knew the language, I had wonderful friends (who remain my best friends today), I drank in everything I could, and I took beautiful photographs that I still treasure.

I was the only exchange student in the country, which had only recently gained independence from the USSR, so I was very isolated. I spent a lot of time walking around the city and speaking with people on the street. That's how I learned Ukrainian.

Living with new families is hard. I rebelled when they insisted that I wear two coats and three pairs of socks even in spring, but after much push and pull I began to soften. I think that my experience living with three very different families ultimately made it easier for me to live with my partner and have a happy marriage.

I was on a high for the first year after my return. Having been an extremely shy and lonely girl before I left, I astounded my classmates and family with my new confidence and was a sort of celebrity in my high school. I even had my first boyfriend. Most important was the fact that I valued myself. I'd done something special and brave. My exchange dramatically improved both my self-esteem and my ability to communicate with all kinds of people.

As a costume historian finishing grad school at NYU, I can see how my year abroad has shaped my work in important ways. I think of myself foremost as a sociologist (albeit one whose work is based primarily on clothing), and I feel that I developed a deeper understanding of human nature from my year abroad. I have always been interested in design, but I think I would have chosen a less sociological focus had I not had that cultural experience.

I returned to Ivano-Frankivsk recently, and it was just as beautiful as I remembered it. Leaving home in high school ultimately made coming back and living in my country a richer experience.

Alyssa Lanz
Hometown: Commack, New York
Destination: Tepic, Mexico
Year: 2003–04 (junior year of high school)

I had a fantastic year in Mexico and continued to learn so much about myself after I came back home. Adjusting to high school in New York was difficult. I felt that my exchange made me grow up an extra five years rather than one. I did not want to get stuck in my old world, where Coach bags and designer jeans were all the rage. I had a new outlook on life and on what mattered most.

There is a part of my life that will never come back again and can never be fully understood by those around me. I'll play my Mexican *banda* music or watch my Mexican *telenovelas* and get an eye roll or a "close your door." I wasn't prepared for the fact that I would have to leave some of my heart and a year of my life in Mexico forever.

I got a scholarship to attend St. Joseph's College. Though I'd always planned to be a teacher, after my exchange I really wanted to get involved in humanitarian work. I'm majoring in Spanish and political science, and thanks to a need-based Gilman International Scholarship, I am currently studying Arabic at the American University in Cairo, Egypt. My experience in Mexico taught me that I should never let fear become an obstacle, and I am excited to learn more about this fascinating culture.

> DON MILLER
> HOMETOWN: AMARILLO, TEXAS
> DESTINATION: LIÈGE, BELGIUM
> YEAR: 1991–92 (SENIOR YEAR OF HIGH SCHOOL)

My friends in high school thought I was crazy to miss senior year, but I had the best experience I could have hoped for. I made friends with people from all over the world and learned so much. Invaluable is how I would categorize life with a host family. They even came to my wedding sixteen years later!

My exchange in Belgium changed my educational path completely. I started off in the college of business administration at the University of Colorado, then transferred to the University of Texas, where I majored in French, Italian, and Spanish with a minor in Portuguese. I currently speak six languages fluently and love using each one as often as possible.

While in college, I put together my own study-abroad program that enabled me to spend a year studying archaeology in Italy. After graduation I did law school at UT Austin, which has a dual program with Université de Paris X, so I have law degrees in both countries. I've spent the last few years living in Paris, where my practice focuses on cross-border mergers and acquisitions.

I do not want to be trite about the overall impact a year of traveling, meeting new people, and learning can have on a teenager. I left an awkward kid and returned a well-rounded . . . perhaps not a man but an individual. Instead of being wrapped up in whether I was with the "right" crowd, I was able to get to know people without all the superficialities associated with high school.

I would not change a single thing about that year. My advice to anyone thinking about it is to *go*. The people you meet and the adventures you will have are like cramming four years of positive high school experiences into one year.

JESSICA BRAMS-MILLER
HOMETOWN: BETHLEHEM, PENNSYLVANIA
DESTINATION: LISIEUX, FRANCE
YEAR: 1997–98 (AFTER HIGH SCHOOL GRADUATION)

My time abroad helped to mold me as a person. I was a little bit of a brat when I left, and when I came back, I had learned how to adapt to situations more quickly, be a better student, and accept people for who they are. I learned a lot about concentration and studying, which helped me go from a B student in high school to having straight As a couple of times in college, and eventually I graduated with high honors from Lehigh University.

My exchange quite literally opened my eyes to my future: I became passionate about architecture. I majored in architecture and voice performance at Lehigh and went on to get a master's in architecture from the University of Pennsylvania School of Design. I spent the spring semester of my sophomore year in Vicenza, Italy, traveled to Ireland, England, Russia, Israel, Germany, and Switzerland, and returned to Paris as a teaching assistant with my master's program. The more I travel, the more I marvel at the impact my exchange has had on my life.

RACHEL LEWIS
HOMETOWN: KAMIAH, IDAHO
DESTINATION: GRINDSTED, DENMARK
YEAR: 2000–01 (SENIOR YEAR OF HIGH SCHOOL)

I come from a logging town of 1,200 people in rural Idaho, far from any city, and international travel had always seemed like a remote and exotic thing. I absolutely would not have had this opportunity had it not been for the financial support that Rotary provided.

I was the first exchange student ever to go from my high school, so there was no precedent to receive credit for any classes I took while studying abroad, and I graduated a year later than my classmates. Despite this, the experience was absolutely worth it!

After I returned, I attended Washington State University and graduated from their business department and the Honors College with a degree in business administration and marketing. Now I live in Seattle and work for a global independent risk consulting company.

I would advise anyone thinking about studying abroad to go for it, despite any delay it may have in your "official" education. The experience that I had abroad helped me to gain the personal independence and maturity needed to excel when I returned from the program—in college, in work, and in life.

PHILIP STOREY
HOMETOWN: HOUSTON, TEXAS
DESTINATION: RIO TERCERO, ARGENTINA
YEAR: 2001–02 (AFTER HIGH SCHOOL GRADUATION)

During my senior year of high school I decided that I wanted to spend a year abroad before going to college in order to learn Spanish and see what another culture was like. I was student body president and valedictorian of my high school and the only student in my class who didn't go straight to college. Nobody understood what

I was doing! However, I had learned that I could defer my full scholarship to Vanderbilt University, so I decided to just go for it.

Armed only with a cowboy hat and a grin, I stepped off the plane in Rio Tercero. On my first day of class I introduced myself as a Rotary Youth Exchange student to the entire student body through a reverberating microphone. My sincerity was met with universal laughter, as the students found my poor Spanish and American accent hilarious. While I felt hopelessly lost at the beginning of my exchange, I gradually became part of the community and was very close to my soccer team, friends, and family. By the end of the year I was no longer Philip the American but *"Fee-leep, un Argentino más"*—one more Argentine.

When I entered college a few months after returning from South America, all things lingual and international fascinated me. I was torn between the biomedical engineering major I had always planned on and the cultural path I found so enthralling. I chose to pursue both programs, which required doing intensive science semesters and summer school so that I could also study abroad in Germany, France, Spain, and China. I graduated Phi Beta Kappa and received honors in the Spanish department for writing a thesis on the health status of Latinos in the United States and the role of language in the doctor-patient relationship.

After finishing college, I received a Rotary Ambassadorial Scholarship, which allowed me to study at the University of Sydney in Australia and earn a master's in international public health. I then went on to study French in Senegal, West Africa, as a last hurrah before beginning medical school at Johns Hopkins University. I have absolutely no doubt that my youth exchange and subsequent experiences made me a much stronger candidate for scholarships and medical school placement.

Since 2001 I have lived a combined four years abroad, traveled to more than sixty nations, studied on six continents, learned to speak five languages, and made friends all over the world that I will have until the day I die. I am now beginning a career in medicine with the hope of impacting international health and serving some of the people whom I have met in my travels.

Going on exchange was the single best decision I have ever made.

It's clear that a yearlong high school exchange can affect your student positively and dramatically for *the rest of his or her life*. In the next section you'll learn about the distinct advantages of sending your student abroad in high school rather than waiting until the traditional junior year of college.

> **Old School:** worrying that a yearlong exchange during (or right after) high school will put students *behind* their peers
>
> **Bold School:** knowing that a yearlong exchange can send students far *beyond* their peers

WHY TIMING IS EVERYTHING

> It has been my observation that most people get ahead during the time that others waste time.
> HENRY FORD

When children are very young, their brains are aflame. Our desire to help our infants and toddlers fully develop their frontal lobes prompts extravagant purchases of educational toys and enrollment in all kinds of preschool programs. We expose them to a rich array of sensory experiences and social situations because we are completely committed to giving them every opportunity to absorb the world around them.

So it's strange that we don't put as much stock in a later but equally important five-year stage of life: when our kids are between the ages of fifteen and twenty. After all, it is during this stage that our adolescents develop the skills they need to become adults. Their brain development in this period will affect them for far longer than the decade of childhood they were preparing for as preschoolers.

For all the effort we put into the first five years of life, we tend to wind down as our kids reach high school, expecting that their brain development—in all its depth, breadth, speed, and glory—will be assured as long as they show up in class and maybe sign up for a few activities.

School. Club meetings. Practices. Part-time jobs.

These are the magic beans we're throwing at our kids at a critical period of their development? That sucking sound you hear is your student's brain crying out for *more*.

Just as young children blossom when given a chance to play with their sense of discovery, adolescents thrive when given a chance to play with their brain plasticity. Late adolescence brings with it some very special gifts—but they're not always the ones we like to open. Students at around age fifteen develop an increased ability to rationalize and argue; they begin to recognize life's inconsistencies. More annoying: kids begin to focus their new skills of analysis on their parents' not-so-logical ideas and rules—and they're *good* at it.

Fun for everyone.

But don't blame your student. It's just that his brain is engaged in the process of playing a new kind of assessment game. At this age our kids develop their own radar for hypocrisy and explore the razor-sharp edges of cynicism. Their sense of humor can swing wildly from childlike silliness to dark satire. We know that high school is marked by gossip and an overall cynicism that can be both cruel and contagious, but what we don't see is the underlying reason—and our role in perpetuating the conditions that keep our kids' high school experiences so much like the teen movies they watch.

Our kids' brains are ravenous for content that will lend itself to analysis, and yet we're sticking them into a world that is so limited that they are reduced to examining hairstyles and hook-ups instead of more challenging fare. Instead of analyzing culture, politics, or world affairs on a daily basis, they're prognosticating about prom dates. They zero in on the fit of their jeans rather than on the fit of a cultural identity within a larger population, and they devote hours to enhancing the clarity of their skin instead of the clarity of their thinking. They are digging into a plate of pettiness because that is precisely what we've served them. They deserve—and are ready for—so much more.

So do we give them a traditional high school experience—or unusual opportunities to learn more about the world? Good news: we can offer *both*! Let them cheer at games and get caught up in the social dramas of high school for a couple of years, and then take *one major step* to assure that they will accelerate their brain development. It helps to do some math: add up the number of games, dances, parties, and other events a student is likely to experience during a year of high school. Now multiply that by *four*. Missing just *one* year's worth of these activities isn't likely to stunt their growth. In fact, replacing one year of traditional high school with something completely different is a very smart move indeed.

Don't believe me? Let's ask a science guy.

Dr. Jay Giedd is a neuroscientist who specializes in the adolescent brain, which will come in handy when his own four kids reach that stage. He explains that the brain during the second decade of life is going through a rip-roarin' period of both growth and pruning. "It's a critical time for brain sculpting to take place," says Dr. Giedd. He describes the brain as being something like a block of granite at the peak of the puberty years. As he puts it, "The art—or in this case, the individual—is created by what remains after the chiseling is finished."

This chiseling is going on right now: the activities our adolescents choose to engage in (or the ones we offer them) will significantly affect their brain development. According to Dr. Giedd, what occurs during this period of life can profoundly influence a young person's perspective and develop a bigger tool chest for later problem solving. "If a teen is given the chance to spend time adapting to new ways of living, communicating with others in another language, and seeing himself and his culture from a completely different point of view, that behavior is likely to become hardwired in the brain."

Consider how your student's brain is being hardwired *today*. Perhaps she is memorizing facts for a test, practicing her sport, or working at a part-time job. Or maybe she is sitting on the sofa, texting her friends, and complaining about her homework. Most likely she is doing a combination of the above. It's all perfectly normal high school stuff.

We would never expect our five-year-old child to learn all she needs to know about herself and the world in a setting that emphasizes standardized academic courses, structured competitive activities, and limited opportunities for exploration, and yet that's exactly what we expect our fifteen-year-old student to do. What would it look like if we treated our fifteen-year-old with that same concern for her brain development we had when she was *five*?

Well, we'd go deeper, broader, faster. We'd make sure she had the chance to meet a diverse range of individuals—mentors, teachers, and friends of all ages and backgrounds—and expose her to as many learning experiences as possible. There would be much greater emphasis on gaining independence and developing an understanding of the world around her; exposing her to other cultures—through music, food, dance, art, and literature as well as travel—would become far more important than surrounding her with that which is familiar. Most of all we would recognize that beneficial brain-sculpting life experiences aren't likely to happen while she's sitting in study hall or scooping ice cream at the mall.

❑ **Smart Move**: Wise parents understand the importance of doing everything possible to maximize their student's prime adolescent years and recognize that staying put and keeping things the same is severely limiting them at a time when exposure to new environments is precisely what will help them most.

Preparing your kid for college? Snooze. The real challenge is helping your student hardwire his brain for young adulthood. And though I'm not one to get overly urgent or dramatic about such things, the fact is that time is a-wastin'—*and so is your student's brain.*

Going on a yearlong exchange during or right after high school is the optimum way to set that adolescent brain on fire and launch a life-changing period of reflection and connection. Sure, your son or daughter could wait until college, and I highly recommend going abroad while earning credits toward that university degree. (Chapter Seven will show you how to avoid the pitfalls and help your student get the most out of that experience.) But there is a *dramatic* difference between spending a year in another country at twenty or twenty-one and doing it at sixteen. It's never too late to experience life in another culture, but there's definitely a sweet spot at which learning and maturation are amplified.

This is the time to go global.

Compared to a typical junior in college, a typical junior in high school is:

- ❏ less attached to a particular view about how things are supposed to be
- ❏ less fearful of making mistakes and more willing to try new things
- ❏ less locked into a set of identity markers such as graduation class, college, teams, clubs, dorms, roommates, and achievements
- ❏ less committed to a particular field of study and therefore open to discovering new talents and interests
- ❏ less likely to have psychological barriers to learning and speaking a new language

But here's the most important thing: the younger student who spends a year abroad is more likely to be *transformed* by the experience, leading to even greater adaptability and an enthusiasm for taking on new challenges.

Bold parents recognize that the advantages of sending kids abroad during college pale in comparison to the advantages of sending kids abroad at a younger and more malleable age. If you want to give your high school student the very best chance to metamorphose into a mature, confident, flexible, and outrageously global young adult in a short period of time, get ready to wave good-bye.

In the next section you'll learn all about the surprisingly predictable cycle of highs and lows your exchange student is likely to experience—and why you should be celebrating every struggle.

> **Old School:** going abroad for a semester during the junior year of college in order to experience life in another culture
>
> **Bold School:** spending a year abroad during high school in order to hardwire a student's brain for flexibility and language learning

BOO HOOS AND WOO HOOS: WHAT TO EXPECT

> When you have completed 95 percent of your journey, you are only halfway there.
>
> JAPANESE PROVERB

Dr. Joe Dispenza has studied the human mind for decades and is the author of *Evolve Your Brain: The Science of Changing Your Mind*.[1] If you've seen the movie *What the Bleep Do We Know?* you might remember him as the guy who talked about waking up in the morning and spending a few moments creating his day by intentionally visualizing the way he wanted it to go. As both an expert on the ways we change our brains through new experiences and as a father, Dr. Dispenza has been fascinated to observe some adolescent brain hardwiring in his own daughter who studied abroad in Switzerland during high school. He told me:

INSIDER INSIGHT

Studying in Switzerland was a remarkably enriching and life-changing experience for my daughter.

As a scientist, I know that the brain is organized to reflect everything we know in our environment. All of the people we've met, every thing we've owned, all the places we've visited, and all the experiences we've embraced throughout the different times in our lives are patterned as diverse but orderly neural networks in our brain. To be placed in a new environment requires an inward dance of the mind with the new stimuli of the external world.

Our greatest learning occurs through transformation and change. As a result of being outside our comfort zone, we must think and act in new ways that totally disrupt everything we have known and continue to adapt and respond until the external world becomes familiar to us. This new information becomes integrated into our nervous system and we are no longer the same.

As a father, I was a little concerned initially when I saw my daughter struggle to adapt to the cultural differences. Then over time I was very pleased to see her grow in so many ways. She truly flourished and became more confident, mature, broad-minded, and worldly. She was *different*.

Spending time abroad during adolescence literally transforms the developing mind and brain. We know that novel experiences grow brain circuitry by making more enriched synaptic connections. If a student breaks away from a routine and predictable environment in order to embrace new social, cultural, and political conditions, his or her mind—and brain—will be profoundly shaped by those opportunities for growth.

The biggest challenge for parents is letting go and trusting the process. Parents must look beyond their own limitations and the prejudices that they might project onto their sons and daughters. Seeing great potential in our children is exactly what we always wanted someone to see in us! Our brain is plastic enough to adapt to new and unique circumstances, and when it does, it always flourishes. This is our greatest gift as humans.

Most parents of exchange students are stunned and thrilled to see their kids become far more independent and responsible than they'd ever imagined possible. The kids have no choice—and ultimately, that's really the point at which *all* of us step up and become young adults. And as in most worthy adventures, there are likely to be a few storms and setbacks.

Culture shock.
Homesickness.
Saying good-bye.
Reverse culture shock.

These are difficult but *absolutely essential* elements of the yearlong exchange.

FACT: Only about 4 percent of Rotary Youth Exchange students on the yearlong program **come home earlier than their scheduled return date**—and this includes those who come back early in order to graduate with their classmates, attend a family event, or start summer school, as well as those who are dealing with homesickness or culture shock.

Dennis White knows a lot about culture shock and its evil twin, reverse culture shock. As a Peace Corps volunteer in Iran between 1968 and 1970, he experienced firsthand the challenges of cultural immersion and reintegration. Now he is a psychologist who specializes in reverse culture shock.[2] He works with Peace Corps volunteers, missionaries, and exchange-program coordinators across North America in an effort to teach others about the profound emotional and mental changes that are experienced by those who spend time living abroad. Although Dr. White has trained members of numerous organizations over the years, he is especially proud to have served as a member and chair of the Rotary International Youth Exchange Committee, an international panel that advises the RI board of directors on all aspects of the RYE program.

During his years of working with thousands of students, parents, and exchange organizers, Dr. White discovered that, though each individual's experience is unique in many ways, students go through a few very predictable stages while living abroad. In addition, he has seen that those who experience reverse culture shock when they come home are the ones who were most fully immersed during their exchange and are most likely to reap the benefits of their time abroad in profound and lifelong ways.

In other words, tussling with the culture shock twins is a *good* thing.

Dr. White has some advice for those who think sending students to live abroad for a year sounds like a superfun vacation:

INSIDER INSIGHT

I tell parents that if they want to send their kid on a trip that will have them coming home the same but happier, they should buy a ticket to Disney World. A yearlong exchange is a life-altering experience, and parents need to be aware of the extraordinary maturation process that their kids will undergo while they are away.

Anyone who has traveled extensively is familiar with culture shock—a temporary disorientation that comes from being exposed to a different place, a different language, and different customs. *Living* in a new place for an extended period is like turbocharging the experience. Those who go through culture shock aren't doing anything "wrong"—in fact, the opposite is true. Many would argue that the most rewarding exchanges are those that are characterized by a cage-rattling case of culture shock, followed by an even more identity-melting dose of reverse culture shock upon returning home.

According to Dr. White, there are four main stages of culture shock, and—here's the kicker—they might repeat themselves in cycles depending on the student and the host culture. Here's the way he breaks it down:

1. Excitement and Enthusiasm
The honeymoon period. Everyone's great, the place is amazing, and everything is fantastic! This initial stage may be repeated in shorter cycles as the student learns new skills, develops more proficiency with the language, or becomes more independent as a traveler.

2. Irritability
The honeymoon's over. Things are starting to get annoying. The student begins to notice real differences (beyond the food and the language), and though they may try to accept the way things are, they can't shake the irritability. They may not understand why they feel the way they do and may attribute their annoyance to particular incidents or people (host families are often caught in the crosshairs) rather than to their own experience of culture shock.

3. Adaptation
Reality check. This is the longest, most difficult, and most rewarding stage, when students accept that they will have

(continued)

to adapt if they are going to be successful in their host culture. They start dedicating themselves to learning the language and making friends. Things start to come more naturally, and they become more comfortable with the elements that were difficult to accept in the beginning.

4. Biculturalism

High five! This stage may come very near the end of the stay or even after the student returns home. They realize that they have become competent in another culture and can function from a very different perspective.

Dr. White explains that those who spend time abroad are moving from *ethnocentrism* to *ethnorelativism*. All cultures are ethnocentric and teach their members that their ways of doing things are the preferred and appropriate way. So naturally our first response, when faced with different values and behaviors, is to feel defensive and view our practices as right and the other culture's as wrong, strange, or just plain ridiculous. Over time we open up to new ideas. "Ethnorelativism is the awareness that develops as one realizes there are other valid ways of dealing with the world, whether we agree with them or not," says Dr. White.

He offers this helpful condensed version of the process:

- I don't like the way they do this—it's stupid!
- But they seem to be doing okay doing it this way.
- If I want to survive here, I'd better learn to do it this way.
- Now that I can do it this way, it doesn't seem so bad, even though I may still prefer to do it my way.

The best exchange programs require students to live with at least two families during the course of the year (though it may not be possible in remote areas). That way they can develop greater flexibility, adjust to the rules and routines of each household while getting to know more people in a very intimate way, and avoid assuming that one family defines the culture. And though changing host families is by design a very difficult part of the exchange experience, it's an extremely important learning process and in many cases the most rewarding opportunity for personal growth.

I hope you can see the value of sending your son or daughter on a high school exchange, but if it's just not going to work for you or your student (or it's already too late), going abroad before, during, or after *college* can provide some outstanding benefits as well.

In the next chapter we'll take a look at how college students can study in other countries cheaply, safely, and in a manner that is most likely to lead to cultural immersion, a deeper appreciation of the world and its diversity, and terrific opportunities to live and work abroad.

Old School: thinking that those who experience culture shock or reverse culture shock are weak, inflexible, or overly dramatic
Bold School: recognizing that those who experience culture shock and reverse culture shock are deeply immersed in their experience and are fully processing their brain-boosting learning opportunity

CHAPTER SEVEN

How to Save Thousands on College Study Abroad

THE SHOCKING NUMBERS—AND WHO IS TO BLAME

> Not doing more than the average is what
> keeps the average down.
>
> WILLIAM M. WINANS

It might seem as though every college student is going abroad these days, but that's not the case at all.

Fact: *Less than 2 percent* of all American higher education students study abroad.[1]

And that's on the *high* end—the exact numbers depend on who and how you're counting. I'll keep it simple: about 205,000 U.S. students studied abroad *for credit* during the 2004–05 school year—*less than 1 percent* of all students enrolled in U.S. higher education.** (Check out the Institute of International Education website at www.iie.org.)

But that 1 percent figure doesn't tell the full story. You see, it counts *all* American students in higher education, and the reality is that nearly 60 percent of those who go abroad do so for doctorate-level research; about 20 percent of all U.S. study-abroad students are taking courses for their master's degrees; and *only 16 percent* **of all American study-abroad students are undergrads.**

It's true that community college enrollment numbers are skewing these statistics, but it's a mistake to assume that study abroad isn't a viable option for those who are enrolled in two-year institutions. In fact, as you'll learn in this chapter, going abroad as a community college student has some distinct advantages, and *all* students—whether they're studying economics, computer graphics, philosophy, music, or cooking—can benefit personally, academically, and professionally from studying in other countries.

International ed cheerleaders are quick to point out that many small private universities have study-abroad rates as high as 80 percent, and some schools, like Goucher College in Maryland, are choosing to make study abroad a requirement for graduation. This is good news, but it points to another disturbing issue—the lack of diversity among study-abroad students and their destinations. (Most common profile: the white female humanities major who chooses to go to Europe.) Hope might come in the form of new governmental policies—organizations like NAFSA: Association of International Educators are calling for the adoption of the Simon Act, which would dramatically increase both the number and diversity of U.S. students who study abroad. (Learn more at www.nafsa.org.)

Hundreds of millions of dollars are being spent each year to promote study abroad for U.S. college students, but the results are decidedly disappointing. There's a lot of blame to go around, but let's focus on the two biggest obstacles that are preventing students from heading to the international departure section of the airport, passport in hand:

▶ The study-abroad packages being promoted by most universities are very expensive.
▶ Most universities do not offer advice or alternatives to students who can't afford the premium options recommended.

Good thing we've got some strategies to deal with these challenges.

Let's take a look at how the very important lessons we learned in the last chapter correlate with current trends in study abroad. **We know that when it comes to brain-boosting study-abroad experiences, the best choice is to:**

- ◗ **go early** (junior in high school as opposed to junior in college)
- ◗ **stay longer** (one year as opposed to one semester)
- ◗ **choose unfamiliar destinations** (and foreign languages)

And yet according to the Institute for International Education, **among the undergraduate college students who do manage to study abroad:**

❑ The most popular year to go is the **junior year of college.**
❑ The most popular length of stay is **less than eight weeks.**
❑ The top destination is the **United Kingdom.**

See the problem here?

We may not feel up to fighting the behemoth forces making it difficult for U.S. students to study abroad, but sometimes it's just smarter to figure out how to go *around* an obstacle instead of spending time and energy smashing it to bits. What you need to know is that there are some tricky ways to jump over the big fat dollar signs in the road, and best of all, there are students who are already high-fiving on the other side and waving for us to come on over.

That's a party we want to join—and we'll get there—but right now we need to see how we *parents* are contributing to the fact that the two-month London pub crawl has been the favorite U.S. college study-abroad option for years. After that we'll happily explore the very simple process that will help students get more depth, length, and learning from their study-abroad experience while saving *thousands* of dollars in the process.

> **Old School:** believing that most U.S. college students are choosing to study abroad
> **Bold School:** knowing that only a tiny fraction of U.S. students study abroad at any time during their higher education, and that those who do tend to visit familiar locations and stay for short periods

FIRST, LOSE THE CRUISE MENTALITY

> Freedom lies in being bold.
> ROBERT FROST

We've gotten terribly soft over the years.

Back in the 1970s student travel was synonymous with backpacking. Think hostels full of world travelers, hitchhiking, and cheap market food. Most college students paid a nominal fee to study abroad or sometimes paid no tuition at all in the case of a direct student swap. Many did not get credit back in the United States; it was more about the experience of being in another culture. Study abroad was not seen as a second-mortgage type of proposition, even in Europe. The most expensive part was the airfare, which was proportionately much pricier back then. Those who went abroad for a semester or an extended journey viewed it as a thrilling and enriching adventure instead of a cushy vacation.

Things are different these days.

Now students are more likely to see study abroad as a chance to take Italian in Rome with a group of other American college students who happen to have $20,000 to spend on a semester in another country. Students choose from among programs that offer everything from van pick-up at the airport to complimentary cell phones during the length of their stay. They favor English-speaking destinations that offer familiar food franchises and accommodations with around-the-clock Internet access allowing them to check their e-mail, Twitter, or Facebook accounts on a daily basis.

Our brave ocean-crossing ancestors must be rolling over in their graves.

It's fine to plan a vacation that involves nothing more challenging than ordering another beer (in English) from the pool bar, but that's a stunningly shortsighted approach to picking a study-abroad option. If you're looking for a global experience that will propel your student far beyond his cannonballing peers, it's critically important to blow past the boxed-set thinking. The innovative leaders of the future—those who will be snagging those creative class jobs (or making their own) all over the planet—aren't simply meeting in the lobby for their daily scheduled bus tour. Instead, they're embracing the bold-school approach to study abroad: **go solo, go long, and go deep.**

According to a 2007 study conducted by the American Council on Education, the Art and Science Group, and the College Board, 55 percent of college-bound students say they are "certain" or "fairly certain" they will study abroad before they graduate from university. (Learn more at www.acenet.edu.) Once they get to college, however, they discover that they have to cough up as much as twenty grand for a semester abroad (or up to $50,000 for a year), if they selected a university that charges its students full room, board, and tuition even while they are in another hemisphere. The price tag pushes study abroad to the never-mind end of the spectrum, so students lose out on the most vitally important experience to prepare them for the global economy.

Good news: study abroad doesn't have to be expensive. In fact, the study-abroad period (whether it's a year or a semester) can and should be the least expensive part of your student's university experience.

Can. Should. But there's a little problem we need to talk about.
I hate to be the one to tell you this, but we parents are part of
the reason that college and study abroad cost so much these days.
It's time to sing our theme song again: *We're afraid.* We are worried for our students' safety, even when they go to places like
London and Paris. We watch the news, get scared, and think it's
just better to keep our little darlings close to home unless they can
go with a packaged program to a place that is safe and familiar.

Many American parents are convinced that studying abroad is
going to be less safe for their kids than spending time on a U.S.
university campus, and while it's true that tourists everywhere are
always bigger targets for crime than locals, the risks for students
can be dramatically reduced through increased awareness. What
gets tourists of all ages into trouble is the vacation mind-set—
engaging in I'm-on-vacation behavior like drinking excessively,
taking unfamiliar drugs, going to clubs with strangers, and not paying attention to surroundings. And while gruesome movies about
hostels from hell and mysterious disappearances fuel our American parental fear, you may find it interesting that parents in other
countries consider the United States, with its easy access to guns
and history of school shootings, to be one of the most dangerous
destinations in the world for their own children.

Binge drinking. Accidents. Date rape. Overdoses. These are
happening on nearly every American college campus, and yet we
panic at the thought of our kids getting pickpocketed (the most
common crime against travelers) or losing their passport (the most
common "emergency" abroad) while in another country.[2] Our fear
spikes the prices for study abroad: program organizers add amenities that give us the illusion that our kids will remain protected,
and we're willing to pay for them.

It's not just our (largely unwarranted) fear of crime; we're
afraid of allowing our kids to be *uncomfortable*. In a frenetic
world we seek comfort, and that usually translates into spending
more money on trappings. This escalation in comfort and style

spills over into the college and study-abroad experience as well. It's no wonder college students today are dazzled by schools with spacious new dorms and state-of-the-art fitness centers—we have trained them to appreciate ample personal space, natural light, plenty of storage, and sleek styling.

The pressure is on to feel like good parents (fear of not doing enough!), and so we go all out to feather our freshman's nest. We worry that our kids might end up in a not-so-comfortable house or experience awkward moments during a home stay in another country, so we encourage them to stay in the study-abroad dorm, where they'll have plenty of amenities and a chance to socialize with other American students. Our own need to ensure our kids' comfort—and the fact that they're used to having their own space and stuff—is precisely what pushes up the costs for both college and study abroad.

It's time to wake up and smell that Starbucks double latte in London:

THE PRICES FOR BOTH COLLEGE AND STUDY ABROAD ARE MARKET DRIVEN. As long as we're willing to pay for that gleaming new student union building or part-of-the-study-abroad-package flat with a lovely view of Hyde Park, universities will continue to charge big bucks for the campus experience or semester abroad.

MANY STUDY-ABROAD PROGRAMS ARE LITTLE MORE THAN OPPORTUNITIES FOR STUDENTS TO PARTY INTERNATIONALLY FOR COLLEGE CREDIT. Parents who would never consider spending $20,000 on a vacation for the whole family are taking out substantial loans in order to enroll their students in a "safe" and "comfortable" semester abroad that consists of several nights out on the town each week with fellow Americans. In many cases college students go abroad before they are of legal drinking age in the United States. There's a reason that American college students have a worldwide reputation as loud, sometimes indecent, and often drunk party people—they've earned it. The rest of the world's students don't view travel as an opportunity to get trashed. It's as American as apple pie.

Study-abroad coordinators and universities around the world are falling all over themselves in an effort to attract U.S. college students to their programs.
Two reasons:

1. They know that Americans expect education and study abroad to be expensive.
2. They know that Americans are interested in—and willing to pay for—extra support services because they are not used to being in places in which other languages are spoken.

Simply put, we're a great target market because **we don't question high prices** and **we're too scared** to go abroad on our own. How embarrassing.

Few countries in the world charge as much for college as the United States, and most non-U.S. citizens are incredulous to learn how much the average American university student pays for a college degree. In 2007 alone students in France, Germany, Israel, Mexico, India, and Canada (among other countries) staged protests against tuition hikes of as little as $800 per year. On most U.S. campuses an increase of $800 barely warrants a *scowl*. We've come to expect that college will be crazy expensive, and so we don't question it. The same is true for study abroad.

Most students choose their study-abroad program based on what sounds fun and easy. For years the United Kingdom has been the top destination for U.S. students studying abroad. (This is changing due to the weakened dollar—check www.iie.org for updates.) There's no language barrier! The food is recognizable!

Parents, wanting their kids to be *comfortable* in a *familiar* place, breathe a sigh of relief when their son or daughter chooses to go to the U.K.

In-the-know student travelers and professors sometimes refer to going abroad with a group of others from your own culture as "submarining"—yes, you're immersed, but there's very little chance of getting wet. College students *should* have fun while they're abroad, and of course all parents want their kids to be safe, but here's the thing: a semester-long party with American classmates—whether it's in Glasgow or Gdansk—is not going to teach students much about the culture or themselves except maybe the preferred drink in the country they visit and their own physical tolerance for said beverage.

Staying in the American bubble while abroad costs *a lot* more and results in students barely dipping a toe into the culture. And don't expect a packaged program to impress future employers. After all, they're looking for students with cultural understanding, confidence navigating on their own, and language fluency—characteristics far more likely to be developed by independent study-abroad students ("indies") than those on a group tour ("groupers").

❏ **Smart Move**: To save money on study abroad, connect with the culture, and earn the respect of those who value global experience, students must play an active role in creating a *personalized* study-abroad experience.

This chapter will show you how to help your student design a fulfilling and affordable study-abroad adventure that offers plenty of fun, yes, but also relevant learning and worthy challenges that lead to more independence, creative thinking, and awareness.

Ready for some stories? In the next section we'll hear from those who've hit the road on their own.

Old School: viewing study-abroad packages as the only option for college students
Bold School: viewing study-abroad packages as the high-end "cruise" option designed for those who value comfort, structured activities, and simple choices

THE REWARDS OF INDIE STUDY ABROAD—AND WHAT STUDENTS NEED TO THRIVE

> The most successful people are those
> who are good at plan B.
> JAMES YORKE

In universities around the world, students from many countries simply show up as international students without the "benefit" of being affiliated with any sort of program or package deal. Many Europeans, for example, are not overwhelmed by the idea of struggling momentarily in the process of enrolling and getting settled, even when they don't speak the language of the country they're visiting. Of course, they're also outraged by the notion that anyone would charge thousands of dollars extra to "help" them study abroad, because they know plenty of students who have done it on their own.

❏ **Smart Move**: Instead of signing up for an overstuffed study-abroad package, students can apply to the foreign university *directly* as an independent international student.

Indies pay more than the local students in that country, but *far* less than what a standard study-abroad program will charge. Thousands of students are already enrolling as independent international students and setting up their own living situations in every corner of the globe.

A Look at the Possibilities

Bronson Pettitt figured out how to study abroad on his own, and he has a few tips to share with other indies:

BOLD STATEMENT

I really wanted to study in Mexico to learn Spanish, but I couldn't find anything that was within my budget. Every program (whether through my school, Minnesota State University/Mankato, or through an independent carrier) was too expensive and in some cases charged double tuition—that is, home tuition at MSU *plus* tuition at the host university.

After two months of searching, it finally dawned on me that I could directly enroll at the language school, Escuela para Estudiantes Extranjeros, through La Universidad Veracruzana in Xalapa, Veracruz, and save loads of money. I simply sidestepped the middleman. Unfortunately, many students don't know that's an option and end up wasting insane amounts of money. Once they get there, they realize that they could have enrolled directly and saved a ton, since tuition is dirt cheap compared to what they're being charged. They also learn too late that many packaged programs lack organization and structure.

I've met many students who regretted not enrolling directly. The problem is that study-abroad offices tend to promote university-organized programs before telling students they can enroll directly, and students are discouraged and left thinking that going on their own is extremely difficult, dangerous, risky, and a waste of time and money since their credits will not transfer.

In my case, MSU's study-abroad office helped me quite a bit when I was making my own arrangements. Luckily, MSU allows its students to take "dummy" credits— that is, maintain enrollment and avoid having to drop out, reapply, and re-enroll. (Check to see if your college has this option.)

Prior to leaving, I had to:

❑ prove that the university was accredited
❑ ask my adviser for permission to get credits upon returning
❑ show class syllabi
❑ find my own living arrangements (easy enough to do—just check the Internet for roommates or families who might host you)

In the end, I had to put up with a few hours of bureaucracy, but it was worth the $10,000 I saved. Besides the obvious financial benefits of going independently, you have to ask yourself this: are you going abroad just to look good on paper, or do you truly want to learn the language and understand the culture? Therein lies the motivation.

I loved Mexico so much that I decided to return after graduation. Now I am working in DF [Mexico City] as a translator/proofreader/English teacher at a law firm (I call myself an *etceterista* because I do a little bit of everything), which pays decently. I live in an 1880 house with a museum vibe (the owner is a painter and has all kinds of art and knickknacks) along with about eight others my age. It's a really creative setting, and every day is a great learning experience.

Here are a few tips for others looking to study abroad independently:

❑ Associate as much as possible with locals and avoid Americans if you want to learn the language and culture.

(*continued*)

❑ Always keep a small notebook and pen with you. You never know when you'll see or hear an unknown word or phrase or observe something strange and later remind yourself of it.

❑ Buy an unlocked cell phone and get a prepaid SIM card in the country you are visiting rather than getting an international plan (probably expensive) for your existing monthly mobile service; try putting your service on hold or sweet-talk your carrier if you are under a contract.

❑ Try reading newspapers. It's one of the best ways to improve your language skills and a good way to know what makes the locals tick.

❑ Find out how much your bank charges to withdraw money. I paid five dollars each time, which can add up amazingly quickly. It's usually smarter to take out larger amounts less frequently—as long as you can keep your money stored safely and don't feel the temptation to overspend.

❑ When in Rome, do as the Romans do. Eat where the locals eat, watch the shows they watch, go to the bars, museums, and sporting events they go to. Assimilate yourself and put your nationality and judgments on hold.

Many students like Bronson discover the advantages of independent study abroad by simply questioning the prices and options presented. Once you begin to pull that thread, it can lead to surprising opportunities and great deals. And thanks to the skills they acquire while making their own connections, many indies find interesting ways to live and work abroad after graduation. Given the wide range of study, travel, and work possibilities around the world, there is sure to be a combination that's perfect for your student.

Let's review our vocabulary because we're about to add a few more terms. **Bold schoolers** intentionally create their own education experience; they tweak or sidestep the standard **four-by-four plan** (four years of high school, four years of college) and make room for lengthy study abroad and intense language learning in high school and college. Because they've already flexed their individuality and learned to deal with **fego** (fear and ego), they are more likely to become enthusiastic **indies** (independent study-abroad students who apply to foreign universities directly rather than go with a packaged plan) and intrepid **solo travelers** (those who set out on their own to go abroad).

Keep in mind that it's certainly possible to go solo without being an indie and vice versa. For example, a student signed up for an expensive study-abroad package might embark on the trip alone, turn out to be the only American enrolled in that particular college that semester, be assigned to a home stay, and have a support organization in the host country—in other words, be a **grouper** who is going solo. And it's also possible to be an independent study-abroad student (saving thousands by enrolling directly), meet other American students the first day who have signed up for a packaged plan and have lots of contact with Americans in classes or dorms—be an indie among groupers. By doing a little research and making informed decisions, students can pick and choose from a variety of options. (You'll see how it works later in this chapter!)

You should also know that plenty of students toe the four-by-four line all the way through school (without making a single bold-school move) and then have no problem whatsoever diving into independent study abroad or solo travel. And because it has become so easy to connect online with others—including Americans who are working in other countries—an increasing number of recent college grads (with or without study-abroad or travel experience) are considering internships and employment options beyond the U.S. borders.

Here's a look at the current trends.

Those who move abroad on their own and find corporate jobs once they're there are sometimes called **halfpats**. Unlike traditional older middle-management expatriates who are transferred abroad by their companies and often accompanied by their spouses and kids (requiring substantial relocation, housing, and education allowances), halfpats tend to be solo travelers who are in their twenties or early thirties, single, childless, and cheaper to employ. Halfpats move to a particular country *first* because they're interested in living there and learning the language, and then apply to companies hiring international workers. Because halfpats have already arrived and settled in, they are very attractive to firms looking to limit their expat packages. (The "half" refers to the fact that these workers cost employers half as much.)

Young **globals** who *already* have foreign language skills and experience living abroad may choose to start out in the U.S. home office of a multinational company with the hope that they will be transferred to an office in another country. They know that many American corporations are looking for young employees who are single, bilingual, and ready and willing to work outside the United States. Those on this global path recognize that it may be smarter to schmooze the bosses at the mother ship than to hand a résumé to the receptionist at a satellite office.

Then there are the **freestyle** global workers who set out without a clear plan (or job offer) and find employment along the way. Jennie Barham started out as an indie study-abroad student, became a solo traveler, worked as a freelancer in various countries, and ended up being hired and relocated to London by an international firm. It all began with a little online research back when she was in college. This is her story:

BOLD STATEMENT

I was born and raised in Raleigh, North Carolina, and had my first chance to travel when I was a student at the University of South Carolina.

I planned my study-abroad experience myself, from start to finish. I decided I wanted to go to Australia, so I searched the Internet to find out what schools had music performance degrees and read up on the piano instructors. From the two best music universities, I chose the one with access to beaches, mountains, and the "raw" Australia.

Everything about Tasmania sounded amazing—the landscape, the history, the ruggedness, and especially the fact that it wasn't the popular or easy choice. I started e-mailing and calling to learn more, wired the money to the school for the dorm and my expenses, and started planning the details of my adventure. At the time the U.S. dollar was strong and the Australian fees pretty cheap. My airfare, room and board, and tuition together totaled less than a semester at my U.S. school!

After learning all about Australian culture and just living the heck out of life, I headed back to South Carolina. I had very understanding advisers and professors who bent the rules a bit so I could graduate on time, and five months later I was facing a much bigger world with many possibilities.

I took the chance to travel to South Africa and wound my way back to Australia, working as a waitress and piano teacher along the way. Later I volunteered at a school in Malaysia, then tried out postgraduate study in South Africa for a few months. After realizing that I didn't really want to spend the rest of my life in a classroom as

(*continued*)

a teacher, I found a job with a company that sent me off to London. Now I live there and travel throughout Europe for my work and absolutely love it!

Note that I chose destinations that allowed me to speak English. My greatest disappointment in myself is that at twenty-nine I am monolingual. I did study Latin in high school, which is a good base, and then Spanish after college on my own, but I am not fluent in anything but English.

Fortunately I am really good at picking up the first bit of a language. For me, it's two things: (1) my ear is very good from music, and (2) I just believe that I can understand what someone is saying. My personal theory is that when you get over that initial fear of hearing another language, you are free to realize just how much you can actually register with only a little effort.

In London I work for an international online self-publishing company. I am surrounded by German, Dutch, Italian, Spanish, and French in my daily work life, as I have coworkers from all of those places. I have convinced many people that I'm fluent in these languages just because I take a little time to learn the basics and then just listen and watch body language. Don't get me wrong—if I were fluent in at least one European language, my job would be immensely easier, and I am successful only through sheer determination.

The greatest benefit I gained from studying abroad and traveling was that I learned people. I have not attended business school, taken economics classes, or had any technical training, but I know how to quickly pick up cultural cues. For example, I've learned that during a business meeting in the U.K. there is relaxed conversation for a while before getting to the serious business. In the publishing world in Spain there's a resistance to change, so it's important to present new ideas in a positive, non-threatening way.

Living and working abroad has taught me to pay attention to these details. By doing so, I know that I can figure out how to work best with people no matter where I am. This is something no class or textbook can teach you.

Jennie wasn't a bold schooler—she did the four-by-four, didn't go abroad until college, and never became fluent in a language besides English. But because of her experience as an independent study-abroad student, she became a confident solo traveler and freestyle worker able to find ways to make money wherever she went. She's a great example of what can be set in motion by simply deciding to strike out and explore a corner of the world on your own.

Are you beginning to see the possibilities for your own student?

❏ **Smart Move**. Savvy parents whose kids didn't participate in an exchange program in high school recognize that it's even *more* important for their sons and daughters to choose to study abroad independently during college.

Getting Used to the Idea

I've met dozens of happy indies who had never even boarded a plane before they set off to study abroad on their own. They are making their way in foreign countries by connecting with locals and other travelers who can help them discover more about *where* they are and *who* they are. Even on the most trying days these indies surprise themselves and everyone around them by overcoming obstacles and developing new skills.

Will your student thrive as an indie? Probably. Here are a few things to keep in mind.

Students considering independent study abroad need the following:

- good communication skills (native language)
- comfort with spending time alone
- skill at connecting with people through e-mail (more details ahead)
- flexibility about eating and sleeping habits
- decent navigation skills (ability to use a map, good sense of direction)
- reasonably mature decision making regarding health and safety
- the ability to ask for assistance when needed
- a willingness to travel lightly and live without the usual comforts of home
- the ability to share space (bedroom, bathroom) in a respectful way

Students with these skills will do very well, and even those with a couple of iffy areas are likely to be just fine on their own. But as we've learned, it's not just the *students* who have to be okay with the idea—parents need to know (and stretch) their comfort zone as well.

As a parent of an indie, you'll need:

- the understanding that you will not see your student for a semester or longer
- the ability to go a week or more without any contact from your student
- a willingness to allow your student to make important choices about where, when, and for how long he will be abroad

- the ability to segue into a mentor role that requires sid side planning instead of top-down management
- trust that your student will find the assistance and support she needs from others while abroad

Parents of prospective indies will need to give at least a grudging if not an emphatic nod to all of the above. Relax—I'm going to help you move along that continuum toward cheerful endorsement. You'll feel better after you've read the rest of this chapter and learned how to help your student study abroad independently, get full credit for it, and gain confidence in traveling solo. Let's begin by hearing from an expert who knows all about the challenges, thrills, and advantages of setting out on your own.

When it comes to solo travel, Doug Lansky is one happy guru. He has visited more than one hundred countries during the last ten years and has been living abroad for an additional six. Doug became America's youngest nationally syndicated columnist; his weekly "Vagabond" column grew to reach over 10 million readers in forty major newspapers. He also had a nice five-year gig as the regular world-travel expert on NPR's flagship travel program, *Savvy Traveler*.

These days Doug has a sweet life in Sweden with his wife and three little girls, but several months each year he hits the U.S. college lecture circuit to offer "Get Lost," his fast-paced and funny multimedia presentation that gets students pumped up to travel solo. Doug's written a bagful of get-lost books, including the Signspotting series (his pictorial laugh fest featuring the world's most absurd signs), and his hilarious anthology *There's No Toilet Paper . . . on the Road Less Traveled: The Best of Travel Humor and Misadventures*. He follows his popular lectures with question-and-answer sessions and has just the thing for those who don't know how to get started: his book *The Rough Guide First-Time Around the World*.

Doug is very familiar with the concerns expressed by students who aren't sure if they're ready for the adventure of the global road, and his story is especially inspiring to anyone dreaming of getting paid to travel. There are plenty of students with both stars *and* dollar signs in their eyes, and they tend to ask him how to make money while traveling to one hundred countries. Doug shared a few thoughts on that question and described the benefits of solo travel at any age.

INSIDER INSIGHT

I get asked about my major all the time, but only by students who are curious to know if there is some magical major you can pick that will somehow train you to be a travel writer. (It was international political economics, if you must know, and I only picked it because it was the one major that didn't require a thesis.) I've never been asked to produce a transcript or asked if I ever, in fact, attended college. When it comes to freelance writing, editors want to know where your previous work has been published, if the story you're pitching them is a good fit with their publication, and if you're a strong writer.

For me, travel didn't just provide material for writing—it shaped my opinions of the world, my own country, and myself. Solo travel is especially valuable because when you're alone, you find out who you really are. With a friend you often encourage each other to tick off the list of must-sees. On your own, if you don't feel like seeing a church or museum, you can skip it and no one will be the wiser. This freedom is more revealing than you might imagine.

Traveling solo doesn't mean you don't meet people or make friends along the way. In fact, you're more easily approached by friendly strangers when you're on your own (as long as you're not plugged into your iPod), and you're more likely to get invited or drawn into a cultural experience. Plus, you read more, listen more, and learn self-reliance.

Of course, I had no idea about any of this when I set out. I thought I was just going for six months. That's the beauty of it—the detours can be the most interesting part of any journey, and being open will lead to more learning than will sticking to a fixed itinerary.

Travel is the world's biggest classroom, but only if you approach it with the right mind-set. It can also be an endless beach party or a superficial sightseeing trip. I get tremendous satisfaction from speaking to students across the United States about how not just to see the world cheaply and safely but to make it an enriching experience.[3]

Whether you're still on the fence or ready to drive your student to the airport, I've got some info that's sure to melt resistance. In the next section you'll learn how to help your student spend less than $5,000 for an incredible semester abroad as an indie and discover why going solo is likely to be *safer* than traveling with a group of other American students.

Old School: believing that students do best when they go abroad in groups

Bold School: recognizing that students zoom ahead when they go abroad independently

HOW TO STUDY ABROAD FOR LESS THAN $5,000 PER SEMESTER—AND WHY IT'S SAFER TO GO SOLO

A wise parent humors the desire for independent action, so as to become the friend and advisor when his absolute rule shall cease.
ELIZABETH GASKELL

Not long ago I met an American in Buenos Aires who was studying law at an Ivy League university. I asked what brought him to Argentina, and he told me he was spending a semester studying law in a program arranged by his profs back in the United States.

Being nosy about study-abroad experiences of all kinds, I asked him about the details. It didn't take long before he told me about his frustration with the "program" and how he had ended up arranging everything himself. His story:

BOLD STATEMENT

I don't have a liaison of any kind from my university down here. I had to find my own apartment. I bought my own cell phone. I even handled my student visa details. I'm okay with all of that—it wasn't that difficult.

But it *really* pissed me off when I discovered that the university here is free to anyone. *Free.* I mean, I could have just come down here and walked into these classes and not paid a single dime or peso. That would have been great.

The problem is that I am paying $20,000 in tuition back in the United States for this semester. I wish I knew where that money is going, considering I could have done all of it—including my travel and living expenses—on my own for about $4,000. Unfortunately I had to pay that *on top* of my tuition payment.

I should have come down here and done this before I entered law school, since it's not part of my regular JD program anyway. I'm just kicking myself for not figuring this out ahead of time, but I really had no idea what to expect and assumed that for the price I was paying, I'd be getting a lot of extras and special treatment. What a joke. Unfortunately, I'm not laughing.

When I told him that I was writing a book about helping high school and college students get a global education that doesn't cost a fortune, he said, "Well, maybe your next book could be about how to avoid getting hosed in graduate school." (Tip: Many U.S. students are figuring out that there are plenty of well-respected master's degree programs abroad—taught in English—that cost less than $10,000 total.)

Right now, all over the world, *thousands* of students have similar stories of paying top dollar back home for programs that they could have easily arranged themselves for far less.

We can fix this situation. The first step is framing the problem in terms of a question that invites a solution.

Why Do Study-Abroad Packages Cost So Much?

Most programs are outsourced. The U.S. university contracts with an organization that does all of the work—developing a relationship with the college in the host country, hiring a local coordinator who can set up home stays and other housing arrangements, and scheduling things like airport pick-ups and excursions. It's great for the U.S. colleges—they become affiliated with the program, pay a fee per student enrolled, and may even collect full tuition, room, and board from students while they are thousands of miles from campus.

Some U.S. universities send a professor or administrator with the students and play a larger role in determining what courses and outings are included, but most colleges find it far easier (and more profitable) to steer students to one of these programs and let the provider take care of everything.

This outsourcing is a good deal for the host universities abroad as well because they can get students who wouldn't normally consider enrolling and can charge the international student rate, which is often double, triple, or quadruple what they charge the local students. But though these programs make study abroad easy and profitable for the colleges involved, *the losers in the equation are the parents and students who are stuck paying for it all.*

Bottom line: students end up paying a U.S. university price for a non-U.S. university program. It varies from country to country and college to college, but in general the packaged programs will charge students anywhere from **three to ten times** the tuition the host university requires from international students—plus housing expenses, which can be double or triple what students would pay on their own.[4]

To encourage students to sign up for their affiliated programs, some colleges are insisting that they will not honor any other credits earned abroad. Worse, many students are told that in order to study abroad on their own, they will have to drop out and re-enroll, and in some cases *it is implied that they may not be allowed back in as a senior in order to graduate!* This inexcusable scare tactic results in students reluctantly taking on debt to study abroad through affiliate programs—or avoiding study abroad completely.

❏ **Smart Move**: To save money, avoid choosing a college with the tight-fisted policy of refusing credits from nonpartner programs or charging full room, board, and tuition while students are studying abroad.

There are plenty of universities that are quite happy to cater to indies and accept the credits they present—provided they submit the proper paperwork.

If your student is *already attending* a university that is refusing to give credit for nonaffiliated programs, there are three options:

1. **Challenge the policy.** Universities are facing mounting pressure to reform their study-abroad policies; expect some changes in the near future.[5]

2. **Arrange to do an independent study for credit.**
   (You'll read tips on this in the next section.)
3. **Go abroad *after* graduation.**

If you're not yet caught in the sticky our-way-or-no-way study-abroad net spread by unscrupulous universities, be grateful! You've just saved a ton of money.

Tips on Timing

MAKE SURE TO ASK ABOUT STUDY-ABROAD POLICIES DURING THE COLLEGE-APPLICATION PROCESS. Administrators need to hear that parents and students are becoming much more informed about their options and are less likely to get duped into overpaying for programs they can duplicate for far less. Some study-abroad coordinators may tell students that their financial aid will not cover any study-abroad programs other than the ones offered through their university's affiliated programs. This is almost never the case. Check with the financial aid office for details.

GO ABROAD DURING THE YEAR BETWEEN HIGH SCHOOL GRADUATION AND ENTRANCE INTO COLLEGE (GAP YEAR). Thanks to the stress and exhaustion inherent in the traditional college-application process, many students feel burned out by the time they get their high school diploma and want nothing more than a reprieve from the classroom. This is a very sad statement about education, but it's a great excuse to spend a year abroad! A year of exploration at this point allows students to see the world and themselves more clearly prior to college—and they're more likely to be excited and directed once they do start classes.

The gap year, common in Europe, is becoming more popular among U.S. students, and as a result many organizations are offering services to help those putting together a year of volunteer, travel, and work experiences. Warning: it's easy to spend as much as $30,000 on a packaged gap-year program, and many organizations charge shocking amounts for volunteer opportunities abroad. Fortunately there are options that are reasonably priced—or follow the tips later in this chapter to create a personalized and affordable gap-year experience.

It's smart to incorporate study abroad during the gap year and get credit while gaining valuable skills and a more global perspective. In addition, students are more likely to get their study-abroad credits accepted if they apply after their gap year as a *transfer* student than if they study abroad on a nonsanctioned program once admitted. (My daughter, Tara, will explain more later in this chapter.)

STUDY ABROAD THROUGH A COMMUNITY COLLEGE INSTEAD OF A STATE OR PRIVATE UNIVERSITY. Most study-abroad programs provided through community colleges (often the very same destinations and schools provided through state or private college plans) require students to pay the basic package price *plus tuition*—but the tuition is far cheaper than what a four-year university will charge. This means that going abroad for a semester through your local community college (you have to be a student there) will cost many thousands less than an almost identical package through an expensive private school or even a state college. In addition, some community colleges have special short-term study-abroad programs designed for students with work or family responsibilities, and many offer funding as well. Community college students—especially those receiving financial aid—may qualify for additional scholarships for study abroad. Check with your local community college to learn more.

A Look at the Real Costs

Most packaged programs charge thousands of dollars more than the sum of their parts. Prices will vary depending on the particulars, but *in general,* for the same destination and in many cases the same classes and living arrangements, this is a typical range:

Indie semester abroad: $5,000 (as low as $2,500 for those who choose certain Central American/Caribbean locations)
Community college semester abroad: $10,000
State university semester abroad: $15,000
Private university semester abroad: $20,000

What do the group programs offer for the extra money? Usually they'll promise a combination of the following:

- *Airport shuttle service*
  Alternative: Every airport has options for new arrivals, and indies connect with those who can share info or even meet them when they get in.
- *Someone to help arrange a home stay or dorm*
  Alternative: Many universities with international student departments routinely handle this aspect at no extra cost. Indies use the tips in this chapter to make their own arrangements.
- *Day trips*
  Alternative: The majority of these outings can be arranged easily and enjoyed more fully in small groups at a fraction of the price the programs charge.
- *Cell phone distribution*
  Alternative: Cell phones don't cost much in most destinations and are easily purchased, along with prepaid phone cards. Indies ask the locals for recommendations.
- *Health insurance*
  Alternative: This can be obtained online within minutes at competitive rates. (We've used www.WorldNomads.com, recommended by Lonely Planet.)

- **Orientation by a local coordinator**
  Alternative: Plenty of people are happy to do this at no charge. (Keep reading!)
- **Internet access at the local coordinator's office**
  Alternative: Most destinations have conveniently located Internet cafés with reasonable rates.
- **Assistance getting a student visa**
  This varies from country to country, but as we've seen in both Mexico and Argentina, "assistance" often means that a big bus will take a group of students to the immigration office, requiring very long waits as each person goes through the process individually. In other countries, getting a visa can be as easy as making an appointment and showing up to sign a few papers.

  Alternative: Those who have recently obtained a student visa in that specific country can often provide additional helpful information. Indies do research, ask directly, find out what they need, and avoid spending hours waiting their turn in a crowd.
- **Website and home office in the United States**
  In some cases having a middleman can result in confusion and unnecessary expenses. I know a number of students who spent hundreds of dollars (and many hours) preparing recommended documents prior to their departure, only to discover that nobody at the host university had the slightest interest in looking at them.

  Alternative: Often going direct is simpler, in addition to being cheaper. Being in e-mail or phone contact with both locals and current students may be a better way to get relevant information than relying upon web copy that might be outdated or U.S. office staffers who have not gone through the process in that particular destination recently.
- **Volunteer opportunities**
  Many programs offer the chance to volunteer for an additional fee, part of which is considered a donation. I've talked to U.S. students who played with kids at orphanages or hospitals for a

total of twenty hours (over the course of several weeks) and paid as much as $2,000 *extra* for the privilege.

Alternative: Indies contact a local church, club, or university group to join their volunteer efforts, giving them a chance to make friends with locals, contribute their time in meaningful ways, and make a direct donation if they choose to do so.

❏ **Smart Move**: Indies know that they can duplicate the services included in most study-abroad packages for a fraction of the cost.

While it's certainly true that there are excellent program coordinators around the world who provide great services to students studying abroad, you will have to decide if you are willing to pay between $5,000 and $15,000 *extra* for the benefits they offer. (And remember, it's not the hard-working coordinators in the host country who are getting the bulk of this money—it's the university back in the United States.)

No matter what you choose, there are no guarantees that everything will go perfectly. Those in organized programs are likely to have just as many (if not more) home-stay disappointments and other frustrations as indies do—but indies have the freedom to make changes, *and* they tend to know more locals who can help them out.

What About Safety?

Humans have a long history of socializing in groups, and we tend to believe there is safety in numbers. However, study-abroad students who move about in large clusters of Americans are much more conspicuous and therefore more obvious targets for theft and other crimes than individuals who are visiting sites with only one or two international students or locals. Those who spend time with trusted locals instead of other new arrivals will learn more about what's safe (and what isn't) and avoid the places that attract tourists and the thieves who prey upon them. Students who spend most of their time in a large group of Americans, on the other hand, are often more likely to:

- be distracted and unaware of their surroundings
- engage in behavior that attracts attention

Unsavory characters who are looking for an easy target zero in on telltale tourist cues—public drunkenness, flashy clothing or jewelry, cameras and other equipment, English spoken loudly to others—that informed indies who make an effort to blend in generally avoid.

Right now, thanks to the favorable exchange rate, Argentina (and Buenos Aires in particular) is a hot destination for college students. We've certainly seen our share of groupers out on the town, and we've heard a number of sobering morning-after stories about stolen items. In the last two years our family of six (each of us frequently heading out alone) has experienced crime just once—Teal's purse was stolen from the back of her chair *while she was dining in a restaurant with a group of American students.* (She was smart not to carry anything of value, and she felt a little better when, months later, one of the Bush twins had her purse stolen at a restaurant in Buenos Aires despite the presence of the Secret Service.) Tom and I have never once had anything stolen or even felt threatened in any way, but several of our friends who were visiting for only a week or so have had a piece of jewelry or a bag taken from them while they were exploring crowded tourist locations with other Americans.

I don't mean to be an alarmist. The truth is that even the most clueless (and drunk) American students stumbling around the streets of Buenos Aires (or anywhere else) aren't likely to suffer much more than a stolen backpack and a bruised ego. My husband and I feel our daughters are much safer in Argentina than they are in the United States, and they certainly agree that they *feel* safer. This is because they:

- generally avoid going out with groups of Americans
- know how to pay attention to reduce risks

These practices are good for students no matter where they go.[6]

❑ **Smart Move**: Never assume that being part of a group program is more likely to insulate students from negative elements.

It's not the program that will protect them—it's their own awareness of their surroundings. Groupers tend to learn this *after* an unfortunate incident (or two or three) among their members, while indies learn right away how to stay safe because they spend time with locals who show them the ropes. (Groupers may hear a safety spiel from a caring coordinator, but groupthink takes over and students forget about the risks once they're out—and drinking.)

Other Benefits

We've talked about price and safety as advantages for those who study abroad independently. What are the other benefits?

- **Indies have more control.** They are choosing (as opposed to being assigned) where to stay (and with whom) and can pick where and what to eat. Plus, they meet locals who will tell them where to find great bargains on everything from phones to concert tickets.
- **Indies get more respect.** Groupers are awed (and yes, irked) to learn that someone has figured out how to get the same experience for much less. They are simultaneously smacking their foreheads and offering high fives. In their intensive Spanish classes at a local university here in Buenos Aires, our daughters sat next to groupers from top U.S. universities (including Ivies) who were paying over $8,000 in tuition *for the very same course* that cost our girls (and other

indies) about $1,200. Indies have the inside scoop, and those who will be paying their study-abroad debt for the foreseeable future are hungry to hear it.

Here's a tip for groupers: consider staying for a second semester as an indie. This will make it possible to double up the time you spend abroad without breaking the bank. The costs will be much less than the first semester because the plane ticket is already paid for (make sure to check into change fees), and you will be able to take advantage of alternate housing and food options while paying reduced tuition as an independent international student.

By making wise choices about the timing and destination of study abroad and recognizing the role of awareness in personal safety, students can create a very affordable experience that provides extraordinary learning opportunities and supportive relationships with those who can offer advice and protection.

But what about getting *credit?* We'll address that in the next section.

> **Old School:** paying thousands of dollars *more* for a packaged study-abroad program that may actually increase risks while limiting students' options
>
> **Bold School:** paying thousands of dollars *less* for an independent study-abroad experience that is likely to be safer and far more flexible

TOP TEN TIPS FOR GETTING CREDIT FOR STUDY ABROAD

> Let us never negotiate out of fear. But let us never fear to negotiate.
>
> JOHN F. KENNEDY

Many students who go abroad in a packaged program are surprised to learn that they have to do some negotiating with their own college in order to get their credits transferred. Although there are exceptions, most partner programs still require students to work with their home college to ensure that they get credit for the courses they take while abroad. In general, students will get a one-page description of the course they will take and instructions to go talk to the registrar. (They should do so *before* the trip!)

In this section you'll learn some valuable tips to help your student get credit for time spent studying abroad, even if they're already attending a university that's persnickety about such things.

How hard is it to get international credits accepted by a U.S. university? Let's ask the Transfer Diva. Our second daughter, Tara, has become an expert on smuggling credits from one country to another.

BOLD STATEMENT

I am not sure if I should be referred to as the Transfer Diva exactly, but I *can* say that I am very good at getting *lo que quiero*—probably because I have a helluva backbone and am not afraid to ask for what I want. That's key.

Also, I've had plenty of chances to practice my craft. I've taken courses from six—count 'em, *six*—universities in *four* countries in *three* languages in a little more than two years, not to mention spending a year in Brazil during high school (in yet another language). Still, I managed to graduate from college almost two years ahead of my high school classmates, which just goes to show that no matter how much you skip around, you never have an excuse to whine about it being too hard to get back on track in order to graduate. You may have to bust your butt a little more than your peers in their thrice-weekly drunken stupor, but it is totally and completely doable.

(*continued*)

I will tell you this: the most important thing is *persistence*. Notice that I did not say patience. See, patience will get you nowhere, and I possess none of it. Occasionally you might have to raise a ruckus, but only after you've turned on the charm and done everything possible to get things done while being nicey-nice. The best strategy is to be cheerful and helpful and to play *sweet* hardball.

I'm not really into video games, but I have to say that I do rock at this game I call Credit Quest. I have been known to get a little obsessed about going to the next level. Hey, there are worse things to geek out about.

Here are my top ten tips for becoming a Credit Quest champ:

1. YOU CAN NEVER HAVE TOO MANY SIGNATURES, SEALS, STAMPS, OR OTHER OFFICIAL-LOOKING DOODADS ON ANY TRANSCRIPTS YOU ARE TRYING TO TRANSFER.

When I was in Brazil, my parents were hounding me to go to my local high school, have them draw up a list of the classes I'd taken, get it stamped and signed, etc. They were relentless. I groaned, I talked back—I even started to refer to credits as "the C word." I really did not want to go through with it, because for one thing it annoyed the *hell* out of the school staff since they had no idea what I was talking about. So I didn't get it all put together (it took several attempts) until the last couple of days prior to my departure from Brazil, which was extremely nerve wracking.

But I am *so glad* I did it—that signed, stamped, and sealed little beauty got me out of my last year of high school and allowed me to start college early. With college credits, the same thing applies—do whatever you have to do to make sure your transfer certificate positively *glows* with authenticity. You won't be sorry.

Heads up: *Get things in writing before you leave the United States.* I had an awesome high school counselor, Ms. Long, but my parents wanted to be sure I was covered in case she quit while I was in Brazil. She wrote notes on my transcript about what I needed to complete in order to graduate, then signed it. She kept a copy, and my parents kept a copy. This strategy works in college too.

2. **Make friends with those in the admissions or registrar's office at every college you attend.**

These people can really help you, and you need to get to know them. Do *not* pester them or waste their time with inane questions! Instead, learn about the processes they handle, let them see that you are more than willing to do your part, and show some love—they work really hard and don't get a lot of pats on the back. I make a point of chatting up my admissions peeps, dropping in to say hello at the registrar's office, whatever it takes.

When my two younger sisters and I were going to a university in Buenos Aires, we always went into the office *together.* We became known as "*Las Hermanas.*" If you don't happen to have a spare sibling or two nearby, always go with the same fellow student who is also trying to get transcripts. The office people will be more likely to remember you that way than if you were just a random single student. Plus, you keep each other strong and you get to take turns playing good cop/bad cop.

3. **Connect with a professor on your campus to set up an independent study *before* you leave the country.**

You need to have an ally who knows where you're headed and what you plan to study. It should be someone

(continued)

affiliated with that particular foreign language or maybe your major, depending on what you'll be studying. I strongly recommend that you set up an independent study with a prof *before* you go—that way you can get the credits through the classes you're taking, and with a little extra work (doing some interviews, writing a paper) you can get additional credit when you come back. This is good insurance and can really maximize your time. If you get overwhelmed, you can always choose to skip the independent study once you get back, but at least get it set up.

4. ALWAYS TAKE THE MOST TIME-INTENSIVE CLASSES AVAILABLE.

Yes, you can sign up to take one hour of class per day, but really that's pretty lame. It's much smarter to pick the classes that are four hours a day. There are still twenty more hours left—you'll have plenty of time to get out and do things. You might as well get the biggest bang for your buck if you're flying all the way there.

Heads up: *The very best way to score in Credit Quest is to take summer classes.* Doing one or two summer terms puts you *way* ahead since you can get up to a year's worth of credit for only three months of study! The pace is really fast and intense, but the professors are laid back, you become closer to your classmates, and it beats getting some pathetic summer job that pays minimum wage. Besides, future employers are far more likely to be impressed by the fact that you finished college *early* than by that summer you spent answering phones in an office. Go abroad, stay on campus or study online, but do *not* skip the summer term—unless, of course, you are totally fine spending many more thousands of dollars and another year or two taking classes.

5. WHEN YOU GET BACK TO YOUR HOME UNIVERSITY, DON'T TAKE NO FOR AN ANSWER.

What usually happens is, students go back to their college, present their transcripts, and then just accept the calculation offered. *No, no, no.* See, they almost always lowball it. If you have an intensive class that was worth, say, eighteen credits but they only give you twelve, don't just nod and smile. Remember your backbone!

Point out why you should be getting eighteen credits (nicely, remember). Talk about the number of hours per week, the number of weeks, anything special you did, and so on. Do not roll over without a reasonably cheerful fight. Most of the time all it takes is a two-sentence explanation, and they'll say something like, "Oh, well, in that case, let's mark it as eighteen credits."

If you don't push, you will lose out. This has been true every single time I have tried to transfer a credit. I would have had to spend another *year* in college if I'd just said "Oh, okay" each time someone told me their initial assessment of my credits. Don't get me wrong—I *love love love* learning, but taking bonehead classes to make up for "lost" credits is tedious and leads to burnout.

Heads up: *The more high-priced the college, the more likely they are to scrimp on your credits.* Come prepared to do some sweet-talking—and back it up with whatever documentation you can think of,

(*continued*)

including showing them your term papers or even your notebook full of class notes in another language (always impressive).

6. IF YOU CAN'T GET ANYONE ON YOUR SIDE IN YOUR REGISTRAR'S OR ADVISER'S OFFICE, GO TO THE FOREIGN LANGUAGE DEPARTMENT AND GET SOMEONE THERE TO LOOK AT YOUR TRANSCRIPT AND BECOME YOUR ADVOCATE.

Sometimes people are just confused by something on the transcript, like the way the credits are counted. A native speaker can help you out here by lobbying for you and clarifying things by saying, "Yes, see in that country, they count semesters *this* way, so it really does add up to eighteen credits."

7. FIND SOMEONE WHO GOT CREDIT AT THEIR UNIVERSITY FOR THE VERY SAME CLASS.

Did you meet other students in your class abroad who are getting credit for it at their U.S. school? Make sure to mention that. In some cases, someone at your registrar's office can just call that other university and sort things out. They might try to drop a credit or two, but *keep pushing*. If it's worth eighteen credits at one university, it should be worth the same at your school. Beg, plead, and buy flowers to say thanks.

8. IF YOU HIT A WALL, GO FOR THE INDEPENDENT STUDY OR CLEP TEST.

If it looks like you can't get credit for the class you took abroad, appeal to your new foreign language department buddy (see number 6) and ask if there is some way he or she will sponsor your independent study after the fact. Ask if you can read a book, write a paper, give a speech, or do *anything* that will show that you've learned something and should get credit for it.

It's amazing how many students return with pitiful language skills because they spent the whole time abroad with other Americans, but if you *really did* gain some language skills, you should have no problem taking a CLEP test to get to the next level of the foreign language you studied. Ask your foreign language prof about this or other ways to bump up to a higher level.

9. Don't be too attached to your major or minor.

If you're doing the liberal arts thing, your major isn't that important. Seriously. Don't be afraid to get strategic. I have changed my major several times (four, to be exact), not because I am a total flake who can't make up my mind but because sometimes it is advantageous to do so. Changing your major might allow you to condense requirements in interesting ways. The key is to go with the major that fits the list of things you want to take and *have already taken.*

If you are being forced to take a ridiculous class when you know it's more beneficial (and challenging) to take a different one, get in there and start lobbying for your— here's the key phrase—*well-thought-out alternative.* Plan it out, baby! Get double duty out of a course so that it gets counted for your major as well as for a university requirement. Don't just moan about how you have to take an extra semester because you can't get into that one last course you're supposed to take. Get creative and be persistent. The goal is to keep learning and move *forward.*

(*continued*)

Heads up: *If you don't want your study abroad to mess up your credits for your major, I highly recommend going abroad before you start college (one last cheer for Rotary!), during a gap year or during your sophomore year of college.* This way you can change your mind about your major early on instead of after you return from that life-changing junior year trip to Utopia.

Oh, and guess what? It may be much easier to get credit for indie study-abroad courses when presenting them as part of a *transfer* package. See, they're more likely to offer you credit up front to get you to enroll (get this in *writing!*), but once you're in, they know they've got you over a barrel, and they'll make it harder for you or charge you major coin even if you want to create your own study-abroad plan. The squeeze is on—but if you're smart and persistent, you can slip right out of that tight grip.

10. DON'T SCAM CREDITS.

I know how to work the system, but I'm not *scamming* the system. I've been granted (nearly) every credit I've earned, but I've also *earned every credit I've been granted.* Scammers just make it harder for those of us who are trying to do things legitimately. That's not cool. Anyway, if you screw the system, you screw yourself. It doesn't matter how quickly or cheaply you go through college—if you don't learn anything, what's the *point?* I am a self-proclaimed nerd—I study like a madwoman and learn like there's no tomorrow. I would be seriously offended if someone suggested that I am scamming. Um, no. I. Work. My. Ass. Off. Well, that and I rock at Credit

Quest. Now that you've got the rules of the game, get out there and start playing!

Got a student who tends to move at the speed of light? Go with it. Though it may require Cirque du Soleil levels of flexibility on your part, remember that start-and-stoppers are far more likely to discover their passions than those who simply plod along on a prescribed path. Keeping Tara reined in would have ruined her; jumping around was precisely what she needed in order to continue her lickety-split learning and keep her engine revved. Tom and I kept our advice to a minimum and reserved our recommendations for times when we were concerned about safety (hers), savings (ours), or sanity (everyone's). That's likely to work for you too.

Tara learned very quickly how to collaborate with others, which is a key component of the bold-school approach in general and the indie study-abroad plan in particular. You're about to find out how easy it is to connect with those who can help your student put the study-abroad pieces in place. A big part of the process is learning how to follow a thread to see where it might lead.

We've got the Internet, and we know how to use it. Get ready to create a terrific list of resources—including colleges and personal contacts—**within a half hour online.**

Old School: being passive about getting your credits from other countries transferred to your home university

Bold School: becoming your own advocate to get every single credit you deserve

CHOOSE A COUNTRY, PICK A COLLEGE, AND FIND CONTACTS—IN THIRTY MINUTES OR LESS

> Every person is a new door to a different world.
>
> JOHN GUARE, *SIX DEGREES OF SEPARATION*

Remember Gabrielle Wallace back in Chapter Five? She created her own study-abroad experience by going online to check out the possibilities in the Dominican Republic and used the same technique to find a home stay in Brazil. And the reason you read her story in this book is because she found my blog and contacted me directly about my advice for those coming to Buenos Aires. We got to know each other via e-mail, and Tom and I were happy to have her stay with us during her first few days in Argentina. It all started with a little research.

It's amazing what you can learn online within a half hour.

I'm going to walk you through the process that Gabrielle and many other indies have used to build a list of contacts and partners for a uniquely personalized study-abroad experience.

It's a great idea for parents and students to go through this search separately and then get together to compare notes. Each person will naturally wind along different paths, and that will lead to even more discoveries and connections.

Fire up the computer! We're about to begin our thirty-minute challenge.

1. CHOOSE A COUNTRY.

Obviously you want your son or daughter to be excited about the destination and elated about the opportunity to study there. However, this is a critical time for parental guidance. You're going to ease up once this decision has been made, but first it's your responsibility as a parent to emphasize a very important point:

The key to *maximizing* any study abroad experience is selecting a country in which English is not the native language and the culture is unfamiliar.

This is about *learning*, remember? Unless you're okay with the idea that your student is heading off on a great vacation, you need to be very clear about the fact that *going global requires a stretch*. It's a *good* stretch, but it's a stretch nonetheless.

Study abroad is a far more brain-sculpting affair when language learning is required, and just as important as learning to converse is experiencing what it's like to fumble around and see oneself as a person who isn't always able to do things flawlessly or effortlessly. Being humbled is powerful. Struggling helps develop compassion for others. This is what will elevate your student to new heights personally and professionally.

So, skip the U.K., Australia, New Zealand, and South Africa—for now. Those are fantastic destinations well worth exploring, and once students have studied abroad, it will seem super-simple to visit these places on their own later. (Parents, rejoice! This is what we want: kids who can travel on their own *and* figure out how to pay for it.)

❏ **Smart Move**: For the best deals, go where the dollar is strong and veer off the student-beaten path.

In general, European universities (and those in South Korea and Japan) will cost much more than most Latin American, Eastern European, Southeast Asian, or African colleges.

Pick a country. It doesn't have to be "the one"—you're only going to spend thirty minutes on this, so you can consider it a dry run if you like.

Got it? Continue.

2. PICK A COLLEGE.

No need to reinvent the wheel. We're going to go with some easy choices that allow for independence and significant savings but also provide support and just a bit of familiarity. Here's where we're going to capitalize on the research and affiliations that already exist.

❏ **Smart Move**: To find universities abroad that cater to international students, piggyback on the groundwork already done by the organizations that offer packaged programs.

First, I'm going to offer a tip of my hat to two top study-abroad programs in the United States: ISA (pronounced *eee-sah*) and ISEP (*eye-sep*). And then we're going to take their info and *run* with it. Keep in mind that there are likely to be other Americans (as well as students from other countries) studying at universities that are affiliated with these programs, but each student can choose how much time to spend with them outside class. (Rather be the only U.S. citizen taking the course? Great! Keep reading for tips on how to connect with those who can point you to less popular options.)

▶ **International Studies Abroad** (www.studiesabroad.com) has been providing study-abroad programs for U.S. college students since 1987, and they do a good job for those willing and able to pay the price. On the ISA home page, click on the country of your choice. Take a look at the page that features options in that country—full year, semester, and short intensives or summer programs. Click on one (longer stays are better!) and read a description of the host universities and the courses.

You're looking for universities that are already familiar with the process of welcoming international students from the United States and handling their transcripts and credits, so this is a *great* shortcut. Bookmark this page and write down the names of the host universities in your chosen destination. Cruise through the options and build your list.

▶ Now head over to the website for **International Student Exchange Programs** (www.ISEP.org). This is another good site for information about countries and colleges that are already offering courses for international students. Click on "Directory of Universities," and you'll see a long list of colleges around the world that offer programs for U.S. students who attend ISEP-affiliated schools. Even better, it includes a link to the website for each university. Find the country you're interested in. You're likely to see several universities that the ISA site did not feature. Add them to your list!

▶ Next stop is **Transitions Abroad** (www.TransitionsAbroad .com). This site is packed with information for those interested in studying, working, volunteering, or living abroad. Click on "Study Abroad," and browse through the options for your country. Write down the names of the universities listed in various programs and any links provided. Onward!

▶ The **American Institute for Foreign Study**, founded in 1964, is one of the oldest, largest, and most respected cultural exchange organizations in the world. Check out its programs (and note the colleges) in your selected country by visiting www.AIFS.com.

▶ Last but certainly not least, the **Center for Study Abroad** is committed to providing quality study-abroad programs at a much lower cost and with a great deal of flexibility to meet the needs of each student. CSA is one of the most reasonably priced programs I've found—check out their prices and compare them to what it might cost for independent study. Their programs are open to all adults eighteen or over—no need to be enrolled at a college, no GPA requirement, and they offer housing options for a range of budgets. Visit their site at www.CenterforStudyAbroad.com and flesh out your list of schools in your chosen country.

3. FIND CONTACTS.

You've got a country and at least half a dozen colleges. Now you're going to see about connecting with real people.

Go back and take a look at each of the **websites for the colleges you selected.** (You may have to Google the university if you don't have the website already.) Find the international students section on each college site, and see what kind of contact information is listed. Is it in English? (This usually means someone there is willing to respond in English.) Is it a standard info @blahblahu.edu, or do you have the name of the person and their personal e-mail address? Note how much information is provided—phone number, fax, any personal info about those who can help you. Add relevant details to your list of colleges. You're looking for names whenever possible and getting a sense of the colleges and programs that are appealing.

Of course, you'll want to spend some time reading through the websites and learning more about the colleges and the programs offered, but save that for later. With your list of colleges handy, let's move on to the next step. It's time to search for the following:

- *American students* who have attended courses at that college recently or who are currently enrolled
- *expats (Americans or other English-speaking individuals from around the world)* who live in the community in which the college is located
- *locals* who write blogs with photos or offer podcasts that provide a glimpse of life there
- *places to stay* when you first arrive

Start with Google and do a few **blog searches** using key terms like the name of the university, the city, *ISA, ISEP, study* *abroad, semester abroad,* or *language program.* Search a few individual terms and combinations and see what comes up. Blogs are a far better source of information than websites because you can see how recently they've been updated and you'll find personal opinions and stories instead of simply sales copy. You're looking for blogs that have recent posts and, more specifically, ones that provide an e-mail address so that you can contact the blogger directly without having to leave a comment. Follow the trail. Check out the blog links listed on the blogs you like—if that person's contact info isn't provided, you can probably find names and e-mail addresses for others who blog on a similar theme. Your list is growing!

Don't forget **podcasts.** Check out www.LearnOutLoud.com for easy 1-click subscriptions through Apple iTunes that feature music, tours, and commentary (in English or the native language) related to your country. Pick one and add it to your list.

Next, see if you can find **English-speaking expats** who live in the community. Expats have had to do a lot of detective work in order to build a life in a new country, and they tend to know other expats as well as locals. They are a good source of valuable information and warmly welcome young indie students to the community. Go back to my favorite site at www.TransitionsAbroad.com and this time click on the "Living Abroad" tab. You'll get a list of all kinds of online resources for expats living in that country, including articles about everything from what to bring to where to stay, insider tips on low-cost outings, great locals-only restaurants, and much more. In addition, most countries have **online forums for expats** where anyone can ask a question or get advice from those who live there. Add the contact info for those you think might be helpful—including any names and personal e-mail addresses—to your list.

Head over to **Facebook** or your favorite social networking site and do a search using the same key terms—the name of the university, city, country, and so on. You'll find students who are studying there right now or have recently returned. Don't get sidetracked—just do a scan to see what kind of possibilities you might look into later. (There's a new social networking site just for expats called InterNations—check out www.internations.org.)

By now, you should have a list of at least **four or five bloggers** (local and expat), **a podcast, a forum or two,** and **several Facebookish possibilities.**

Check out CouchSurfing, at www.CouchSurfing.com, and find the country you've chosen. Scroll through and see photos and comments from **those who are willing to host**—at no charge—students and other travelers who are passing through the city in which your selected college is located. Get a sense of the ages, interests, and accommodations represented. Not everyone has extra space for overnight guests—some people simply offer to meet travelers for coffee or show them around. No need to join yet (but it's free when you do)—this is just an info search to give you an idea of what's available and who you might connect with prior to your arrival so that you can make sure your first few days are covered while you get settled and look at more long-term options. Many countries and cities have CouchSurfing forums and events, which makes it easy to make new friends (and meet more potential hosts) once you arrive. (Facebook has a CouchSurfing application, which means that you can add it to your profile and easily find other Facebook members who are interested in hosting.) Another site to check out is www.GlobalFreeloaders.com, which tends to attract a slightly older crowd of travelers and hosts (some with nicer accommodations to offer), but you'll have to take a few minutes to register before you can view the options.

Bonus tip for parents: Just for fun, skip on over to www.HomeExchange.com, a terrific site for people around the world who want to swap homes with someone in another country. Take a look at the photos and descriptions of the people and homes available in your student's destination.

The reason I love Home Exchange is that it reinforces my faith in the goodness of people. Surfing through the Home Exchange site is a delightful way to see how others live, but it's also a potent reminder that there are warm, friendly, generous, trusting, and helpful people everywhere. You don't have to swap houses, but do take a look and recognize the folks who would likely be very happy to meet your student or help her if she needed anything. Feel better?

Time's up! Unless you got distracted, that whole process took less than half an hour. You've got names, e-mail addresses, websites, comments, and impressions of the people and places. You know where to find out about the best neighborhoods, restaurants, and excursions. Your list has links to people who can answer all kinds of questions about everything from visas and health care to concerts and nightlife.

❏ **Smart Move**: Indies can save thousands of dollars and create a richer experience by making *direct contact* with the people who know and love the place that will become a home away from home.

See how easy this is? Next step: reach out and touch someone—via e mail.

This is where you give your student a gentle poke and then step back. You can cheer her on (better than nagging), but it's *your student's* job to make the connections—not yours. Of course, if you happen to stumble upon a contact you think could be helpful, it's okay to pass that along.

No two individuals will make the same connections and have the same experience, even if they are headed to the same location. That's the cool part—this approach *guarantees* that each student's trip will be unique.

How much planning is required? How much lead time is needed?

I've done my share of seat-of-the-pants, no-plan travel, and so have my kids. I love the exhilaration and serendipity of it. But this isn't just travel—it's study abroad. If the goals are to save money, make connections with locals, find decent housing, *and* get credit for courses taken, it's *absolutely essential* to do some planning.

Parents, this next part includes extremely important information. I've written it specifically for students, so please read it yourself first and then pass the book to your son or daughter.

TIPS FOR INDIES

❑ **The two most critical items for anyone abroad: a current and correct visa and passport.** I cannot emphasize this enough: it is not the university's responsibility to make sure you have the right stuff—it's *yours*. Read the legalese online, but make sure to check with the university, your online contacts, current students, and anyone else who can give you the most up-to-date info on visa requirements. Some colleges abroad will not provide transcripts to students studying on a *tourist* visa, and you won't be happy to learn after the term is finished that you were supposed to have a *student* visa!

Visitors from around the world are facing increased scrutiny upon entering the United States, and other countries have responded by tightening their visa requirements for U.S. citizens.[7] Things change rapidly and surprisingly; a young man I know was recently detained for nearly two weeks—*in jail*—in Japan following a year of teaching English there because his visa had expired two weeks earlier. He'd been assured that the country's long-standing thirty-day grace period would allow him to fly home three weeks after his visa's expiration date, but the rule had changed in the previous few months. There's nothing like being deported (and having to pay a steep fine) to put a damper on your whole experience. Listen, I'm not trying to scare you—I'm just wearing my expat hat and telling you to take your visa *very seriously*. Some countries are strict, some are lax, but if you assume that every destination requires you to follow the rules to the letter, you won't go wrong.

Please note: ninety days is *not the same* as three calendar months! Do the math on your visa dates, or you might be in for a very unpleasant surprise when you try to leave the country.

❏ **Next, focus on the school.** Contact the college, check the start dates for your semester, and get as much help as possible from the university directly, including tips on housing and, again, your student visa requirements. Plenty of indies simply fly to their destination a few weeks or even days in advance of the semester start date and put everything into place once they get there, and some choose their school *after* they've had a chance to visit the campus and talk to students and administrators. This can turn out beautifully—or very badly. Yes, be spontaneous and arrive without a contact or a clue if you're traveling just for fun, but don't try this with study abroad if you want to get credit for it.

❏ **Begin connecting with your contacts about three months in advance of your arrival.** You are not likely to get help if you say that you "might be coming sometime next year," but don't wait until a week before you get there to start contacting people either. Most will be happy to assist you if (1) you're definitely coming, (2) you're arriving in the not-too-distant future, and (3) they're not pressured or rushed to provide information.

❏ **Keep your e-mail messages short and clear,** but be warm and show gratitude in advance for any help. If you can

(*continued*)

use your foreign language skills (or get help from someone else), by all means do so! (This is assuming that you have the ability to understand the response and continue correspondence.)

❏ **Don't be afraid to resend a message** if you haven't heard anything for a week. Glitches happen. If you really want to know if your message has been received, you can sign up for a free trial at www.DidTheyReadIt.com and get read receipts for up to ten messages. Still nothing? Focus on others on your list. The key is to keep several irons in the fire.

❏ **Be open to possibilities,** such as offering English lessons or some other kind of assistance to someone in exchange for room and board. There's room for creativity here! (Keep it legal, please.)

❏ **Go for the low-hanging fruit.** Check out the resources online for activities you love, like local yoga studios, hiking clubs, cooking classes, or even a gym in your chosen destination. Nonverbal activities are great for beginning language learners! Just one enthusiastic response from someone is all you need to get started building a relationship and learning more.

❏ **Do not bombard any one individual with queries!** Spread the love—and your questions—among the people on your list of current students, local bloggers, expats, social network connections, and any friends of friends.

❏ **Get a good travel guidebook** for your destination (*Lonely Planet* and *Rough Guide* are my personal favorites) and read the whole thing. This alone will make you more informed than the average grouper, and you'll go beyond the basics when talking to the locals. And don't forget novels, memoirs, biographies, movies, and music. You can learn a lot about the country before you arrive by doing some sleuthing and studying on your own.

The adventure has begun—and the rest is up to you. You don't need me, your parents, or anyone else to hold your hand once you've made contact with those who can help you connect the dots.

❏ **Smart Move**: Being independent is cool, but being collaborative is *cutting edge*.

Go forth and connect.

Old School: feeling confident about a study-abroad program based on the claims posted on the organization's website

Bold School: feeling confident about creating an individualized study-abroad program based on direct connections with people who live, work, and study there

CHAPTER EIGHT

The Full-Family Deal

SABBATICAL OR SELL-IT-ALL?

HOW TO SAVE THOUSANDS FOR COLLEGE (AND GIVE YOUR KIDS GREAT GLOBAL SKILLS) BY LIVING ABROAD

> There is nothing like a dream to create the future.
> VICTOR HUGO

High school exchange. Independent study abroad. Solo world travel.

At this point, you might be asking yourself various versions of the following:

- Do I have to wait until my kids are in high school or college to give them the advantage of going global?
- How difficult is it to take my kids out of school for a couple of months during the school year?
- Can I really just sell everything and move abroad with the whole family?
- Is it possible to live abroad while making enough money to support my family and even save for college?

Or my personal favorite:

▶ Hey! Why should my kids have all the fun?

Once these questions have popped into your head, you're going to have a hard time shaking them loose. If you find yourself fantasizing about spending time abroad as a family, you're going to *love* this chapter.

When we tell people that one of the reasons we moved abroad was to save money for college, they don't believe it. Of course, the biggest reason was to experience life abroad with our kids and give them a chance to gain some global skills. If you don't want to wait until your kids are high school or college age and you want to spend time abroad *with* them, a sabbatical can be a fantastic experience for the whole family. And though it won't be the same for everyone, for us moving abroad turned out to be an unbelievably effective way to reduce our monthly expenses so dramatically (while maintaining a much nicer lifestyle) that we were able to pay for three simultaneous college educations.

But I'm not going to write this next part. I'll let my husband, the number-cruncher, take it from here. This is your chance to hear from a poor put-upon father of four teenage girls in suburbia—and how life is much, much sweeter these days.

INSIDER INSIGHT

I was fortunate to learn some important lessons about money by the time I turned thirty-two. I was very busy as a homeowner, business owner, father of four, and investor in a couple of small commercial properties, and we had hit the six-figure income level for a couple of years. But even though I had a pretty relaxed schedule compared to my peers, I realized that my kids were not going to be young forever, and I wanted to spend a lot of time with them.

(continued)

So Maya and I decided to really focus on being together as a family during the next decade. We knew we
could always make more money later. We lived very well
with less and showed our kids that they didn't need a lot
to be happy. (This made it much easier for them when
they started living independently.) We taught them to be
smart about money, save time, reduce waste, and think
independently, and we made sure they knew how important it is to do what you love to do.

At the end of that wonderful decade, we were staring
at the high school years. Suddenly it seemed much more
difficult to manage the increased demands of raising kids
in suburbia. (We'd been living in a small town until Taeko
hit her freshman year.) The pace was faster, the expectations were higher, and wherever we turned it seemed
there was yet another expense or obligation. Though
Maya and I were very good at saying no, and our kids
were far less acquisitive than most, clearly this was going
to be a challenging stage for everyone.

What's it like to raise four teenage girls? Parents have
to aim for a constantly moving target—what may work
with them one week will not work the next. With an endless barrage of emotional pleadings coming at you, it is
nearly impossible to make the right decision every time,
and you learn very quickly that you rarely please everyone. Should I be loving, strict, logical, compassionate, or
a hard-ass? I went for a little of everything. These are the
kinds of comments I found myself making:

▶ "You need $20 for a birthday gift for Brittany? I thought you
weren't talking to her. Oh, that was last week. Hold on, last
week you got $20 for a gift for Courtney. I thought we

agreed that we will pay for one birthday party a month. Oh, several of your very best friends have birthdays this month? I see. She invited how many to her party? Fifty? That's a lot of presents. Maybe you don't need to bring one. Fine, here's $20. What? You need a ride to the mall? Fine, I will take you with your two sisters, who also have to buy birthday gifts."

▶ *"Seven hundred dollars* for a three-day trip to Disneyland? Oh, it's a marching band competition. Don't they have them in our state? I thought so, since we paid $100 last month for that one. I see, you are 'required' to go to get a good grade."

▶ "Of course, I will be happy to drop you at the dance at eight p.m. and pick you up at eleven. Oh, and take you to Red Robin afterward where you are meeting your friends? Uh, sure. Oh yes, and wait for you to finish and then take you to your friend's house to spend the night? Of course, what else would I be doing?" Keep in mind that this night is a $180 gift—$25 for the ticket to the dance; $25 for hair, makeup, and manicure; $100 for dress/shoes/jewelry; $30 meal—that requires me to wait in my car in the dark.

I was constantly questioning whether all of these pressures—to buy, sign up, attend, compete—were doing anyone any good. We all want to be the best parents we can be, and we want to give our kids every opportunity to "succeed." But the most important thing we can do for our children (beyond providing a loving home) is give them a good education, and yet most of the costs and frustrations we encountered had *nothing to do with education!*

While most families plan their vacations based on the proximity to a theme park or sunny beach, I turned to the ever-helpful section of the World Atlas where it lists

(*continued*)

the income per capita for any given country. For the cost of that three-day Disneyland band trip, I could live for a year in Nepal (average annual income: $400) and still have enough for a few $20 birthday gifts.

Cheap travel hint for families: when the kids are young, stay away from luxurious accommodations. Our kids have been happy in almost every place we have stayed, and we made sure to leave plenty of room for improvement. In fact, our best family memories seem to center on our worst accommodations—including one night at a rat-infested teahouse that provided inspiration for countless school essays in later years.

Travel should be a great adventure for kids. Sleeping in a fancy hotel room is fun on occasion, but it's not exactly the kind of experience they'll tell stories about for years to come. Besides, if they start their travel life getting used to high-thread-count sheets and heated pools, then they will not enjoy traveling at budget level, which means:

- you will be financing some very expensive trips
- they will see travel as a luxury they can't afford on their own later in life.

"Getting away from it all" is not a good enough reason to sell everything and leave—well, it is, but it might not sit well with the kids. So our logic was that if we went someplace relatively inexpensive (Mexico), we could save enough each month to pay for a month of college expenses. The girls understood this immediately. We played up the fun and discovery aspect while never glossing over the fact that it was bound to get tough at times.

The Internet had reached the point that putting my

business online (wholesale product to retail stores) took just a few days. Accounting, customer database, inventory, fax, and phones were all made virtual. Employees were thrilled to work from home, and the fulfillment company I used did a far better job of receiving, inventory management, and shipping than I did. Within two months of moving to Mexico, my sales doubled from the year before. New motto: concentrate on what you do best and let others handle the rest. Duh.

How much did we save?

Your savings might be much more or much less than ours; it all depends on your starting point, your destination, and your lifestyle choices. Here's what it looked like for us as a family of four in Mexico (Taeko was in college in Canada, Teal was on exchange in Brazil):

Mortgage: We still had a house in the United States that we were renting to a friend (he bought it from us a few months later), and his payment covered the mortgage. Our rent in Mexico was half the cost of that mortgage. **Savings: $750 a month.**

Transportation: Our two cars in the United States were paid off, but we were paying about $350 a month in insurance, gas, and maintenance. In Mexico we had no cars—we walked, rode the bus, or took open-air taxis along the beach road for a total of less than $50 per month for the entire family. Best of all, the girls had a lot of independence—they could go anywhere they wanted without relying on us for rides. **Savings: $300 a month.**

(continued)

Phones: We had three cell phones, a landline, plus cable in the United States. In Mexico we bought cheap cell phones with prepaid cards (we usually used free text messages), had no landline, and paid for cable, which covered our Internet and VoIP phone setup as well. **Savings: $200 a month.**

Utilities: Gas, water, electricity, and garbage service for our house in Oregon had cost us about $200 a month, but it all ran less than $50 a month in Mexico. **Savings: $150 a month.**

Food: We shopped for groceries at several different stores in our suburban area, had inexpensive lunches out four times a week, and took the family out for dinner a couple of times a week. We went out every day in Mexico—often more than once a day—and shopped locally (within blocks) for produce, coffee, fresh tortillas, and other supplies. **Savings: $800 a month.**

Health insurance: In the United States we paid $500 a month for high-deductible health insurance that covered us if we spent $7,500 or more a year, so really it covered nothing. Our out-of-pocket costs ran about $3,000 per year. In Mexico we bought traveler's health insurance for $100 per month but never made a claim. We did go to the doctor and dentist, but the cost was negligible. **Savings: $800 a month.**

Entertainment, activities, club memberships, etc.: The biggest savings came in terms of our family's activities. The best part was that I always felt generous—"You need twenty dollars for dinner, a night of dancing, and taxi fare? For *both* of you? Sure!" It was great just to relax about money and know that Tara and Talya were learning the language, making new friends, discovering the culture, and having fun for about the cost of a moronic movie they'd go see with their friends back home on a Saturday afternoon (not counting any refreshments or the shopping afterward, of course). **Savings: $1,000 a month.**

My original estimate that we would save a thousand dollars per month was low. Though I did not keep careful track (things were so cheap I didn't even bother), it's safe to say that **we saved around $3,000 a month and had an infinitely better lifestyle.**

Moving abroad changed me and affected the way I am with my kids. Instead of whiny, negative, sarcastic Dad, my kids got happy, positive, sarcastic Dad. (One can only change so much.) In the three years we have lived abroad with our family, I cannot remember saying no to my kids more than about five times total, and that's counting many, many requests for all kinds of outings and events. There was never a question about money—the activities were cheap and generally educational in some manner.

Though we were tentative at first in the big city of Buenos Aires, we put our kids on a pretty long leash and were never disappointed. In fact, once the girls realized we were going to let them use their best judgment, they were happy to regale us with stories of the places they went (including clubs and parties) and the people they met. Our only rules were "Absolutely no drinking and driving" (not a problem since everyone takes taxis and they rarely cost

(*continued*)

more than five dollars), "Always come home with a sister or friend in the taxi," and "Text us midway through the night to let us know everything is fine."

Other cultures have a different idea about independence—they don't try to structure every minute of their kids' activities as Americans do. Parents know that kids need to be with their friends and that spending six hours dancing is a good way for them to enjoy themselves and relieve stress, so they provide places with reasonable guidelines to assure safety but also a great time. In fact, the underage clubs in Buenos Aires keep the kids dancing until dawn so they are not out wandering the streets at night—they emerge when it's daylight.

We've had many postclubbing Sunday breakfasts with our kids, after which they sleep for several hours before we head out as a family for the traditional three-hour Sunday afternoon meal at one of many restaurants in our neighborhood. We spent our Sundays in the United States doing yardwork or running errands, and our kids were scattered among various friends' houses and required a lot of pick-ups and drop-offs. Even our hikes required driving! Our lives are very relaxed in Argentina, and we spend a lot more time just hanging out as a family.

From the beginning Maya and I felt that keeping our girls debt free through college graduation would allow them to devote themselves to work they *wanted to do* that might not pay well in the beginning. We decided that this would be our gift to them. Our youngest will graduate by the end of 2009. I am elated—and relieved.

The best years of my life (so far) have been the past three while living abroad. I am not richer financially, and I pay myself far less than I did in the United States, but to be honest, I don't care much about my net worth anymore.

It just does not hold the importance that it once did. I have watched my kids work to their potential, speak second (and third) languages, and become fearless.

Maya and I have a fantastic lifestyle and great friends we see very regularly. We are far from broke (even after paying for college), we own our home outright (plus another apartment we rent out for extra income), and it is all due to moving abroad. The two of us feel incredibly fortunate to have shared this experience with our girls, and we look forward to years of continued creative living while spending as much time as we choose visiting our daughters and other places around the world. We have never been happier or healthier. My only regret? I wish we had done it sooner.

There are all kinds of ways to live abroad, and settling in one place isn't the only option. Some families move around quite a bit, and others create a lifestyle that puts them in a new location almost every *day*. The constant for these families is homeschooling—it allows them to take their "school" with them wherever they go.

Maybe you're more intrigued by the idea of having a thrilling family adventure than simply living abroad and saving money for college. (There are degrees of expat life, and truth be told, ours is on the tame side of things.) Many people dream of selling everything they own in order to live on a boat and sail to exotic islands. Some lease a boat for a year at a time, and others have a sell-and-switch approach: sell the house, buy a boat, sail around, sell the boat, do something else. If you plan it right, you can actually save a lot of money and not have to work much at all while you're off playing Ponce de León.

You're about to meet Cindy Lesher, who, along with her husband and two kids, spent *four and a half years* sailing around the Caribbean. Were they experienced sailors when they started out? Nope. But they did it anyway. Here's their story:

INSIDER INSIGHT

Ten years ago, if you had told me we were going to quit our jobs, sell everything, buy a catamaran, and go cruising with our two elementary-aged children for over four years, I would've said, "Yeah, right—I don't think so!" But that's exactly what we did, and I am so grateful that we made that decision. It was so liberating to sell it all and begin a new lifestyle that featured plenty of family time together and a whole new idea of living.

The seed of the idea was planted early on. Back in the early 1980s, when Randall and I were dating, he was laid off from work as an aviation mechanic. Deciding to take advantage of the "time off" coupled with the ability to purchase discounted airline tickets, he packed his backpack and spent seven weeks in Hawaii, Australia, and New Zealand. When he returned, he said, "Cindy, someday we are going to move onto a boat and go sailing. That would be the way to travel and see places."

My response: "Yeah, right—I don't think so!" But the idea kept surfacing through the years. We got married, and within a few years, Randall's career in aviation flourished— he went into sales and became a branch manager selling aircraft parts. I was in radio advertising sales and traveling all over central Pennsylvania for my work. The idea lingered.

By the 1990s we had two babies and were acting as general contractors on a three-year project to build our dream home. In the middle of it Randall changed his career! We wanted marble and granite in our house, and long story short, Lesher's Marble and Granite was born in our basement. Still, the sailing idea was calling to us.

A few years later, when our kids were six and eight, the marble and granite business had expanded to a ten-thousand-square-foot facility that Randall and his brothers owned together. Life was very busy, and the sailing idea became even more appealing.

We started visiting boat shows in Maryland, but I still couldn't imagine how we could possibly do it. We didn't live near the water (we were landlocked in Hershey, Pennsylvania), we had never owned a boat before, and our sailing experience was limited to a few childhood vacations and Randall's quick outings on a Hobie Cat. We'd certainly never been sailing together, let alone lived on a boat. No one in our family or among our friends was rallying around us—they didn't want us to leave town at all, and certainly not on a boat!

But we'd been meeting people at the boat shows in Maryland who actually did own boats, lived aboard, and went cruising for extended periods. These people were more than happy to share their experiences with us! Gradually my fears were disappearing (Randall had none) as we met families who pointed us in the right direction. Because he had been a mechanic, Randall was sure he could handle the ongoing maintenance of the boat. It no longer seemed like such a crazy idea.

For me, the biggest remaining question was education, but following some advice from the cruisers we'd met, I went to a homeschool curriculum fair and learned that there are all kinds of wonderful resources available. We ended up choosing the Calvert curriculum—everything you need for the entire year (including lesson manuals and erasers) comes in the Calvert box for each grade.

And so in the summer of 2002 we sold everything—the cars, the furniture, the accumulation of junk, and the dream house we'd built. We quit our jobs and bought our new home—a 47-foot Catana Catamaran named *Duchesse*.

(continued)

With a captain guiding us on our maiden voyage, we left heading south toward warmer weather! Before we knew it, we were on our own, connecting with fellow cruisers (many with families) and sailing from island to island in the Caribbean. We'd decided to give it at least six months and pack it in before six years had passed.

People often picture sailing as a really solitary activity—spending weeks at sea, living in cramped quarters, and getting lonely. Our experience was nothing like that! For one thing, our boat was very comfortable—the kids had their own rooms and shared bathroom, and Randall and I had a master suite with full bath.

Lonely? No way. The social life was fantastic! We were never alone unless we wanted to be. There is a whole cruising community out there that is like family in the islands. We had barbecue dinners on the beaches, organized potluck dinners ashore, dinner parties on each other's boats, dinghy floats at sundown, parties with more than twenty guests on our boat, inland tours, games, and the list goes on and on. We have friends from Spain, England, France, Canada, and all over South America and the United States with whom we will always share a special connection.

Most cruisers head "down island" before hurricane season, so there are hundreds of boats in the Bahamas and a huge concentration anchored around an island called Georgetown for an annual boating regatta. There are children of all ages, games, sports, and all kinds of activities. After that some cruisers head back to Florida, and others meander to leisurely explore various islands. We always kept in touch with the other "kid boats," and our first year we got together with a group for a graduation party for kids from kindergarten to eighth grade in St. Martin, a French island.

My days were happily spent with the children doing schoolwork from nine A.M. until about one or two P.M. Once I sent my son, Austin, over to another boat for his reading lesson about King Arthur; the couple from Britain was more than happy to elaborate on the subject! Another time, when we were reading about Robinson Crusoe, we happened to be sailing along the coast of Tobago, the island where he was shipwrecked. Talk about a field trip!

We ate most of our meals on board, going out occasionally for a break and to check out the local cuisine. After the kids did their studies, we had plenty of time to go snorkeling or fishing or would often go for a stroll through town or a walk on the beach together.

One thing about living on a boat is that there is a lot of maintenance and repair work to do. Whenever anything broke, Randall had to fix it immediately—if he didn't, the work would have been even more overwhelming. From the freezer to the GPS navigation system, it all breaks at some point, no matter how new your boat is. The more electronics you have, the more you have to fix. We had it all. Lesson number one: Keeping it simple may be better!

Of course, if something breaks (and it will), you can rest assured that someone will have advice, a spare part to offer, and all kinds of assistance. Every cruiser is willing to go the extra mile to help you. One time our water maker broke while we were in Los Roques, off the coast of Venezuela, and our cruising friends shared with us on a daily basis, allowing us to enjoy the most remote and pristine beaches I've ever seen.

It was an incredible lifestyle and we enjoyed it enormously, but after four and a half years we decided to sell the *Duchesse* and spend some time exploring South

(continued)

America on land. We traveled through Patagonia and stayed in Buenos Aires for a few months. Compared to the thriving homeschool community we'd had while cruising, we found it harder to connect with other families in the city. Most expats send their kids to the American school, but eventually we found another homeschool family and the kids were able to do some fun things together.

As I write this, we're spending a few months visiting friends and family in the United States, and then we plan to explore Central America. I'm not sure where we'll go or what we'll do exactly, but that's part of the ongoing adventure! I can't imagine what our lives would have been like if we'd never kept that idea of sailing alive. It changed everything for our family.

Are you excited yet? No matter what you're dreaming of doing with your family, there are likely to be others out there who are doing (or dreaming of doing) the same thing. With the Internet, it's easy to connect with them and begin the process of defining and designing your own family adventure.

Of course, moving abroad isn't for everyone, and starting out with a sabbatical is a great way to test the waters. It helps to know that there are different levels of immersion (and commitment) and plenty of room to find what will work best for you. In the next section I'll share some tips for families considering a sabbatical or a major move.

Old School: assuming that those who move abroad must be wealthy
Bold School: understanding that middle-class families may actually save money while living the life of their dreams in foreign countries

THE TEN COMMANDMENTS FOR FAMILIES
HEADING ABROAD

> Control is never achieved when sought after directly.
> It is the surprising outcome of letting go.
> JAMES ARTHUR RAY

I have lived abroad as a single person, a newlywed, and a mother of toddlers. I've experienced the joys of taking four elementary-school-aged kids on sabbatical for three months, and then went for the brass ring, selling everything and moving abroad while the girls were teenagers. My one regret is that I did not spend even *more* time living abroad at each stage.

People often ask me about the advantages of each period, and I can see them struggling to decide what to do. Should they go abroad before they have kids? Should they live abroad when they have babies? Should they take their elementary school children on an exciting adventure? Or should they move abroad as a family when the kids are older?

My answer: *yes* to all of the above.

It's never too early or too late to live abroad, but there are definitely times when it is *easier*. You need to know yourself, your partner, and your kids in order to create an experience that's enriching for all of you. Just as one educational path might be exciting for one student and excruciating for another, one family's fantastic voyage may be another family's nightmare. Have many relaxed, meandering family discussions about what's appealing—and what isn't—long before you buy those airline tickets. Wait for the this-will-be-awesome adrenaline to die down, embrace the are-we-nuts stage, and don't get so soaked in fego that you allow worries about your kids' education to shut out your family's opportunities for mind-expanding cultural expeditions.

With very few exceptions, I can't think of a reason *not* to spend time living abroad, and I especially recommend going when kids are between the ages of about five and ten—when they are young enough to be very flexible about making new friends and learning new languages but *old enough to remember the experience*. Having babies in Japan was a wonderful (and wild) experience for us, but our two oldest girls don't remember it at all and never let us forget how we robbed them of the chance to be raised bilingual by leaving when they were too young to talk.

Almost every day I get e-mails that go something like this: "I just found your blog and I'm so excited! My husband and I are really into education and travel, and we want to give our daughter the experience of living abroad for a year. We're planning to arrive in three months. Can you recommend any top schools in Buenos Aires? Our daughter is four years old."

(Sigh.) A four-year-old does not need a "top school" abroad—she needs a chance to get silly with her parents, play with local kids, and fully enjoy being a four-year-old sponge in a new and stimulating setting.

❏ **Smart Move**: Wise parents on sabbatical choose to focus on their children's *development* rather than on their education.

This is true for kids of all ages but especially for those under ten. Parents need to emphasize exposure to new cultures and languages (and happy times spent with the family) rather than academic rigor. Going on a sabbatical is a wonderful opportunity to evolve the brain (as Dr. Dispenza described it) in all kinds of ways, but enrolling a kid in a highly competitive school abroad so he won't "fall behind" misses the point entirely.

Though I encourage you to follow your instincts, you're likely to be a lot more relaxed (and possibly less clueless) if you have a few simple and well-tested guidelines to follow. I offer this list of ten commandments (more like loving-but-firm suggestions) for families considering a lengthy sabbatical or move abroad without connections, corporate ties, or diplomatic perks.

1. **THOU SHALT NOT GO ABROAD UNLESS THY PARTNER IS IN FULL AND REASONABLY ENTHUSIASTIC AGREEMENT ABOUT THE DESTINATION, TIMING, AND LENGTH OF STAY.**

Almost every early-return case I've ever heard about has been precipitated by one person being totally wrapped up in the wonder of the experience and ignoring the fact that the other person is sulking and miserable. This does not end well. If one of you is determined to go abroad and the other is hesitant, keep talking to each other. You've got to reach a compromise about the destination and timing *before* you go. For couples, this is important, but for families it is absolutely *crucial*. If Mom and Dad aren't getting along, everyone will suffer. It's normal for one person to be more worried than the other, but both of you need to be pretty excited about the whole thing before packing your bags.

2. **THOU SHALT NOT GO ABROAD WITHOUT DOING THY RESEARCH.**

This is key if you happen to have health issues, a child with special needs, a passion or hobby you can't live without, or a pet that you can't imagine boarding. Oh, you can still go abroad, but you will save yourself a lot of headaches if you check things out before you arrive. Connect with a few people (don't take one person's word for it) who can answer your questions and lead you to the right resources.

3. **THOU SHALT NOT GO ABROAD IF THY CHILDREN ARE ABSOLUTELY ADAMANT ABOUT NOT GOING.**

Everyone must understand *and be okay with the idea* that it will be difficult at times. Try to reach consensus, but consensus with misgivings may be as close as you get.

(continued)

That being said, if your son or daughter is bolting the bedroom door and refusing to budge, this is a huge red flag.

Reality check: You can completely avoid this problem by going when your kids are too young to bolt doors! And why do you have a bolt on your kid's door anyway?

4. THOU SHALT NOT GO ABROAD WITHOUT BEING FISCALLY RESPONSIBLE.

Plenty of parents plan a six-month sabbatical but end up going home by the third month because they run out of money. They were in vacation mode, but having never been on a six-month vacation, they had no idea how quickly things could add up. Get some *realistic* advice about expenses from those who live in your destination, and budget accordingly.

5. THOU SHALT NOT BRING THY AMERICAN STUFF AND LIFESTYLE.

Bringing a mountain of luggage, all of your kids' toys and gadgets, and a bunch of framed photos, art, and keepsakes with you? This is your chance to leave all that stuff *behind* and see if you even miss it. Chances are you won't. Store your beloved items if you must, but pack light. It's nice to have an occasional blast of home, but if your selling point to your family is that "Everything will be practically the same there!" you might as well not bother.

6. THOU SHALT NOT INVITE ALL THY AMERICAN FRIENDS AND FAMILY TO VISIT WITHIN THE FIRST THREE MONTHS.

A lot of people who go on sabbatical or move abroad view it as a chance to show off their new home and adopted country. Within days of arrival they invite their extended clan to come for lengthy stays, and they host a steady stream of visitors the entire time. Although this can be great fun and it's certainly a good deal for your friends and relatives, you must keep in mind that the point of the experience is to spend time away from the United States to see what it feels like to be a tight family unit in a new and fascinating culture. Go on vacation with your siblings and buddies if you like, but *do not* bring them along on your sabbatical. *Wait for several months* before hosting any visitors if you've just moved abroad; your kids will have a much harder time adjusting if life is a never-ending series of greetings and good-byes to loved ones. Once they've got their feet firmly planted, they'll love showing others around.

7. Thou shalt not cocoon.

It's easy to stay inside the house and avoid going out, but this defeats the purpose of being abroad. Yes, it's confusing and uncomfortable at times, but remember that this is a learning experience. Staying in, watching movies, playing video games, talking to friends back home online—these are coping mechanisms that should be employed sparingly.

8. Thou shalt embrace thy inner dummy.

You must fully expect to make several embarrassing mistakes before lunch. You will butcher the language, commit a cultural faux pas, get lost and buy the wrong items on a *daily* basis—at least in the beginning. The great part is that you will see improvement quickly and master small tasks, and this will boost your confidence—until you make the next blunder, that is. It will be a lot easier if you and your family members can let go of the idea of yourselves as competent at least temporarily.

(continued)

Good news: Your goof-ups will become your most treasured and hilarious family stories.

9. THOU SHALT NOT BEGIN EVERY SENTENCE WITH "BACK IN THE UNITED STATES . . ."

You will naturally want to compare everything in your new place to things back home. This is good for developing critical thinking skills, but if everyone gets in the habit of repeating the same "it's way better back in the States because" line, things will go downhill very quickly. Reduce your verbal comparisons, and find interesting things to appreciate about your new location.

Good family discussion starter: What cool/funny/unusual/beautiful thing did you notice today?

10. THOU SHALT NOT CLING TO THY IDENTITY.

In the United States our identity is closely tied to our work, and we're used to introducing ourselves by talking about our jobs. In many other places in the world, your occupation is a topic that might not come up for a full fifteen minutes or more of conversation. Frankly, nobody cares much about what you used to do—they care about what you think, why you're there, and what you want to do *now*. We can smell fresh-off-the-plane Americans a mile away by sniffing out their earnestness and listening to their "I'm a [insert position here] for [insert company here]" introductions, followed quickly by the question, "And what do *you* do?" It's okay to leave that behind. In fact, it's a relief. Try it.

Going abroad will be a much happier experience for everyone if you follow these ten commandments. But how do you decide whether to go for a sabbatical or to make the big jump to living abroad permanently?

Try doing it in stages. In the next section you'll learn about the differences between short-term and long-term stays and what to expect from each.

Old School: worrying about your timing, travel agenda, and children's education while abroad

Bold School: focusing on your family's happiness and children's development while abroad

SHORT STAY OR BIG MOVE: A LOOK AT THE DIFFERENCES

If you lived here, you'd be home now.

UNKNOWN

Should you start with a two-month trip or a two-year stay?

Well, you can make either experience work, but suffice it to say that a two-month sabbatical is going to be a *much* easier sell than packing and leaving "forever."

Going on a sabbatical as a family can be a terrific way to get a taste of living abroad, but it has its own challenges as well as a few cheater-type advantages over the sell-it-all option.

Here's what you need to understand about the sabbatical experience:

▶ **It's temporary**. This is what makes it easier for everyone involved to digest, and why it's a much better first option than leaving the country for good. At the end of it all you will be *coming home*. Your house, your friends, your family, your kids' schools, and in most cases your work will still be there. Although you will have gained some insights about both your temporary home and your own culture, within a few weeks your routine will be back to normal, and you'll be left wondering if it was all just a dream.

♦ You're likely to travel more and spend more money on sabbatical than you would if you spent the same time living there under different circumstances. It's one of those while-we're-at-it situations—you've already come this far, and who knows when you'll ever get back to this place? So you book that extra excursion or add an extra loop of sightseeing activities. While the permanent expats are budgeting for long-term expenses in their adopted country, the daily sabbatical budget tends to burn a lot more financial fat.

♦ Kids view a sabbatical as an exciting adventure that they can tell their friends about when they get home. They focus on documenting their experiences and sending e-mails back home to their classmates, and they look forward to returning with great stories to share. Kids who *live* abroad, on the other hand, recognize that their stories aren't likely to be told anytime soon, and they have to make a mental shift to thinking about daily living in their new home. They've got bigger issues to worry about than sending postcards or buying souvenirs; they must go through the process of making a completely new group of friends. To add insult to injury, they have to go to school and do homework (perhaps in a new language) and do chores while the sabbatical kids are splashing in the pool without a care in the world.

Sabbatical kids are less likely to get bored, lonely, or frustrated than those who move abroad, which is *precisely* why you absolutely must take your kids on sabbatical! You will see your children at their very finest, and they'll see you as cool-adventure Dad or funny-goofball Mom—as long as you've followed the ten commandments, that is. This is an unforgettable treat for everyone.

It was relatively easy to talk our girls into moving abroad because they had so many happy memories of our sabbatical. That three-month experience transformed our family; it was definitely a matter of opening Pandora's box. (Consider this fair warning.)

In 1998 my husband was a consultant helping U.S. companies export goods to Japan. When the Japanese economy tanked, we decided to seize the day. Tom put his business in a coma, we liquidated our vintage/used clothing store, sold our snowboard/skateboard business, and took off to visit his host families in India.

Time from decision to departure: six weeks. (This seems to be our favorite time frame.) We'd just finished a five-month remodel of our home, we had plenty of bills to pay, and yet our instincts told us that this was the perfect time to go.

Most people's instincts told them we were insane. Our daughters were seven, eight, ten, and eleven at the time. Take four little blond girls to *India?* We were warned that they'd get horribly ill or maybe even kidnapped. It wasn't *safe*! What were we thinking?

❑ **Smart Move**: If you're considering taking a family sabbatical, talk to those who've actually *been* on one instead of those who have concerns about the idea. Even better, find an enlightened educator who has spent time abroad. This will ease your mind and pave the way for conversations with teachers and colleagues.

Fortunately we had a tipping-point conversation with a school administrator. We talked to the principal at Taeko's school about the fact that we were considering traveling in Asia. What did he think about our plan to take our daughters out of school for three months?

And Dr. Rob Thomason—bless him—said this: "Go. Go. Just *go!*" He'd lived abroad with his family and knew how wonderful it can be to spend time with your young children in another country.

In India we were guests in the homes of various host parents and host siblings with whom Tom had stayed when he was sixteen. We traveled by train, explored the wonders of each new city, and spent our thirteenth wedding anniversary watching our girls dance in the grass at sunset with a view of the Taj Mahal in the background. After two months in India we spent a month in Nepal, where we laughed together for hours each day in Kathmandu and took breaks to play cards and admire the breathtaking vistas while trekking in the Annapurna range.

It was a pivotal experience for our family; we still divide our lives into "before India" and "after India." We learned how little we need to be happy (we brought just a small carry-on backpack each) and how much fun we could have together when we were exploring new places and learning along the way. We discovered that obstacles are opportunities to get creative, and we remembered that what matters most is spending time together.

Our kids went from riding elephants in the jungle in Nepal one week to riding the bright yellow school bus on country roads in Oregon the next. And while we were reacclimating to our American lives, we were determined to hang on to the things we'd learned while on our trip.

But over the next few years we felt the sabbatical and its lessons slipping between our fingers. As the girls started shuffling through middle school, their friends were signing up for all kinds of sports and other activities. We resisted.

Without the need to rush, our lifestyle—despite having four teenage daughters—was very relaxed. We chose to move into a much smaller house than we could afford that was within easy walking distance of schools because we wanted to keep things simple, convenient, and cozy. This was partly an environmental thing, but it was also based on our memories of our trip together and on the fact that having less to take care of gave us more time and money to do whatever we liked. And then, as we were helping our daughters get readjusted to American life when they returned from their exchanges, we learned that there were ways to complete high school without actually going all four years, and that tech tools were available to make our businesses virtual. And so the big question emerged: *Why do we have to stay here?*

That was all it took to get the ball rolling. First stop, Mexico. We knew it would be inexpensive to live there, and we wanted to be near enough that we could come back in case of any business issues or problems with our widowed mothers. (Note: They are happier, healthier, and more independent now than before we left. Apparently we are not as indispensable as we thought.)

Once we got settled into our apartment in Mexico, we developed a routine—morning walks on the beach, coffee in the courtyard, breakfast together, working online, sharing a midday meal when Talya came home from school, taking a siesta, and gathering with the neighbors in the plaza. Every day we laughed until we cried. Life was just so funny—we made embarrassing mistakes with the language, and the Mexican people were so warm and cheerful that we spent our days smiling and enjoying the whole crazy experience. (Well, mostly. There were some very trying times—you'll read Talya's story later.)

Misconceptions About Expat Life

There are a number of misconceptions about expat life. Let's smash a few:

MISCONCEPTION 1: EXPAT LIFE IS LIKE A VERY LONG VACATION. Things might feel a little vacationy at first, but eventually reality hits: you must start from scratch to build a new life and identity for yourself. Some people do really well with this challenge, while others struggle to feel comfortable with a very stripped-down persona and a new community. Who are you *without* your job, house, stuff, hobbies, and friends? Well, this is your chance to find out, but not everyone likes what they discover.

MISCONCEPTION 2: EXPATS LIVE IN COMMUNAL CLUSTERS OF OTHER EXPATS. This is often true for corporate families and retirees, but unless you're moving to a huge enclave of Americans (and they exist), you will be a minority and will live in a neighborhood with mostly locals. Of course, you can still have lots of expat friends, but don't expect to be surrounded by them. Some expats pooh-pooh the idea of mixing with other expats—it does hinder your language learning and cultural understanding if you spend every waking hour with other English speakers—but most have a combination of local and expat friends.

Here's a rule that has really helped us become integrated into our community: we pay for people instead of stuff whenever possible, and we buy everything as close to home as we can. For example, though it's cheaper in the long run to buy a washing machine, we take our laundry to Katsuo and Sumiko, the Japanese Argentines who own the laundry service on our block. This gives us a chance to support our neighbors while getting to know them. (We chat in a weird but totally understandable blend of Spanish and Japanese.) Instead of buying any kind of fitness equipment or joining a big health club, I have private Pilates sessions three times a week with Rita just two doors down. She is a forty-six-year-old Argentine grandmother who speaks no English. We have become great friends. Though we could shop at any number of large supermarkets nearby, we buy our vegetables from Elizabeth, the Bolivian produce vendor on our block who flirts with Tom and makes sure to stock extra cilantro for him. Nearly all of our transactions are very personal, direct, and within two blocks.

Our neighbors don't know where we've worked, where we went to school, or where we've lived prior to moving here. They're much more interested in what we think about the latest strike, the unseasonably cold/hot/humid/dry weather, or the renovation of the building down the way. We admire the babies, pet the dogs, and gossip about the celebrity who lives in our building, a popular television hostess who wears huge sunglasses even at midnight. You know—neighbor stuff.

Misconception 3: Expats live exciting lives full of exotic travel. Our daily routine isn't exactly edge-of-your-seat thrilling. We do our work at home, go out to cafés, chat with neighbors, and go for long walks. Several times a week we get together with friends for hours-long conversations over coffee or dinners that go until two or three in the morning. I have met more fascinating people in Buenos Aires—both Argentines and expats—than I have in the rest of my life put together. This is partly due to the creative culture but also because people make time for thoughtful dialogue. (The wine helps too.)

Sure, many of us are solopreneurs or freelancers who have the flexibility to make our own hours, and we've made a conscious choice about where in the world we want to live, but we laugh out loud when our friends back home refer to us as "globetrotters" or "world travelers." You see, those who decide to live abroad tend to be more interested in the rhythm of life in their community than in adding to a long list of destinations visited within that country. Most expats we know don't travel back to their home country very often either (perhaps once every year or two), and those who do consider it more of an obligatory hassle than a pleasant vacation. Like most of our friends, we try to limit our travel and plan our routes to allow for much more time in each place and much less moving around once we're there. If we can't visit a country for at least a month or two, we won't go. It certainly helps that we can work wherever we are, but just as important is.

- consciously avoiding a frenetic pace
- eliminating the thousand-places-to-visit list

MISCONCEPTION 4: EXPATS LIVE LIKE ROYALTY ABROAD. Though some buy extravagant penthouse apartments or elegant mansions and live lavishly, most expats we know around the world are living simply on a small budget. That being said, depending on the location, it may be possible to have a fabulous lifestyle that doesn't cost much. We spend much less than $2,000 per month, and that includes luxuries we'd never spring for back in the United States. (A month of private Pilates sessions with Rita—a total of twelve hours—costs less than *one* hour-long session in the United States.) Though this is definitely an appealing part of living abroad, it's not the only reason we (or our friends) have chosen to make Buenos Aires home. The relatively low cost of living might have inspired us to come in the first place, but we all choose to stay because we love it—and we're not deterred by inflation.

Once you've sold everything you own, you realize that you don't need much to be happy. This changes the social landscape considerably; there's much less emphasis on buying and maintaining things and much more on spending time with others. Those who make the break and set up a new life tend to be low-key types who value friendship, creativity, and community.

MISCONCEPTION 5: EXPATS WHO WORK ABROAD ARE CORPORATE TRANSFERS, DIPLOMATS, OR THOSE LUCKY ENOUGH TO BE ABLE TO DO THEIR U.S. WORK VIRTUALLY. It used to be that those who lived and worked abroad were corporate executives, diplomats, military people, journalists, or travel writers. But as you learned in the last chapter, there's a new type of expat these days (younger and very independent), and many never *expected* to live abroad. Thanks to the Internet, many expats can continue doing their U.S. work from anywhere (and continue getting paid in dollars), and plenty are finding or creating work in other countries that is completely unrelated to their specific training or education. The "slashes"— people who have had more than one career (this/that)—view their expat experience as yet another opportunity to reinvent themselves. The creative class is scattering around the world and surging ahead precisely because they are not afraid to explore new territories, both literally and figuratively.

We know expats ranging in age from twenty on up to ninety-two (she recently published her fourth novel—and didn't start writing until she was in her eighties) and who hail from well over a dozen different countries. All of them are carving out their own niche and reveling in an environment in which they can cultivate interests that they've never allowed themselves to consider. Here's a list of a few Americans we know here in Buenos Aires:

- a retired biology professor/conservationist from Los Angeles who produced a booklet featuring butterflies of the area
- a university librarian from Tennessee who offers book and website design for authors
- an Illinois businessman with two young children who started a cookie business that supplies cafés all over Argentina
- a tango dancer/actress/psychologist from Washington, D.C., who sees clients in her apartment and sells vintage clothing online
- a Chicago man who is helping his Argentine wife bring the family farm into the 21st century
- a chef/sommelier from New York who operates a closed-door dining establishment
- a business coach/actress/grandmother of three from Arizona who is writing a children's book
- a Portlander with a degree in film who started a wine-exporting business

And on and on it goes. You'd find a similar range of talents and work choices among expats in any major city in the world.

Though it requires some research into possible barriers and isn't likely to shoot you to millionaire status, creating a life that allows for significant travel or an extended stay abroad is easier than ever. It's not necessary to have a certain major, background, or job experience in order to make things work. All you need is:

- **creativity**
- a dash of **boldness**
- some **basic skills** that you can barter for cash

♦ **flexibility and good humor**
♦ and **an ATM card** linked to an adequately funded bank
account

That last one is pretty important. Do your research regarding costs, visas, and housing/work options *before* you set out, and make sure you have enough for your first few months of living expenses. Then bust out your best connecting moves, and start meeting and contacting people. That's how you'll learn about opportunities wherever you go.

So expat life can be fantastic for adults—but what about the *kids?*
The truth: most of our friends listed above *do not have kids living with them.* It's not that it's impossible to do it with kids—it's that not many parents know it's a viable option or how to go about doing it. (That's why I'm writing this book!)
Young children who go to a preschool or elementary school, even in another language, can adapt very quickly. But unless they go to an American high school abroad (and isn't that what we left behind?), older students will find it challenging to make friends in a new country and in a new language. We've found that even international schools aren't likely to have many expat students who were not raised there, and most tend to be bicultural and bilingual.

❑ **Smart Move**: Going on sabbatical or moving abroad is exciting and challenging for everyone, but families considering it must understand some simple math: *adjustment period* multiplied by *the number of people in the family* PLUS *the adolescent factor* equals *total flexibility required.* If you can handle this equation with humor and your kids are willing to communicate with you very openly throughout (even when you'd rather they didn't), you'll all thrive abroad.

In the next section you're going to get the inside story on what it's like for high school students to move to another country without the benefit of the relatively easy transition to an American high school.

Fasten your seat belt.

> **Old School:** believing that living and working abroad is reserved for corporate types, diplomats, military folks, journalists, or travel writers
>
> **Bold School:** understanding that almost anyone who is creative and flexible can find a way to live and work abroad

"YOU'RE DRAGGING ME *WHERE?*": BRINGING THE ADOLESCENTS ALONG

> Heredity is what sets the parents of a teenager wondering about each other.
> LAURENCE J. PETER

Going abroad on a high school exchange is a great experience for students, but going with the family is another thing entirely. What's appealing about going on exchange is *getting away from your parents and being independent.* Going anywhere with Mom and Dad at the age of sixteen isn't generally high on the list of cool things to do, and having to leave your friends behind in order to do so is like pouring salt in the jagged wounds. Remember what you learned in Chapter Six about the adolescent brain needing to chew on something meaty? Well, taking your adolescent abroad will give them a big chunk to chew on all right, but you might not like getting it spit back into your face.

I don't want to suggest that taking adolescents abroad is too horrendous for words, but neither do I want to paint a totally rosy picture of expat life for high school students. That's why I'm letting our daughter Teal tell you what it's *really* like. Teal has the sunniest of dispositions under normal circumstances and thrives in new social settings—but a perfect storm of adolescent angst factors can blow even the most rock-solid and cheerful kid off course for a while. See for yourself.

BOLD STATEMENT

Whenever I tell someone about my high school years and the fact that my parents just *decided* to move abroad for the heck of it, I get one of two reactions. The first reaction is "Wow, I would've *killed* my parents if they'd taken me away from my friends in high school," and the second is "Wow, I would've *loved* to have my parents take me out of high school!" Before any of the moving took place, I probably would've answered more in line with the second option.

It's one thing for a high school student to choose to go on exchange for a year, like I did, but it's another thing to have your parents make you move to yet another country right after. Basically, the idea of exchange for me was fantastic—I was excited to go and even more excited to come back and see how much I had changed in a year. I managed to accept that they were going to be living in Mexico while I was in Brazil and that I wouldn't be coming back to Oregon. However, when they decided to move to Argentina (a place much farther from my U.S. friends and completely new to me) and it dawned on me that I'd have to start all over again in a new country and language, well, let's just say I was less than thrilled.

I made no effort to hide it from my parents. In fact, I was a total bitch. *All* the time. For about three months straight. Impressive, I know. It turned out to be rather exhausting for everyone, especially me. I came to my senses and realized that by acting this way, I wasn't making my life any better. Once that epiphany hit, I never looked back on my "dark age" and actually took advantage and enjoyed the rest of my time abroad with almost no regrets to this day.

For me, high school is divided into three eras: American, Brazilian, and online/Argentine. I got to live in three countries, learn two foreign languages, and experience things before I reached eighteen that some people will never get to experience in their lifetime. As fabulous as it is looking back on it, I was definitely not a happy camper for a good chunk of the time I lived abroad. With all the amazing highs that I experienced, there were incredible lows that went along with them.

I seriously lacked friends for the first few months in Argentina. It was hard to meet Argentines because I was still learning the language and not attending a school with Argentine students. All the foreigners I met were college students who were only there for about two months at a time to study Spanish. So although I always had people to go do things with, most of my friendships were very short term, with the exception of one: Monica was my only friend who actually *lived* in Buenos Aires during the year I was there. She had arrived from Lebanon due to the war (she and her family were evacuated with just a few hours' notice), and we both felt like lost, lonely teenage girls stuck in Buenos Aires. (Okay, so at least I didn't have to worry about my hometown being destroyed or my friends getting bombed.) We became best friends immediately.

It was rough knowing that my best friends back in my hometown were all hanging out together during our sen-

(continued)

ior year. And as much as I loved going out and dancing every weekend and living in such an amazing city, it just wasn't the same as having a solid group of friends—not to mention I had *just* left all of the great friends that I had made in Brazil!

One of my best friends during my exchange in Brazil was Anna from Germany. She told me about how she had dreamed all her life of being able to live like the girls in American movies—walking down the hallways carrying books in her arms, going to the football games dressed in school colors, and being asked to a dance with flowers and candy. She watched numerous movies and shows portraying the typical American teenager's life, and when she explained her envy for characters in *Mean Girls, 10 Things I Hate About You,* and *The OC,* I realized that I had, in fact, already experienced that.

I went to dances, I played sports (well, one), I went to football games in the fall—I did the whole thing. And to tell you the truth, I loved it. In fact, my two years as a Westview Wildcat were two of the least stressful and most enjoyable years that I can remember. But that's exactly it— they were just so . . . easy. In my family, we tend to look at any situation and ask how we could learn more by going just *one* step further. It definitely keeps life interesting!

Anyway, after a year in Argentina, it was time for me to head back up to the northern hemisphere to complete my college degree. I was really excited to go to a place where I wasn't always stared at because of my pale skin or naturally blond hair and assumed to be rich simply because of my nationality. I couldn't wait to just be *normal*. I was sad to leave the city of Buenos Aires but not exactly sad to leave my life there—I was *so* over online classes and temporary friends. So, off to Canada I went!

Arriving in Nova Scotia was a whole new experience—I had culture shock in my own culture. Everyone spoke English, and everyone was just like me—on the surface, at least. The way of life was completely different, though. I missed kissing people on the cheek every time I saw them, I missed not being able to have a glass of wine with my friends in a bar, I missed not going out dancing, and I even missed the often-harsh honesty of the Argentines. I basically didn't know where I belonged. From the outside I was just another North American, but I was holding on to the things that were Argentine. Despite my identity crisis, I did eventually enjoy being an ordinary kid who blended in.

One of my best friends from Oregon (she had spent her junior year on exchange in Argentina) decided to go to the same college, so we ended up having a fun year together. Also, I later spent a summer in Portland and was reunited with all of my best friends from high school, and it was great to feel like I still had that group despite being away from them for three years. I learned some good lessons about friendship.

Looking back, I am so thankful that I had the experiences that I did in Buenos Aires and in Brazil, as difficult as those two years were, and I long for my old Latino life all the time. I am sure I will always consider Buenos Aires one of my homes, even though I am a foreigner there. There were many times when I could have had more fun and made new friends but I was either too bummed or too overwhelmed to face a couple of hours of struggling in a new (for me) language. But I learned a lot from that, and it made me a much better RA: I was able to reach out to the freshmen in my dorm and make sure they felt connected and cared for.

(*continued*)

Graduating at nineteen gives me plenty of time to decide what I want to do, and I'm really excited about working for Norwegian Cruise Lines and meeting so many people—staff and guests—from around the world. I have no idea where it will lead, but that's fine. No matter what I do next, I am sure to be taking it just *one* step further.

If you have a student who is going through a rough transition and doing a little target practice with poisoned verbal arrows, try not to take things too personally or sling any arrows of your own. As long as the words are reasonably respectful, look upon them as evidence of intense personal growth and intellectual development. Teal kept her sense of humor (even as she cloaked it in a malevolent dark trench coat) and funneled her fury into her academic pursuits—she developed fierce study skills that allowed her to not only finish high school that year but earn two years' worth of college credits via online and on-campus classes.

Bringing your high school student on a sabbatical is likely to be fairly easy (provided you follow the ten commandments), but moving them abroad is going to require some cardiovascular parenting with a full heart. Tom and I have danced the dark culture-shock tango back and forth across several borders with our four daughters (with a few dips and spins of our own), and we know that the sun will rise eventually. But for newbies, it can be very difficult to watch your son or daughter go through a rough patch without knowing for sure if things are going to get better.

I don't know your kids, but I do know that things almost *always* get better. The bigger question is whether you can surf that wave without wiping out.

❏ **<u>Smart Move</u>**: Do *not* talk to friends and family back home about the struggles you and your kids are experiencing abroad.

See, they all want you to return, and any hint of difficulty is going to be met with scarcely concealed glee and various combinations of the following dangerous phrases:

❏ "I told you so."
❏ "Life shouldn't be so hard."
❏ "Just send him/her home for a while."
❏ "Don't you think it's time to move back?"
❏ "We can't wait to see you all again!"

You might not make it through these conversations without caving.

A much better option is to talk with other parents who live abroad with their kids. They've already been through it and can offer advice and support. (Check out the parent resources at www.NewGlobalStudent.com.) Tom and I have met with frantic moms and dads online, on the phone, and in person. Most find my blog and contact me to see if I'd like to "share ideas about raising kids abroad," which I have learned to interpret as "please help us—our kid is miserable, and we're about to lose it." It's always great fun to swap stories with other parents and to feel reassured that we all tend to have good instincts worth trusting.

Not all high school students handle the expat experience the same way (and remember, we're not talking about those who attend American high schools abroad), but it is universally challenging, and even in ideal circumstances (your kid is elated to go abroad with you) there is likely to be a not-so-pretty period of adjustment. Expect some storms and turbulence, hang on for the ride, and know that you'll all break through to sunnier skies eventually.

Bottom line: Go early if at all possible, but don't opt out simply because you've got older kids.

Still not sure it's worth risking a few months with an unhappy student? Allow me to remind you that if you've got teenagers, you are likely to deal with some difficult days no matter where you are. At least when you go abroad, you know that the hardships are hardwiring your kid's brain for flexibility and cultural awareness, which is a lot more than you can say for the social squabbles and dull disappointments of regular high school life.

In fact, the difficulties can become the most memorable part of living abroad. We find ourselves laughing and shaking our heads at many of the experiences we shared in both Mexico and Argentina. Despite the frustrations, the balance tilts *much* more toward hilarious than harrowing when we look back on it. That's almost always the case.

If you're still with me on the spending-time-abroad-as-a-family thing, you'll get a kick out of Chapter Nine's section "Mutinies, Meltdowns, and Other Merriment" (with vivid examples provided). And even if you're *not* ready to pack up the family, you'll benefit from some essential advice that will help you handle criticism regarding *any* education decision—from skipping the SAT to studying abroad independently—like a seasoned (and not too snide) pro.

We'll start "Mutinies" with a little story about our very first week in Mexico, during which we learned that sometimes a mutiny leads to the best possible outcome.

Old School: worrying that moving abroad with a high school student will be a terrible mistake

Bold School: understanding that moving abroad with a high school student will involve a difficult adjustment period followed by a chart-busting boost in confidence, maturity, and appreciation for new experiences

MAKING IT WORK

CHAPTER NINE

The Get-Real Guide for
Bold Parents

MUTINIES, MELTDOWNS, AND OTHER MERRIMENT

> Dare to be naïve.
> BUCKMINSTER FULLER

Even if you and your loved ones aren't ready to consider spending time abroad anytime soon, it's helpful to know that the challenges your family would face in another country are likely to be funnier, more valuable, and definitely more interesting than what you'd deal with on a typical crappy day back in the United States.

One of the most rewarding parts of living abroad with kids is experiencing things on the same level with them. Parents can't pretend to know everything; and for kids, this is an *unparalleled* opportunity to:

- develop skills and confidence
- laugh at their parents

Humbling? Sure. But it's also good fun, and it allows kids to step up and take the reins.

❏ **Smart Move**: Bold parents know that, at some point in the not-too-distant future, their kids will discover that Mom and Dad do not know everything. This is actually simpler (and sillier) for everyone if it happens while living abroad.

Admitting mistakes is a lesson taught far more memorably when parents offer themselves as sterling examples of doofusness. Believe it or not, such admissions cement the family into an unbreakable unit and lead to greater compassion and respect for each other—at least, once the laughter dies down.

Let me give you an example.

Prior to our arrival in Mexico, we had arranged (via e-mail) to rent an apartment for the first two months. We worked with an expat woman who handled rentals, and we found what seemed like a reasonably decent (based on attached photos) house only a few blocks from the school. Talya (almost fifteen) would be attending.

Being experienced travelers, we knew that staying in a sight-unseen place could be risky, but we didn't have much choice in the matter—school was starting within two days of our arrival, and we felt that having an initial landing place would be easier than trying to move between hotels while searching for an apartment.

When we arrived, the house was not exactly what we expected. That is to say, it was ugly, dark, and depressing, and it had a most nauseating smell, thanks to a sewage trench a few yards behind it. Worse, it was on a street that served as the parking area for bus drivers on break, meaning that we had to inhale fumes from engines all day and night.

We assured the girls that we could spruce things up and just make the best of it until something else became available, but we sensed that a disturbing mix of alarm and anger was about to bubble to the surface.

After about five days there—following a violent thunderstorm that, combined with the searing August heat, raised the stink level substantially—Tara and Talya sat us down in the dingy living room for a chat. Knowing only too well our tendency to discount Tara's dramatically expressed opinions about everything, the two had put their heads together and wisely decided to let Talya—level-headed, diplomatic, never-complaining Talya—be the voice announcing mutiny.

After politely stating that she and Tara were dissatisfied with the living situation, she requested permission to go out and find a more suitable option. We insisted that there were no other options out there—we'd been in touch with three agencies, wandered the streets ourselves, and felt sure that we'd just have to wait for something else to open up. But we told them our budget and sent them on their way. We figured it would be a good bonding experience for them.

Within about fifteen minutes we heard them screaming. Tom and I ran outside, expecting the worst. Between squeals, they explained that they had met an American woman (single mother of a young son—one of only two expat families we'd meet the entire year) who led them to a place she was planning to move into—a brand-new complex of charming colonial-style apartments facing a courtyard with a pool and a fountain. There was only one finished apartment—a two-bedroom place—and the owner (a German woman married to a Mexican man) was not planning to rent it out until after the entire complex was completed. But the girls had begged, and she'd told them she would consider renting it after about two weeks. The price was reasonable and the location was ideal—two blocks from the plaza, four from the beach, and near the school. We'd even walked past it without knowing it was there; only a battered front wall with a rusty iron gate (beautifully redone once the apartments were completed) was visible from the street.

After the girls had calmed down a bit, we followed them as they skipped hand in hand to the apartment. We met with the owner, and in no time at all we'd arranged to move into our gorgeous new place. The girls were beside themselves, jumping up and down with tears streaming down their faces, so proud and ecstatic to have discovered this sweet oasis.

Of course, Tom and I would have liked to pretend that the first house was just our parental ploy to get them to take charge, but we had to admit that we'd gone for something quick without really taking the time to look for something fantastic. From that point on we happily allowed the girls to lead in many family decisions. It turns out that humble pie is kind of tasty once you get used to it.

That's how things went in Mexico: one minute we were moaning and distressed, the next minute we were on the moon. But none of us experienced this nearly as much as Talya.

We knew that she would have a hard time in a situation in which she was not the top student but that there were also some extremely important lessons she could learn. Frankly, we felt she would benefit from a little deprogramming in order to relax about her need to achieve, but we certainly didn't want to *torture* her. I'll let her tell her story here.

BOLD STATEMENT

I survived my year in a Mexican high school by accepting the fact that sooner or later I would have to appear stupid. Never one to laugh off my mistakes, I took my responsibilities very seriously and hated appearing disorganized or unprepared. I was always the girl who woke up an extra hour early to pack her lunch and revise her planner just to make sure she didn't miss an assignment. In middle school I was the one who did the extra credit simply to show off my determination. In a sense, I felt my grades could prove to the other students that I was smart and mature for my age.

Considering the person I was in the United States, I

am still surprised that I handled that year so well (in the end, anyway). I started at Colegio El Pacifico speaking absolutely no Spanish and knowing nothing about the Mexican culture. From the minute I stepped into the building, I was clearly the foreigner. In the United States I had made an effort to fit in—I dressed like everyone else, I tried my best to befriend nearly all of my classmates, and I even pretended to agree with my friends. But now, being the only non-Mexican student in the entire school, I could not avoid the stares. For the first time I was pulled out of my comfort zone, and I had no control over the situation.

Although I had taken a few Spanish classes in middle school, I was not prepared at all to keep up with the speed and slang of teenage chatter. I hated appearing stupid, and so for the first three months I refused to speak Spanish in front of my classmates. I was so afraid of mispronouncing the words and having everyone laugh at me. Later, I realized that the only way I could become fluent was by letting my guard down and fumbling my way through—and that meant making a complete fool of myself. Let me tell you, I was still devastated when my classmates mocked my accent or laughed at my language mistakes, but for the first time I had to accept the fact that I wasn't perfect.

After six months of tears, joy, and all sorts of agonizing embarrassment, I was beginning to master the language and adapt to the Mexican lifestyle. My friends would invite me to their homes to celebrate the Mexican holidays, on weekends I would spend days at the beach with my classmates, and I even stayed a whole week with my friend's family just to improve my Spanish. I still felt

(continued)

like a complete outsider, but I was determined to fit in in any way possible.

Once I could actually understand what the teachers were saying, I began to study really hard. I would spend at least an extra hour a day going through my homework just to make sure I made no grammar mistakes. I spent my free time reading my textbooks and underlining words I didn't know. By the seventh month I was surpassing most of my classmates and I was even chosen as the chemistry tutor—in Spanish! My work had paid off, and I was waiting for some kind of recognition.

But while I was working so hard to prove to my classmates that I was smart, I failed to recognize that none of them were studying, comparing GPAs, or even jumping up for joy when they received an A on their exams. Just when I thought I was beginning to understand what it was to be Mexican, I was once more put in my place. What was so foreign to me was the fact that my classmates felt no reason to compete. They didn't care if the teacher read out their grades in front of the entire class and told them that they had failed miserably. Unlike my friends in the United States, my friends in Mexico were not stressed at all about their grades. Although I had been one of those students who was almost obsessive about overachieving, I found it such a relief to be in this new environment.

And then things got even more overwhelming. Of course, everyone knew about the "American girl with blue eyes," and I was chosen by my class as a candidate for Spring Queen. From what I understood, this was just going to be some sort of English festival where I would have to stand up in front of all the parents and give a speech in English. Considering I was the only native

English speaker, this made perfect sense. How hard could it be?

Well, it turned out that this Spring Queen thing was a full-on, highly competitive pageant (it had nothing whatsoever to do with English), for which families prepared and saved for months prior to the coronation. Before I knew it, I was asked to organize a team to collect cans, complete at least three community service projects, and even coordinate an entire caravan of cars to parade through the city (with everyone wearing T-shirts I'd provide) and chant my name! Let's remember, I was barely fifteen and had started learning Spanish just a few months before. Anyone in their right mind would have just walked over to the principal's office and refused to participate as a princess. But not wanting to let my class or myself down, I accepted the challenge.

In fact, I did all of those ridiculous things and even more. I created posters that said *Vota por Talya,* made collages about all the community service projects I did, and even wrote a speech that I read in front of the entire school in Spanish   voluntarily! Despite my complete lack of knowledge about this festival and my role, I had to compete with the other princesses while figuring out the appropriate things to wear for various occasions, including posing and speaking at numerous events, doing press conferences (in Spanish), riding in a convertible during a parade, and curtsying during a formal coronation ceremony for which I had to rent a fancy gown.

Every day was traumatic and humiliating in some way. I'd go to school or an event only to find out that there was yet another thing I was supposed to have prepared

(*continued*)

for (or been in charge of) that I'd known nothing about. My classmates, as first-year students, had no clue and were no help whatsoever, and though my family was extremely supportive, they didn't know what was going on either. I was truly on my own until the last week, when the senior princess (she was later crowned queen) took pity on me and helped me out a little.

Looking back on the insanity of that month-long period, I see that I simply got used to never knowing what was going to happen next. I had to give in to things, which was a gigantic leap for me since I have always been such a planner.

My year in Mexico was by far the most stressful time of my life, but although I went home bawling at least twice a week, I was learning so much about the culture and about myself. Sooner or later I would have to make mistakes, but I learned that I could feel okay in bizarre situations, and that being a complete outsider could teach me to be proud of my differences instead of hiding them.

Although I am extremely grateful for that year and look back on it with so much pride and affection (I have some really happy memories, too!), it certainly was not easy. I would not recommend it to everyone, but I would absolutely respect those who are up for the challenge. I probably would not have agreed to move to Mexico had I known what would be coming, but I am so glad I was so naïve!

I couldn't possibly tell anyone how they will feel if they go to a high school abroad, but I can offer a few tips:

- *Get comfortable with feeling like a fool.* In order to learn any language, you have to practice, which requires a lot of embarrassing mistakes and people laughing at them. If you're like me, the chance to relax your expectations about yourself can be really liberating.

- *Being uncertain is not always a bad thing.* Sometimes when you don't know exactly what is going on, you end up taking risks and doing so much more than you would have had you known what was expected of you.
- *Being an outsider allows you to learn more about yourself.* By not having anyone to compare yourself to, you can focus on how you react to situations and develop your own identity. Not only do you have a clearer image of yourself, but you also gain a lot of self-confidence.

After finishing my year in Mexico, I had to adapt to a new culture in Argentina. Though I felt extremely lost and helpless during my first few weeks in Buenos Aires, looking back, I can see how much I have grown: I created a beautiful life for myself, mastered the Spanish language, made friends with others from around the world, and even found love.

Now, after living abroad for over three years, I am back in my own culture and speaking in my native language. I am amazed at how easy college life in the United States feels! I am so glad to have been truly challenged these last few years. Now I have the confidence and skills to walk into any environment—anywhere in the world—and eventually feel at home.

Watching Talya go through her year in Mexico was one of the most painful and proud parenting experiences of my life. We all smothered her with as much love and encouragement as we possibly could, and as we watched her glide gracefully across the floor in her heavenly blue gown on coronation night, we shed our own tears of happiness as we celebrated her personal triumph. It was never about winning (she came in third); what mattered was that she had fully embraced her experience. Her time in Mexico and Argentina transformed her from a quiet, eager-to-please perfectionist to a confident, relaxed conversationalist ready to stand up for her ideas and herself.

Talya learned how to handle criticism of all kinds while sitting in a bilingual hot seat. You, however, will have a *much* easier time! In the next section you'll learn about the four types of naysayers (and how to deal with each one) and discover that being bold and smart can be a great opportunity to inform and inspire others.

> **Old School:** expecting a year abroad in a tropical location to feel like an endless vacation
>
> **Bold School:** understanding that beyond the beach and sunshine are opportunities for rich and radical personal transformation

HANDLING CRITICISM: THE SNAPPY COMEBACK CHEAT SHEET

> The dogs bark, but the caravan moves on.
> ARABIC SAYING

Whether you're allowing your student to take the GED or buying a catamaran to sail the Caribbean, you're sure to face some criticism. You might as well have a little fun with it.

The hardest part of taking a big leap is not the leap itself but dealing with those who warn you about slipping into a dark and terrifying crevasse. Don't be scared. We *know* that big hole is just smoke and mirrors. Our job is to help other people recognize the illusion or, if that seems impossible, to smile and thank them for pointing it out.

Although some will toast your decision, not everyone is going to be cheering for you. In fact, you may be surprised by the reactions of others when you tell them you're about to send your daughter to study abroad for a year when she's fifteen, have your son head off by himself to Timbuktu on a do-it-yourself study-abroad plan when he's eighteen, or (here's the whopper) sell everything and leave the country with your kids. You might even hear a few comments that will:

- ❯ make your blood boil
- ❯ cut your heart out
- ❯ make you wonder why you are friends with these people in the first place

Good times!

Tom and I have had a lot of practice dealing with verbal barbs, sulking, full-blown fits, and the cold-shoulder treatment—and I'm talking about *adults* here, not teenage daughters. In this section, we're going to share what we've learned so that you'll be much better prepared than we were.

There are two important points to remember at all times:

1. **When you make choices that are different than the norm, normal people will question them.** It's that simple. The sooner you recognize this fact, the less time you'll spend feeling hurt and the more time you can spend on the happy details of your particular choice. If you hang out in a rather mainstream circle of friends, know that they will be likely to question any decision that isn't part of their typical group behavior. On the other hand, if you run in a tribe of independent thinkers, outcasts, and rebels, well, they'll move to the celebratory stage almost immediately.

2. **No matter how people respond to your news, their reaction will almost always be centered upon their concerns for *themselves*.** For example, parents will feel that their own decisions have been called into question when you announce that you are taking your kid out of the very same high school at

which they've been tirelessly volunteering. If your company transferred you to Podunk, USA, everyone would have a big party for you and wave you off at the airport, but if you sell everything and leave the country for no reason other than you *want* to, your family, friends, and neighbors are going to feel rejected.

You can't blame them, really. You'd probably feel the same way. So your best strategy is to understand where they're coming from and respond in a way that doesn't belittle their concerns but that makes clear that you've done your research and you're happy with your decision.

Everyone's different—and you'll discover that you can't predict someone's reaction in advance—but you'll definitely encounter consistent categories of responses. It's actually kind of fun if you let yourself view it as an interesting psychological study.

In general, everyone—loved ones, colleagues, educators, neighbors, and friends—will fit into one of these four boxes, whether you're talking about skipping the SAT or moving abroad:

> ▶ **Shoulder Shruggers:** Either they're really not that interested, or they don't understand why you're doing what you're doing and *don't care enough to ask.* The worst is finding that a good friend or relative—someone you thought would be really supportive—is a Shoulder Shrugger.
>
> **Best defense:** Do nothing! It might sting, but you can't change someone's reaction if they show no interest in having a conversation about it. Save your energy for the others.
>
> ▶ **Eye Rollers:** These people act like they think you're crazy, but this response is often masking their own concerns. They might be wondering if your choice is actually better than the one they're making, but they don't want to give any clues about their lack of conviction. They're a little passive-aggressive; they might not say anything at all except "Good luck." Who knew that could feel like a slap in the face?

Best defense: Disregard the disdain. Eye Rollers tend to simmer in their own sauce. Let them stew while you stride forward.

▶ **Scowlers:** Scowlers come armed with information to shoot down your plans. They will send you links to all kinds of scary articles and shower you with statistics about college-admissions requirements and the competitive job market. They'll tell you about the neighbor who heard about a guy who went abroad and disappeared off the face of the planet. They'll imply that going on a sabbatical could end up damaging your career, your finances, or your home. Remember that most Scowlers are looking for a way to validate their own choices. Listen, if you're saving thousands by sending your kid to community college, a dad who's paying $45,000 for his son's freshman year of frat parties and a 1.5 GPA is going to do some serious digging to find anything that will make him feel better about his decision. Scowlers may mean well, but deep down they're more worried about themselves than about you.

Best defense: Nod at the statistics, let them know you've considered your choice very carefully after doing your own research, and thank them for their concern.

▶ **Gaspers:** It's shocking! It's terrible! How *could* you? Gaspers respond with surprise and then distress, and they take your decisions personally. You're a villain if you take your daughter away from their daughter ("But senior year will be ruined!"), perhaps on a family sabbatical during the prom ("But they've been talking about it since they were twelve!"), especially if she is leaving behind a sport ("But the team is counting on her!"). Teachers might be horrified if your son will be going to community college instead of starring in the high school play ("But that role is made for him!") or if he stops playing first

(continued)

saxophone ("But he would have had some killer solos next year!") or if he decides to go on exchange during his junior year ("But what about the college scouts who might see him play?"). Your choice is affecting *their* dreams, and they can't believe you'd be so selfish as to mess things up for everybody. Gaspers cling tenaciously to their perfect scenarios, and they don't handle change well. Their disappointment tends to be contagious, and pretty soon others start gasping too. Gaspers often adopt the wounded look; after all, you've spoiled their fun. But remember that they are rarely distressed about how your choices will affect *you or your kids*.

Best defense: Keep breathing, and recognize that their hyperventilating is only temporary. They'll catch their breath eventually, and you'll be off doing your thing.

Expect a few reactions of each type, and remember that it helps to sort them by categories. That way you'll know what you're dealing with and can better respond with sass and snark.

Wait, did I say that? I meant humor and grace. Because you see, getting snippy doesn't help anyone and just gives others a reason to peg you as a snob who thinks he's too good to do the same thing as everyone else. Believe me, some people will come to that conclusion on their own (it's a handy one) despite your best efforts, and you don't need to do anything to lead them to it.

The trick is to come up with ways to respond to the naysayers that show concern for *them*. Your mind is already made up, so you've got to turn the tables and make it more about how you can help them understand your decision.

I've made it easy for you with this Snappy Comeback Cheat Sheet. Feel free to add sweetness or snark to taste, but remember that **providing information** to questioners is the best way to soothe any concerns for you (real or fake), appear to be a thoughtful and informed parent, and politely shut them up.

* * *

Get ready for a blast of fego! Here is the undisputed Big Daddy of all questions:

"Aren't You Worried That This Is Going to Make It Hard for Your Kid to Get into College?"

Whether it's in reference to not taking AP courses, enrolling in community college, taking the GED tests, skipping the SAT, opting out of sports or other activities, going on a high school exchange, or moving abroad, you'll hear this question so frequently that you'll begin to think that you are, quite possibly, the worst parent in the world. First take a deep breath and repeat after me: "This person is just seeking information." Do it again. Now, how can you be of assistance?

ANSWER: YOU KNOW, THAT'S A GOOD QUESTION. WE WERE REALLY CONCERNED ABOUT THAT AT FIRST, BUT WE'VE DONE A LOT OF RESEARCH, AND THANKFULLY WE FEEL VERY POSITIVE ABOUT THIS DECISION AFTER FINDING OUT THAT [PICK WHATEVER APPLIES]:

- *Advanced Placement:* **More and more colleges and universities are choosing not to accept AP test scores for credit.** In fact, some high schools are dropping AP courses from their curriculum since it turns out that the focus on the tests often limits the scope of the class and ends up stressing out kids. We learned that the dual enrollment program/IB program [whatever else] is actually a much better option in terms of preparing students for college success.

- *SAT:* **The SAT is really losing ground as a tool for college admissions.** There's quite a backlash against the test because it's really not a very good predictor of college success—in fact, it's less reliable than high school grades! Plus, a growing number of universities—close to eight hundred so far—no longer require SAT scores for admission. Besides, a student who has earned at least a year's worth of college credits during high school can apply as a transfer student to a four-year college and won't need an SAT score at all, since the grades in those college courses are what matter most for transfer applicants.

- **Community College: Community college is the new high school for motivated kids.** Those who are ready to start college early can transfer to a four-year university at eighteen as a junior. Taking college classes early impresses future employers too, since businesses are looking for students who are interested in advancing themselves and have spent time in a more adult setting. The right classes can really give your kid a boost compared to high school. Plus, we're happy about saving several thousand dollars on college costs this way.

- **High School Exchange: Going abroad in high school is the best way to hardwire your kid's brain for language learning and flexibility.** Being fluent in another language and comfortable living in a foreign culture are the two *best* ways to prepare for the global job market of the future. Plus, we've heard some pretty impressive stories from those who've returned and done very well, and it seems like an amazing experience for our son or daughter. He or she could wait until college, but we believe that this is the *optimal* time to develop traits that will become a permanent part of his or her skill set.

- **GED: The GED isn't just for dropouts anymore.** In fact, it's become a tool for advanced kids who want to skip the usual college entrance process and begin taking courses at sixteen or so. Kids who travel a lot for elite sports or other activities are taking the GED these days in order to finish up and take college courses online. And some homeschooled kids are taking the GED as a way to show what they've learned (it includes five different subject tests) and dive into college courses early.

- **Opting Out of High School Activities: College-admissions folks are looking for students who are**

stepping *off* the track in order to learn more about themselves and their community. My child has had a great time with [fill in the blank] over the years but is really excited to try something new. This is such a great opportunity for her or him to have a mentor and develop more skills, and we feel confident that it will be a much bigger advantage than another year of [fill in the blank].

- ***Going on Sabbatical or Moving Abroad:* Living abroad is actually a very big plus on college applications.** You see, colleges are looking for diversity in all areas, and having students with a different perspective (not to mention a different language or two) and experiences in other countries are quite desirable on a campus where many students have never left the United States. Don't worry— there are ways to make sure my child keeps up academically. We feel this is the *best* way to both prepare him or her for college and invest in his or her global education. Oh, and we figured out that if we do it right, we can actually *save more money* for college by living abroad while having a great family adventure!

If that's too much for you to memorize, I've got a simple and effective response that will work with *any* question that gets thrown your way:

- **All-Purpose Response: There's a whole new approach to education that we learned about while reading a book called *The New Global Student*.** A lot of things are changing, and it's actually smarter to do things differently. You should read the stories from the students and parents! Anyway, we're excited about trying this "bold school" approach ourselves because, to be honest, the "old school" way is exhausting, expensive, and way too competitive. We're glad to leave it behind! Have you read the book yet? It might help you figure out the best options for your son or daughter!

A shameless plug obviously, but you'll look smart, it will send them scampering to the bookstore, and you won't have to answer any more questions. Everybody wins!

Ready for question number two?

"Aren't You Worried About Your Kid's Safety?"

This question is sure to get you feeling that you might actually be putting your student at risk (fear!) and that others see you as a reckless and irresponsible parent (ego!). I think it's time for another deep breath, don't you? Hmmm . . . ahhhh. Better.

You won't be able to avoid this question if you're considering a high school exchange, an indie study-abroad option, a sabbatical, or especially a more permanent move abroad. Keep in mind that people who ask this love you and your kids very much. I mean, keep that in mind even if it's not true. You'll be nicer that way.

The best discussions (and breakthroughs in terms of understanding) are likely to occur when you *skip the defensiveness* and *have a broader conversation* about crime, safety, and health care. So no matter where you're going, do some research and prepare some answers that will help others understand your decision and recognize that there are risks in everything we do. Use the following as a template.

ANSWER: WELL, YOU'RE RIGHT, THAT'S A VERY BIG CONCERN, AND WE WANTED TO MAKE SURE WE'RE NOT MAKING A MISTAKE THAT COULD JEOPARDIZE OUR SON/DAUGHTER/FAMILY'S SAFETY. AFTER DOING OUR OWN RESEARCH, WE WERE SURPRISED TO LEARN THAT:

- **By being abroad during this year of high school, our son is actually reducing the biggest risk to his health and safety.** Did you know that the number-one cause of death of American kids ages fifteen to nineteen is car accidents?[1] Well, he will not be driving abroad or riding in cars with young friends in [fill in the blank] as they can't get their driver's license there until they are eighteen. What a relief! Of course, we'll also save on car insurance while he's away!

- **Young students abroad are generally more protected from anti-American sentiment than the average tourist would be.** They have host families, school friends, and other locals who are watching out for them. Actually, I believe these students who go abroad are most likely to change the minds of their peers about what it means to be an American and a global citizen. The world would be a better place if there were more international friendships at an early age, don't you think?

- **Studying abroad independently can be a much safer option than going with a college group.** I know it might *seem* that traveling in a group is safer, but American groups abroad tend to be bigger targets for crime than one or two traveling together, and they tend to go to places that are staked out by those intent upon engaging in crimes against tourists. My daughter is already corresponding with people in [fill in the blank] who are answering her questions and offering all kinds of help, so we feel good about the fact that we have contact information and have even talked by phone with those who are interested in hosting her. By spending more time with locals, she will make friends with those who can help her learn about how to stay safe.

- **Health care in [fill in the blank] is excellent, and she will be fully covered by insurance while abroad.** In fact, we did some research and corresponded online with some Americans who live in [fill in the blank], and they are quite impressed with the clinics and doctors in that country. They have access to top-notch hospitals, and from what we've heard, the doctors are very caring, many speak excellent English, and of course some of them have been trained in the United States. Plus, it's nice to know that in [fill in the blank], the health care is subsidized; hospital stays that would bankrupt someone here in the United States are mostly covered there, even for foreigners. Who knew that [fill in the blank] had more advanced and humane health care than we do here in the United States? (Okay, sorry, but I hope you see that there are creative ways to steer the conversation away from you and toward bigger issues.)

By preparing yourself for these two questions, you can avoid moments of stuttering and look like the smartest parent on the block. Concentrate on slinging out the info, and that way, even if they don't agree with you, they'll have to admit that you have put plenty of thought into your decision.

Now I've gone and overprepared you, but trust me, that's better than being blindsided. Memorize your favorite responses (along with the foolproof book referral), and you'll be ready for anything.

You've got the information you need to help your son or daughter make the best decisions about education and study abroad, but before we close up shop, let's take a look at the big picture one last time.

Old School: letting others' fear and ego prevent you from making your best choices

Bold School: preparing your responses to others' questions in order to allay their concerns and provide helpful information

The *Not So Big* Education

> Don't ask what the world needs. Ask what makes
> you come alive, and go do it. Because what the
> world needs is more people who
> have come alive.
>
> HOWARD THURMAN

Catapult. Zoom. Leapfrog. Blast.

I've used these words throughout this book to suggest that those who make their own best choices can move forward in remarkable ways, but one thing I haven't addressed is what our students should be catapulting, zooming, leapfrogging, or blasting *toward*.

The bold-school approach is less about helping your student get ahead of others than about encouraging him to *get ahead of where he would have been* if he'd made choices that were less personal, intentional, and global.

I wrote this book to help parents and students see that there are some simple, affordable ways to get a fantastic international education and that choosing alternative routes has advantages. But there's another reason: we need a clearer vision of what's possible when we give our children—individually and collectively—opportunities to reach across the world.

Want to help your student fulfill her greatest potential (and avoid a midlife meltdown)? Pay attention *now* to the interests and talents that hint at her most gratifying work, and do everything in your power to celebrate these gifts while downplaying any deficiencies. We need to stop pointing our kids in the direction of the biggest paychecks and encourage them to focus on their natural strengths and sharpen their skills in the areas that most intrigue them. Only in this way can we help them discover their own grin-inducing livelihood. Our challenge is to recognize that **the two most detrimental beliefs shaping our lives** (whether we're fifteen or fifty) are:

- that choosing a traditional or popular path is the best way to ensure that we will be happy and live a good life
- that acquiring and maintaining more and better stuff is evidence that we are happy and living a good life

We can do *our very best work*—for ourselves and others—by cutting out the clutter that blocks our real progress as people. The new cool in the 21st century is to choose to live smart, well, and simply. Conserving resources is hot, but doing so while directing our talent and energy toward making the world a better place (in whatever way we choose) is positively *sizzling*.

Big life, little lifestyle.

When Sarah Susanka moved with her family from the United Kingdom to the United States at the age of twelve, she was shocked by the size of American homes. Her ideas about our needs for comfort—which have little to do with how much space we use—continued to develop over the years and culminated in the publication of her breakthrough book, *The Not So Big House: A Blueprint for the Way We Really Live,* which inspired thousands of people to choose to live in a small, well-built, and comfortable home instead of a McMansion.[1] With gorgeous photos and uplifting prose, Sarah helped us see the value and beauty of being authentic and original as opposed to cookie-cutter impressive.

Now, with seven best-selling books (including *The Not So Big Life*) and a veritable empire based on the *Not So Big* concept, you could certainly say that Sarah's life has become quite big; she has tremendously expanded the scope of her work in terms of reach, influence, and financial security. Sarah has been named an "Innovator in American Culture" by *U.S. News & World Report*, a "Top Newsmaker" by *Newsweek*, a "Fast 50" innovator by *Fast Company*, and a "Power Broker" by *Builder* magazine, and she was included in the "Environmental Power List" by *Organic Style* magazine. And yet her lifestyle has become much simpler and more satisfying than when she was working at an architecture firm years ago. This is what she shared with me:

INSIDER INSIGHT

I couldn't have written the *Not So Big House* book without first recognizing what I needed in my life, which was the time to pursue my writing. I was working as a managing partner of an architecture firm with forty-five employees. I had a lot going on, I was very busy, and one day it became obvious to me that no amount of financial success would fill the void I felt in terms of not having the time to pursue what was most meaningful, what was calling me. And so I decided to carve out time for "a meeting" with myself every Tuesday and Thursday morning so that I could write. It seemed crazy at the time—how could I possibly spend several hours twice a week on writing when I had so much work to do? But once I made the decision to do that, everything shifted to support what I had stated I wanted.

Once the book came out and met with almost instant success, it became clear that leaving my architecture firm

(continued)

was the best way to pursue my passion for the written word without having to juggle and compromise my architectural projects. And though this was very scary, it also felt very true. It allowed me to be much lighter on my feet and go where my life was leading me. I was free to focus on the projects that really resonated, without being overwhelmed by other tasks that weren't such a good fit. This is something I've carried over to my work today.

I often say that the most sustainable thing you can do for your heart and the planet is to do what you truly want to do. And the signs were all around me—I felt that I needed to write, and once I started paying attention to that, everything opened up.

When I went on tour for the *Not So Big Life* book, it felt like a really amped-up version of the *Not So Big House* tour in terms of what people shared. The stories were extraordinary. Astonishing, really. And what people expressed to me over and over again was a sense of gratitude about what they'd discovered about themselves and their lives.

We tend to view the world in such a linear way. Things look impenetrable. Our schedules, our responsibilities, the way we look at the course of our lives—it all looks impossible to change. This becomes a huge obstacle, at least in our heads. But we need to know that this process is not about logic. The intellect believes that things are linear when in fact there are more directions and options and possibilities than we can imagine. Once we see this, the world opens up.

I know that for me the most important advice was (and still is) to follow your heart. Instead of getting caught up in worrying about the best job you can get in order to pay the bills, you need to focus on what fills you, what excites you, and go in that direction. Of course, the trick is to have your sensory apparatus turned on—you've got to pay attention to whatever is showing up, even if that's a credit card bill! But rather than getting stuck in the urgency of making choices to earn big money, the key is giving yourself the time to *hear* what it is your heart is wanting to do. Listen!

In the same way that Sarah's book series inspires people to choose a home that is more **sustainable, soul-filling, and unique,** my deepest hope is that this book will convince parents and students to consider these same qualities when picking an education option or an opportunity to go abroad. Whether you are searching for an alternative to an unsatisfactory high school situation, choosing a great local college despite pressure to head to a brand-name school, or going abroad for self-discovery and global awareness, it's essential to recognize what is tugging at you and then be bold enough to *lean into it.*

Please understand that there is no race to win—at least, not in the old way. Even though I've used language that suggests beating others—getting ahead, stepping forward—I'm really referring to movement toward that which is *most irresistibly magnetic.* We're switching from motivation that is determined by others' expectations to enthusiasm that is cultivated through meaningful experiences. A different deal altogether.

What you're competing with is not your neighbor next door (or in the next hemisphere) but that little do-or-die devil on your shoulder shouting that there is only one right way to get an education and live life. If going abroad at sixteen (or forty-six) doesn't feel right—for whatever reason—there's no need to head to the airport. A traditional four-by-four plan that includes AP courses, SAT tests, and an Ivy League school could be a perfect choice as long as it's based on an understanding of *all* options available. The key is to slow down long enough to pay attention to those twinges and **take the time to figure out if it's *fego* or *fiery passion* that is pulling the strings**. In the beginning of this book, I talked about the fears we face as parents, but you may feel that I've dealt you a whole new hand that stirs up just as much fear as the old one:

- ▶ fear of not speaking a foreign language fluently
- ▶ fear of not spending enough time abroad at an early age
- ▶ fear of not being flexible/aware/curious/trustworthy/self-motivated
- ▶ fear of upsetting the adolescents by sending or taking them abroad
- ▶ fear of missing out on the chance to have a great adventure with the family

Breathe and smirk. After all, these fears are *much* more interesting and defined than the old ones. Instead of an all-encompassing sense of falling short as a parent, you've got some clear starting points for creativity and collaboration. So stash the old fear cards in the back of the junk drawer and start playing with this shiny new deck. You'll come up with your own games in no time.

I share my family's story here not to suggest that our decisions are better than anyone else's but to encourage you to recognize and celebrate the freedom you have to *make your own*. I offer this book as a heart-shaped permission slip to do things differently. I wish you much love, learning, and laughter along the way.

> Begin, be bold, and venture to be wise.
> HORACE

NOTES

TOP TEN REASONS TO READ THIS BOOK

1. "Creative class" is a term used by Richard Florida in his books *The Rise of the Creative Class, The Flight of the Creative Class,* and his newest, *Who's Your City: How the Creative Economy Is Making the Place Where You Live the Most Important Decision of Your Life.* It denotes a group of citizens whose economic function is to create new ideas, new technology, or new content and includes scientists, engineers, architects, designers, educators, artists, musicians, businesspeople, attorneys, health care workers, and entertainers, among others. In the United States the creative class is 40 million strong and makes nearly half of all wage and salary income. Florida, who has done extensive research on this topic, is concerned that the creative class in the United States isn't growing nearly as fast as it is in other countries. In fact, the United States is not even in the top ten in what he calls the Global Creative Class Index. You can read much more on his website—and I highly recommend his blog—at www.creativeclass.com.

CHAPTER 1. CREATIVE, NOT CRAZY

1. Tim Ferriss had not yet written his best-selling book *The Four-Hour Workweek* when we left the United States to go virtual, but it's a great resource for anyone considering streamlining work by using a variety of tech tools and outsourcing options. We figured out how to switch to virtual by literally Googling things like "Quickbooks online." It's amazing what's available, and new resources are popping up all the time. Just go online and start searching!

CHAPTER 2. BEYOND MATH AND MANDARIN

1. From 1985 to 2002 the number of international students enrolled in U.S. institutions of higher learning rose each and every year, for a cumulative increase of more than 50 percent. But after 9/11 (from 2002 to 2005) the trend reversed and enrollment declined. The drop in enrollment from Middle Eastern and Muslim nations was especially severe, and tougher visa restrictions for students from other countries contributed to the decline. However, the number of international students who came to the United States to study in the academic year 2006–07 increased and rebounded to pre-9/11 numbers, and the country maintains its position as the world's top destination for foreign scholars, followed by the United Kingdom, France, Germany, Australia, and China. More than half the international students enrolled in U.S. institutions come from Asia; the top five nations of origin are India, China, South Korea, Japan, and Taiwan. You can find much more info at www.iie.org or www.state.gov/youthandeducation.

   Dr. Mitch Leventhal is the president of the American International Recruitment Council (www.airc-education.org), an organization committed to developing standards and ethical practices pertaining to the recruitment of international students to American educational institutions. According to Dr. Leventhal, there is a common misconception that the U.S. Higher Education Act bans the use of overseas recruitment agents. The use of agents for domestic recruitment is forbidden *within the United States* but is legal abroad. The persistent idea that the use of agents is illegal or unethical has severely limited the growth of U.S. institutions, while other nations are capitalizing on the opportunity to recruit students using agents in strategic countries around the world.

2. Read more about the Center for International Initiatives study at www.acenet.edu.

3. A report issued by America's Promise Alliance (chaired by former Secretary of State Colin Powell) found that only about *half* of the students served by public school systems in the nation's largest cities receive diplomas, and nationally only about 70 percent of U.S. students

graduate on time with a regular diploma. Seventeen of the nation's fifty largest cities had high school graduation rates *lower* than 50 percent; the lowest graduation rates were reported in Detroit, Indianapolis, and Cleveland. This study was based on numbers for the 2003–04 school year. Learn more at www.americaspromise.org.

4. This is a nod to Thomas Friedman's excellent book *The World Is Flat*, in which he describes the ways that technology has leveled the playing field and given individuals everywhere more access to information and opportunities around the world.

5. Richard Florida says that the world is actually spiky: in thriving metropolitan regions talent, technology, and tolerance come together to create a more attractive environment for those looking to collaborate. I play with the term *spiky* here by using it to describe the qualities that bold schoolers are leveraging—being artful, atypical, advanced, and adventurous—to distinguish themselves from what one might call the *flat* crowd of students on a more traditional path.

6. In September 2008 PBS presented an outstanding program called *Where We Stand: America's Schools in the 21st Century,* hosted by Judy Woodruff and funded by the Bill and Melinda Gates Foundation. More statistics on where we stand in terms of global education—and clips from the program—are available at www.pbs.org.

7. You can order the DVD of Bob Compton's documentary, *Two Million Minutes,* and even test your knowledge compared to eleventh-grade Indian students (in English), by visiting www.2mminutes.com.

8. The United States did much better in the 2008 competition, earning first-place awards in photography (Jennifer Hui and Melissa Hui) and interface design (David Roedl and William Odom). But it did not make it into the top three in any of the other seven categories. More at www.imaginecup.com.

9. While this figure has been reported in articles in the popular media, in speeches by policymakers, reports to Congress, and in statements by the U.S. Department of Education, it has been disputed by others, including Vivek Wadhwa, a fellow with the Labor and Worklife Program at Harvard Law School and executive in residence/adjunct professor at

the Pratt School of Engineering at Duke University. In an article in the *Harvard International Review,* he states that the graduation statistics in common use are misleading and based on faulty comparisons. He and others have done research suggesting that this statistic is being used to justify moving U.S. engineering operations abroad, due not to a domestic shortage of engineers but rather to lower costs abroad and the proximity of growth markets. Still, he goes on to say that Indian companies are excelling by focusing on seven key areas of innovative practices in engineering education. The important question is not what the actual number of engineers might be but how the United States can learn from the growth of the engineering programs in China and India. Read the article at www.harvardir.org/articles/1752/.

10. This statistic about honors students appeared in a startling video presentation titled *Did You Know?* put together by Karl Fisch in 2006 as part of a staff training program in his school district in Colorado. In February 2007 it went viral and has now been seen online by more than 10 million viewers. You can view both the original and the updated version at his site at www.thefischbowl.blogspot.com.

CHAPTER 3. FEGO

1. As previously cited, U.S. high school graduation statistics can be found at www.americaspromise.org.

2. According to information available as of January 2008, 46 percent of all U.S. undergraduates are community college students. Read more at the American Association of Community Colleges website at www.aacc.nche.edu/research/index.htm.

3. In an article in the April 18, 2008, issue of *The Chronicle of Higher Education,* Beth McMurtrie interviews several community college leaders attending the American Association of Community Colleges' annual meeting in Philadelphia. Go to www.chronicle.com/free/v54/i32/32a04003.htm.

CHAPTER 4. AP, IB & SAT

1. Education expert Tony Wagner sees a profound disconnect between what potential employers are looking for in young people today (crit-

ical thinking skills, creativity, and effective communication) and what our schools are providing (passive learning environments and uninspired lesson plans that focus on test preparation and that reward memorization). In his new book he explains how every American can work to overhaul our education system, and he shows us examples of dramatically different schools that teach all students new skills. Learn more at www.schoolchange.org.

CHAPTER 5. MEET THE NEW A STUDENT

1. Thomas Armstrong has written extensively on the concept of multiple intelligences, the idea that there are numerous kinds of "smart" and that there are ways to develop each one. I recommend his books *7 Kinds of Smart: Identifying and Developing Your Multiple Intelligences (revised and updated with information on 2 new kinds of smart)* and *In Their Own Way: Discovering and Encouraging Your Child's Multiple Intelligences (revised and updated)*. Learn more at www.ThomasArmstrong.com.

CHAPTER 6. THE BOLDEST ADVANTAGE

1. Watch Dr. Dispenza's videos about the brain at www.drjoedispenza .com.

2. Dr. White has posted articles helping parents and students learn more about culture shock and reverse culture shock at www.yeoresources .org.

CHAPTER 7. HOW TO SAVE THOUSANDS ON COLLEGE STUDY ABROAD

1. The Institute of International Education is devoted to increasing opportunities for students, scholars, and teachers to study abroad in a wide range of destinations. (The IIE oversees the Fulbright and many other scholarship programs.) In 2007 study abroad increased by 8.5 percent to a total of 223,534, according to the **Open Doors 2007** report, published annually by the IIE with funding from the Department of State's Bureau of Educational and Cultural Affairs. The increase in students studying abroad is largely due to the growing number of

short-term trips available (52 percent choose to stay eight weeks or less). Only 5.5 percent of students who study abroad choose to do so for a full academic or calendar year. Read more at www.opendoors.iienetwork.org.

2. Lost or stolen passports may be replaced fairly quickly and easily abroad, depending on proximity to a U.S. embassy. For more information, visit http://travel.state.gov/law/info/info_623.html.

3. Lansky offers tips for solo travelers and wannabe travel writers on his website at www.DougLansky.com.

4. This varies a great deal, depending on the destination. However, you can get an idea of the markup by comparing the rates for a semester at a given university on the ISA or ISEP sites with the rate charged for international students applying directly to the same foreign college. Most colleges abroad charge a triple rate for international students (that is, three times more than the locals pay), but many U.S. private universities charge their study-abroad students the same tuition whether they are on campus or in another country. I'll refrain from getting too specific (and picking on certain universities), but suffice it to say that depending on the two schools in question, the U.S. university may charge as much as ten times the rate required of international students who apply directly.

5. In August 2007 New York State's attorney general, Andrew M. Cuomo, began issuing subpoenas to organizations that provide study-abroad programs to colleges, seeking information about the organizations' business practices and financial arrangements with universities.

An article that same month in *The New York Times* written by Diana Jean Schemo states: "At many campuses, study abroad programs are run by multiple companies and nonprofit institutes that offer colleges generous perks to sign up students: free and subsidized travel overseas for officials, back-office services to defray operating expenses, stipends to market the programs to students, unpaid membership on advisory councils and boards, and even cash bonuses and commissions on student-paid fees." Many compare the cozy relationships between colleges and study-abroad providers to those that have existed between some college financial aid offices and student loan companies.

Parents are getting outraged too. According to *The Chronicle of Higher Education,* James P. Brady, the father of a Wheaton College alumna who studied abroad in South Africa, is suing the school for overcharging his daughter for her study-abroad travels. Had his daughter studied at the South African college as an independent international student, she would have saved $4,500. According to Brady, Wheaton provided no additional services but charged his daughter the full price of an education at the U.S. campus, including room and board. Brady, an attorney, has been quoted as saying, "This is the crudest kind of commercial gouging." Wheaton administrators denied accusations of unfair billing practices, stating that charging students full tuition allows the college to evaluate and oversee study-abroad programs and provide financial aid to needier students.

6. For more information about staying safe abroad—and special tips for young women traveling solo—visit www.info.iiepassport.org/tipsforfemalestudents.html.

7. What started out as a tit-for-tat visa reciprocity issue is now more of a he-said-she-said problem. At the website for the U.S. Department of State at http://travel.state.gov/visa/frvi/reciprocity/reciprocity_3272 .html, you'll read this: "The United States strives to eliminate visa issuance fees whenever possible; however, when a foreign government imposes such fees on U.S. citizens for certain types of visas, the United States will impose a 'reciprocal' fee to nationals of that country for similar type of visas." But if you go to the Europa site at http://europa.eu you'll read reciprocity updates like this: "No tangible progress has been made regarding the USA despite all efforts of the Commission and individual Member States" (July 2008).

In an article in the March–April 2007 online edition of *Academe,* the publication of the American Association of University Professors, Wendi Maloney describes the continued restriction of visas for foreign students entering the United States. She states, "Even though the process required to obtain a US visa has improved recently, travel to the

United States remains unnecessarily challenging, according to a joint statement issued in January by five organizations with diverse interests: the Alliance for International Educational and Cultural Exchange; the Coalition for Employment Through Exports; the Heritage Foundation; NAFSA: Association of International Educators; and the National Foreign Trade Council." Learn more at www.aaup.org.

CHAPTER 9. THE GET-REAL GUIDE FOR BOLD PARENTS

1. You can find more details at www.statisticstop10.com/Causes_of _Death_Older_Teens.html.

EPILOGUE. THE NOT SO BIG EDUCATION

1. Learn more about Sarah Susanka and her work at www.NotSoBig.com.

INDEX

Page numbers beginning with 299 refer to notes.

To read more student stories and updates, get the latest news in global education, and connect with bold schoolers and their parents around the world, visit www.NewGlobalStudent.com.

Maya, Tom
Talya, Teal, Tara, Taeko

About the Author

Maya Frost has taught thousands of people how to pay
attention. Her eyes-wide-open approach to awareness
and creativity has been featured in scores of publica-
tions and websites worldwide, ranging from *Ladies'
Home Journal* to the Italian version of *Elle,* from
MSNBC.com to Match.com. Though she has spent
most of her life in Oregon, Maya and her husband
have lived abroad with their daughters in Japan, Mexico, and Argentina. She can be found chatting in cafés
and exploring the side streets of her beloved Buenos
Aires. Her website is www.MayaFrost.com.